More praise for *Frontiers in Spiritual Leadership*

"Allison, Kocher, and Goethals have succeeded in gathering an all-star team of scholars representing diverse disciplinary perspectives to bring focus to spiritual leadership and its noble, life-giving qualities. *Frontiers in Spiritual Leadership* is an inspired volume that forges new ground and offers much-needed hope and direction at a critically important time."

—Bryan Dik
Associate Professor of Psychology, Colorado State University
Co-Editor of *Purpose and Meaning in the Workplace* and
Psychology of Religion and Workplace Spirituality

"Allison, Kocher, and Goethals' *Frontiers in Spiritual Leadership* is an original and truly interdisciplinary study of spiritual leadership and its impact on the lives of individuals and communities."

—Michael Harvey
Professor of Business ManagementWashington College
Co-Editor of *Leadership Studies:*
The Dialogue of Disciplines

"Leaders are models and mentors, instilling in others the motivation to transcend their current states in order to take actions that would not otherwise occur. Such transcendence is the essence of spirituality and, as such, the understanding of leadership and spirituality are synergistic intellectual pursuits. However, no prior book has integrated these fundamental facets of human life. Creatively bringing together scholars from multiple disciplines, *Frontiers in Spiritual Leadership: Discovering the Better Angels of Our Nature* provides rich, unique, and singularly important discussions of the history, and contemporary significance, of transcendent leadership for enhancing personal thriving and social well-being."

—Richard M. Lerner,
Bergstrom Chair in Applied Developmental Science and
Director, Institute for Applied Research in
Youth Development
Tufts University

Jepson Studies in Leadership

Series Editors: George R. Goethals, Thad Williamson, and J. Thomas Wren

Managing Editor: Elizabeth DeBusk-Maslanka

Jepson Studies in Leadership is dedicated to the interdisciplinary pursuit of important questions related to leadership. In its approach, the series reflects the broad-based commitment to the liberal arts of the University of Richmond's Jepson School of Leadership Studies. The series thus aims to publish the best work on leadership from economics, English, history, management, organizational studies, philosophy, political science, psychology, and religion. In addition to monographs and edited collections on leadership, included in the series are volumes from the Jepson Colloquium that bring together influential scholars from multiple disciplines to think collectively about distinctive leadership themes in politics, science, civil society, and corporate life. The books in the series should be of interest to humanists and social scientists, as well as to organizational theorists and instructors teaching in business, leadership, and professional programs.

Books Appearing in This Series:

The Values of Presidential Leadership
   edited by Terry L. Price and J. Thomas Wren
Leadership and the Liberal Arts: Achieving the Promise of a Liberal Education
   edited by J. Thomas Wren, Ronald E. Riggio, and Michael A. Genovese
Leadership and Discovery
   edited by George R. Goethals and J. Thomas Wren
Lincoln's Legacy of Leadership
   edited by George R. Goethals and Gary L. McDowell
For the Greater Good of All: Perspectives on Individualism, Society, and Leadership
   edited by Donelson R. Forsyth and Crystal L. Hoyt
Executive Power in Theory and Practice
   edited by Hugh Liebert, Gary McDowell, and Terry L. Price
Leadership and Global Justice
   edited by Douglas Hicks and Thad Williamson
On Effective Leadership: Across Domains, Cultures, and Eras
   G. Donald Chandler III and John W. Chandler
Leadership and Elizabethan Culture
   edited by Peter Iver Kaufman
F. A. Hayek and the Modern Economy: Economic Organization and Activity
   edited by Sandra J. Peart and David M. Levy

Conceptions of Leadership: Enduring Ideas and Emerging Insights
edited by George R. Goethals, Scott T. Allison, Roderick M. Kramer, and David M. Messick

Leading Through Conflict: Into the Fray
edited by Dejun Tony Kong and Donelson R. Forsyth

Frontiers in Spiritual Leadership: Discovering the Better Angels of Our Nature
edited by Scott T. Allison, Craig T. Kocher, and George R. Goethals

Frontiers in Spiritual Leadership

Discovering the Better Angels of Our Nature

Edited by
Scott T. Allison, Craig T. Kocher, and
George R. Goethals

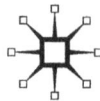

First published 2016 by
PALGRAVE MACMILLAN

The authors have asserted their rights to be identified as the authors of this work in accordance with the Copyright, Designs and Patents Act 1988.

Palgrave Macmillan in the UK is an imprint of Macmillan Publishers Limited, registered in England, company number 785998, of Houndmills, Basingstoke, Hampshire, RG21 6XS.

Palgrave Macmillan in the US is a division of Nature America, Inc., One New York Plaza, Suite 4500, New York, NY 10004-1562.

Palgrave Macmillan is the global academic imprint of the above companies and has companies and representatives throughout the world.

Hardback ISBN: 978–1–137–58080–1
E-PUB ISBN: 978–1–137–58082–5
E-PDF ISBN: 978–1–137–58081–8
DOI: 10.1057/9781137580818

Distribution in the UK, Europe and the rest of the world is by Palgrave Macmillan®, a division of Macmillan Publishers Limited, registered in England, company number 785998, of Houndmills, Basingstoke, Hampshire RG21 6XS.

Library of Congress Cataloging-in-Publication Data
    Frontiers in spiritual leadership : discovering the better angels of our nature / edited by Scott T. Allison, Craig T. Kocher, and George R. Goethals.
    pages cm.—(Jepson studies in leadership)
    Includes bibliographical references and index.
    ISBN 978–1–137–58080–1 (alk. paper)
    1. Leadership—Religious aspects. I. Allison, Scott T., editor.
BL325.L4F76 2016
206′.1—dc23   2015033771

A catalogue record for the book is available from the British Library.

CONTENTS

ACKNOWLEDGMENTS

This book would not have been possible without assistance and inspiration from many friends, colleagues, and loved ones. First, we are indebted to our outstanding colleagues at the University of Richmond, a place we are so fortunate to call home. As this volume is packed with local talent, we are especially grateful to our friends at Richmond, who agreed so graciously to contribute their intellectual gifts to the venture. These generous individuals include Elisabeth Gruner, Henry Chambers, Jennifer Erkulwater, David Burhans, Stephanie Cobb, Peter Kaufman, Rich Morrill, Sydney Watts, and Thad Williamson. We also extend heartfelt appreciation to Ed Ayers and E. Bruce Heilman for taking the time to share their wisdom and unique perspectives by bookending our volume with a Foreword and an Afterword. Thank you, kind sirs.

Other friends and colleagues at the University of Richmond are also deserving of our gratitude for supporting our efforts to illuminate spiritual leadership. In the Department of Psychology, we thank Beth Crawford, Jane Berry, Craig Kinsley, David Leary, Erin Ottmar, Mark Fox, Elyssa Twedt, Cindy Bukach, Laura Knouse, Pete LeViness, Taylyn Hulse, Kristin Jamison, Karen Kochel, Andy Newcomb, Bill Cooper, and Karyn Kuhn. These quality people have provided an ideal environment for encouraging good scholarship and teaching.

In the office of the Chaplaincy, we express our thanks to Emily Cobb, Molly Field, Andrew Goodman, Rizwan Mujeebuddin, Tom Mullen, Karen Redden, and Bryn Bagby Taylor, all of whom embody spiritual leadership in beautiful ways for the University of Richmond community. In the Jepson School of Leadership Studies, we thank Michele Bedsaul, Elizabeth DeBusk-Maslanka, Don Forsyth, Crystal Hoyt, Peter Kaufman, Pam Khoury, Sandra Peart, Terry Price, Tammy Tripp, and Thad Williamson.

We are also grateful to the people who helped financially support our efforts to bring this book to fruition. The lead editor, Scott Allison, was supported by a John Templeton Foundation Grant (#35279). Moreover, Kathleen Skerrett, the dean of Arts and Sciences at Richmond, helped fund a stimulating dinner gathering of this book's contributors. We appreciate this support very much.

Our families, especially, have galvanized us through the long and rewarding process of compiling this volume. Our heartfelt appreciation goes out to Connie Allison, Heather Allison, Robert Allison, Sara Allison, Claire Bergvall, Abby Kocher, Caroline Kocher, Jim Kocher, Sally Kocher, Marion Goethals, Andrew Goethals, and Jefferson Goethals. We are forever grateful for the unfailing love and support given to us from these remarkable individuals. Finally, we give thanks for the special places that lift our spirits, including the Blue Ridge Mountains, the James River, Raquette Lake, and Westhampton Lake.

FOREWORD

"Spiritual" and "leadership"—two words that could hardly be more slippery. The editors of this book are brave to take on both at the same time. They are even braver to examine those words within the context of a twenty-first-century institution of higher education.

It may seem surprising at best to look for the spiritual within a secular university. It is not obvious where the spirit might live in a place that is simultaneously an institution of higher education, a complicated bureaucracy, a business enterprise, an athletics franchise, a nonprofit, a large employer, a wealthy investor, a philanthropic institution, and a large real estate holding.

The place of spirituality may seem especially fugitive in an institution that bore an explicitly spiritual mission throughout most of its history but now does not. The University of Richmond was proudly and explicitly Baptist for its first century and a quarter. Since the 1970s, however, the institution, like counterparts across the nation, has grown steadily more diverse in the faith traditions it welcomes and supports. Today, the chaplain coordinates those who minister to Catholic, Jewish, Buddhist, Hindu, Muslim, and Protestant students. The two chaplains represented in this collection, David Burhans and Craig Kocher, reflect on the experience of presiding over a place that has seen spirituality flourish both in the context of focused denominational vision and in the newer context of a broader diversity of faith.

The place of leadership is also complicated in a university. Shared governance is an article of faith in a university, and yet exactly what is shared, when and how, requires elaborate explication and continuous negotiation. The Board of Trustees has the ultimate responsibility for a university, but the faculty exercise the most important and immediate leadership within an educational institution—determining what is taught and how it is taught, day in and day out, in every classroom for generations. The administration exercises power only on behalf of other people. The president is more a broker than anything else, negotiating among every group that claims an interest in the institution, ranging from students and their parents to neighbors to alumni to staff to faculty to donors to fans to accrediting agencies to bond-rating companies.

Such a complex environment both nurtures and fractures spirituality and leadership. To the surprise of many, religious faith has not registered a steady decline in an increasingly secular world. Rather, it has taken new forms and shapes, often less anchored in formal institutions but vital nevertheless. Young people, in particular, yearn for a kind of meaning that can only be described as "spiritual" even as they sustain only flitting relationships to churches, synagogues, and mosques. A university provides a welcome haven for such seekers, offering the welcome and fellowship of faith without strict confines and commitments.

Leadership, too, flourishes in a university that seems to have no fixed leadership. Students seek out "leadership opportunities" of every sort, finding them in fraternities and sports clubs as well as in student government and in alliance with the administration of the university. Faculty exercise leadership in departments, in schools, and on university-wide committees as well as within their classrooms and disciplines.

Universities are tightly woven into the society beyond its bounds, so that trends analyzed in this collection press on institutions that seem timeless in their architecture and ceremonies. Many people worry, for example, that the neoliberal values described in Jennifer Erkulwater's chapter are eroding the communal values of higher education. Others worry that higher education policies created in Washington correspond poorly with the needs of actual students.

The range of topics explored in this collection demonstrate that American universities early in the twenty-first century, even a relatively small one proudly devoted to undergraduate education, foster broad curiosity and erudition. The specialized knowledge displayed in the pages that follow impressively embody the kinds of knowledge that live in a university and nowhere else.

The chapters in this book thus reflect a paradox: spirituality and leadership can flourish in a university precisely because they are not unitary, not fixed, and not bound there. The very flux that stirs anxiety also stirs creativity and energy.

EDWARD L. AYERS
Tucker-Boatwright Professor
of the Humanities
President Emeritus
University of Richmond
August 2015

INTRODUCTION

Spiritual Leadership: A Fresh Look at an Ancient Human Issue

SCOTT T. ALLISON, CRAIG T. KOCHER, AND GEORGE R. GOETHALS

We are not enemies, but friends. We must not be enemies. Though passion may have strained, it must not break our bonds of affection. The mystic chords of memory, stretching from every battlefield, and patriot grave, to every living heart and hearthstone, all over this broad land, will yet swell the chorus of the Union, when again touched, as surely they will be, by the better angels of our nature.

—Abraham Lincoln, Inaugural Address, March 4, 1861

Abraham Lincoln's iconic phrase, "the better angels of our nature," revealed his belief that the noblest qualities of humanity would heal a divided nation. This book, *Frontiers in Spiritual Leadership: Discovering the Better Angels of Our Nature*, is about the expression of these noble qualities and how leaders such as Lincoln make that expression possible. Lincoln was arguably America's greatest spiritual leader. His words and actions promoting justice, equality, and reconciliation were a spiritual tonic to war-weary citizens yearning for healing and unification. Lincoln exuded charisma with his unique look, confident mannerisms, and deft speeches that often quoted or paraphrased scripture in ways that resonated to his audience (Goethals and Allison 2014). He sprinkled his orations with quintessential phrases such as "a house divided against itself cannot stand." The house metaphor might have had an impact by itself, but surely its spiritual origins gave it additional power. Lincoln's Emancipation Proclamation contained appeals to important values and divine approval, concluding that "upon this act, sincerely believed to be an act of justice warranted by the Constitution, upon military necessity, I invoke the considerate judgment of mankind, and the gracious favor of Almighty God."

What Is Spiritual Leadership?

This volume was inspired by the confluence of the terms "spirituality" and "leadership." These two phenomena appear, at first glance, to be unrelated. On closer examination, they are twin processes. Merriam-Webster's dictionary defines spirit as "the force within a person that is believed to give the body life, energy, and power." Similarly, leadership is said to be the force within a group that is said to give it life, energy, and power. Combining the two terms, we can say that spiritual leadership refers to the process by which a person or persons within a group give it life-affirming aims and the power to bring those aims to fruition. This definition of spiritual leadership is consistent with previous efforts to define the phenomenon. Adopting an organizational behavior perspective, Fry and Nisiewicz (2012) proposed that spiritual leadership "involves intrinsically motivating and inspiring" followers through faith in a "vision of service" within a cultural context "based on altruistic love" (4). These scholars identified two key processes of spiritual leadership. First, spiritual leaders create "a vision in which leaders and followers experience a sense of calling so that their lives have meaning." Second, they "establish a culture based on the values of altruistic love whereby leaders and followers have a sense of membership, feel understood and appreciated, and have genuine care, concern, and appreciation for both self and others" (5).

Doohan (2007) has gone so far as to claim that spiritual leadership is the only acceptable form of leadership in the world today. "The heart of leadership," according to Doohan, "lies in the heart of leaders" (12). From this perspective, leaders are called to consider their interdependence with the world, and not simply their roles within their organizations. Leadership is about the exercise of "moral values, ethics, resources of our hearts and heads, the joy of a leadership mind, the need to face the world with soul, the challenge to bring love, spirituality, and virtue to contemporary organizations" (12). In a similar vein, Benefiel

(2005) defines spiritual leadership as leadership that takes into account the "intellectual, emotional, and relational depth of human character, as well as the continuing capability and yearning for personal development and evolution" (7). Spiritual leadership "manifests itself in humor, compassion, and relational competence" (7). Benefiel concludes that leaders who apply spiritual principles can bring about "individual and organizational transformation" (8).

The significance of transformation is a recurring theme in various treatments of spiritual leadership. Political scientist James MacGregor Burns (1978) proposed one of the first theories of exemplary leadership, although he never directly referred to any of the components of such leadership as "spiritual." Burns identified the highest form of leadership as transforming leadership. Drawing from Abraham Maslow's (1943) humanistic work on self-actualization, Burns believed that transforming leaders play an important role in satisfying followers' lower needs, thereby elevating them for the important work that they, that is, leaders and followers, can do together to produce significant change for the better. As Burns described transforming leadership, individuals engage each other "in such a way that leaders and followers raise one another to higher levels of motivation and morality." Both leaders and followers will be elevated such that the leaders create a "new cadre of leaders." This conception follows Maslow closely, though it makes explicit an idea that is largely implicit in Maslow, and that is that the self-actualized person is a moral actor (Goethals and Allison 2016).

Previous research on heroic leadership suggests that the most spiritually enlightened leaders exhibit high degrees of morality and competence to followers (Allison and Goethals, 2011, 2013). A heroic leader's demonstration of exemplary morality can have an elevating effect on followers. Recent scholarship suggests that moral exemplars evoke a unique emotional response, which psychologist Jonathan Haidt (2003) has, in fact, called "elevation." Haidt borrowed the term "elevation" from Thomas Jefferson, who used the phrase "moral elevation" to describe the euphoric feeling one gets when reading great literature. When people experience elevation, they feel a mix of awe, reverence, and admiration for a morally beautiful act. The emotion is described as similar to calmness, warmth, and love. Haidt argues that elevation is "elicited by acts of virtue or moral beauty; it causes warm, open feelings in the chest" (121). Most importantly, the feeling of elevation has a concomitant behavioral component: a desire to become a better person. Elevation "motivates people to behave more virtuously themselves." A form of moral and spiritual self-efficacy, elevation transforms people into believing they are capable of engaging in significant pro-social action.

Transformation holds the key to the mythic hero's successful completion of his or her journey, according to Joseph Campbell (1949). The ingredients of this classic journey are well known to storytellers. A hero is cast into a dangerous, unfamiliar world and is charged with accomplishing a daunting task that requires assistance from sidekicks and mentors. There are formidable obstacles along the way and villainous characters to overcome. After many trials and much suffering, the hero prevails and then gives back what he or she has learned to society. Success on this journey requires a personal transformation. With assistance from leaders, whom Campbell calls mentors, heroes acquire an important quality that was conspicuously missing, and holding them back, before the journey. All heroes start out "incomplete" in some sense; they lack some essential strength that is crucial to their personal and spiritual development. This missing attribute can be humility, courage, compassion, faith, resilience, or some fundamental truth about themselves and the world.

The discovery, or recovery, of the missing quality produces a personal transformation that enables heroes to rise above their suffering and prevail. Campbell believed that the hero's journey was, in part, a spiritual journey of self-completion and connection to one's self and the world. "The function of myth," wrote Campbell, "is to put us in sync—with ourselves, with our social group, and with the environment in which we live" (19). Campbell (1991) also revealed "the final secret" of hero stories—"to teach you how to penetrate the labyrinth of life in such a way that its spiritual values come through" (34). Most importantly, the culmination of the hero's journey is his or her engagement in spiritual leadership. That is, heroes give back what was once given to them. After having been mentored on their journey, heroes later become the mentor figure to other people who are on earlier stages of their own journey. As Richard Rohr (2014) observes, "transformed people transform people" (126).

Spiritually Intelligent Leadership

We acknowledge that terms such as "morality," "heroism," and "spirituality" can mean different things to different people. This fact suggests that spiritual leadership itself is in the eye of the beholder. In their chapter in this volume, Allison and Setterberg note that if we define spiritual leadership as leadership that serves a higher moral purpose, then we must be mindful that morality can be twisted to serve the psychological needs and goals of the beholder. A sad truth is that many God-loving nations have waged wars against each other, with leadership on each side claiming the spiritually superior upper hand. At the same time, it can be argued that there are clear benefits to living in a time when spirituality can carry with it so many different connotations. A spiritual practice today can include attending a church service, taking a yoga class, beholding a dazzling sunset, watching children play, or even solving a vexing math equation. Astrow et al. (2001) define spirituality as "the search for transcendent meaning" that can be expressed in religious practice or expressed "exclusively in [people's] relationship to nature, music, the arts, a set of philosophical beliefs, or relationships with friends and family" (14).

For many, the belief in a higher power is the centerpiece of spirituality. Such a power need not be divine for people to be transformed spiritually in mind and in heart. Mohr (2006) adopts this broad definition of spirituality by defining the term as "a person's experience of, or a belief in, a power apart from his or her own existence" (378). Kaiser (2000) extends this definition of spirituality to include "a broad set of principles that transcend[s] all religions. Spirituality is about the relationship between ourselves and something larger. That 'something' can be the good of the community or the people who are served by your agency or school or with energies greater than ourselves. Spirituality means being in the right relationship with all that is. It is a stance of harmlessness toward all living beings and an understanding of their mutual interdependence" (78).

Love and Talbot (1999) provided a synthesis of spirituality based on their review of scholarship by theologians, social scientists, and healthcare specialists. Their analysis revealed that spirituality is an internal process of (a) "seeking personal authenticity, genuineness, and wholeness as an aspect of identity development"; (b) "transcending one's egocentricity in the development of a greater connectedness to self and others"; (c) "deriving meaning, purpose, and direction in one's life"; and (d) developing "openness to exploring a relationship with an intangible and pervasive power that exists beyond human existence and rational human knowing" (96). These four perspectives have clear connections to the aims of transformational leadership as described by James MacGregor Burns (1978). Burns identified the ability of transforming leaders to elevate the motivation and morality of followers by instilling them with meaning, purpose, and higher-level values.

One could argue that spiritually gifted leaders possess a high degree of spiritual intelligence. Zohar (1997) proposed that spiritually intelligent individuals are guided by a moral vision and show great humility, compassion, resilience, and an appreciation for diversity. Wigglesworth (2006) argued that spiritual intelligence is essential for effective leadership, stating that the most spiritually gifted leaders possess "the ability to act with wisdom and compassion, while maintaining inner and outer peace, regardless of the circumstances" (31). Emmons (2000) suggested that spiritually intelligent individuals possess "the adaptive use of spiritual information to facilitate everyday problem solving and goal attainment." From this perspective, effective spiritual leaders are virtuous individuals who sanctify everyday experience, possess a socially relevant purpose in life, have a well-developed conscience, and are committed to promoting human values. Over the past decade, scholarship devoted to understanding spirituality and its role in human activities such as leadership is burgeoning in psychology, sociology, political science, economics, philosophy, and religion (Miller 2012; Paloutzian and Park 2014).

The Genesis of This Book

As noted earlier, this book was inspired by our interest in exemplary leadership that incorporates spiritual principles. The three editors of this volume hold positions at three different units within the University of Richmond. The lead editor, Scott Allison, is a professor of social psychology, who studies heroism and villainy. On several occasions he has invited the second editor, Craig Kocher, to give guest lectures in his classes on the psychology of heroism. Kocher is the university chaplain and Jessie Ball duPont Chair of the Chaplaincy. Allison was struck by how much his students resonated with Kocher's spiritual approach to psychological issues pertaining to morality, and one day over coffee the two decided to embark on a book project examining spiritual leadership. While Allison brought his psychological expertise on the topic and Kocher his theological background and his seven years of experience as the university's spiritual leader, the two men realized that the volume would benefit considerably from the many talents of George Goethals, a full-time member of the faculty in the Jepson School of Leadership Studies.

At first, Goethals offered some resistance to the idea of collaborating on this book. With his secular orientation, what could he bring to the table? Allison and Kocher assured him that his long and storied professional background, coupled with his many personal gifts, made him an ideal contributor to scholarship bearing on spiritual leadership. In his career, Goethals has enjoyed considerable success as the chair of the Williams College Psychology Department, acting dean of the Faculty, provost, founder and chair of the program in leadership studies, and editor of numerous academic journals and books. Allison and Kocher knew that during Goethals's effective administering of these leadership positions, he exemplified spiritual leadership at its finest. Goethals, like Kocher, leads with the heart. Building relationships and leading with meaning, purpose, compassion, humility, and warmth have been the signature of Goethals's leadership. These spiritual qualities in both Goethals and Kocher are what attracted Allison to this project and to this special collaboration.

We acknowledge that our tripartite editorial arrangement has its advantages and disadvantages. One obvious benefit, mentioned earlier, is the fact we hail from three different disciplinary units: psychology, the chaplaincy, and leadership studies. Psychology is viewed by many as a key intellectual hub in a liberal arts campus, with its connections to the natural sciences, the social sciences, and the humanities. The Jepson School of Leadership Studies boasts of a multidisciplinary approach to leadership and is staffed by faculty from eight different disciplines. The Chaplaincy's stated mission is "to inspire generous faith and engage the heart of the University." These three diverse perspectives assisted us in bringing fresh ideas, a healthy synergy, and different sets of connections to potential faculty contributors across our campus. The three of us also represent somewhat different age cohorts. Goethals is the eldest and wisest of the three. Allison sits comfortably in middle age, while Kocher is a youthful dervish. In our teamwork, we discovered that the differences in our age and experience had a counterbalancing effect and offered a rich synergism.

The central disadvantage of our collaboration is perhaps obvious. The three of us are middle class, White, European American males, each of whom, much to our amusement and consternation, drives a Toyota Prius. Our recognition of this demographic and automotive homogeneity inspired us to work feverishly to produce a volume with diverse content and spirit. We set out to solicit chapters that provided coverage over as wide a spectrum of spirituality as possible. Our volume is split into two sections; the first half focuses on historical perspectives on spiritual leadership, whereas the second half addresses contemporary approaches to spiritual leadership. Within each section, we sought to cover as much terrain as possible in terms of substantive content and disciplinary perspectives. We believe that we have assembled an outstanding collection of authors who tell a compelling story about spiritual leadership from a variety of viewpoints and drawing from many different spiritual traditions.

Overview of the Chapters in This Book

Our volume begins in rousing fashion with a thoughtful Foreword by our university's most recent former president, Ed Ayers. We hope that you take a moment to read Ayers's short preamble to the book. His unique perspective on our collection of essays reveals him to have been one of our university's most outstanding spiritual leaders. As we have noted, the first half of this volume focuses on historical perspectives in spiritual leadership while the second half addresses contemporary issues. Our historical section opens with a chapter by professor of religion Stephanie Cobb, who writes a thoughtful essay titled "Women's Leadership in the Early Church: Possibilities and Pushbacks." Cobb explores the roles that were sometimes available to women in the early church, along with the ways in which the church—or the culture at large—resisted women's spiritual leadership. Rather than drawing conclusions about what was or ought to be, Cobb's chapter challenges readers to observe differences in discourses and to see the ways various cultural concerns affected leadership possibilities for women in the early church.

In chapter 2, Peter Kaufman from the Jepson School of Leadership Studies writes a compelling piece titled "Clerical Leadership in Late Antiquity: Augustine on Bishops' Polemical and Pastoral Burdens." Kaufman explores the leadership qualities of St. Augustine, Bishop of Hippo, who is widely regarded as one of the most influential theologians and pastoral leaders in the Christian tradition. Augustine faced significant challenges in shaping the character of the clergy and church doctrine amid enormous social unrest and significant personal turmoil. In chapter 3, history professor Sydney Watts offers an illuminating essay titled "The Spiritual Leadership of Madame Guyon and Madame de Maintenon under Louis XIV." Watts focuses on the spiritual leadership of two elite French women, Madame Guyon and Madame de Maintenon, who dedicated their lives to instill in young women a desire for virtue and pure love—spiritual goals that eclipsed the subordinate place women held under patriarchal authority. During the late seventeenth- and early eighteenth centuries, religious identity among French female elites was often caught between the political and ecclesiastic tensions under royal absolutism and the personal demands put upon women as forms of movable property as much as ossified vessels of aristocratic beauty. As the Counter-Reformation brought with it a place for women to engage their intellectual faculties in the salon, many sought new ways to cultivate their spiritual lives by focusing on questions of religious piety and morals.

In chapter 4, University of Richmond School of Law Professor Henry L. Chambers Jr. contributes a cogent essay titled "The President as Spiritual Leader: Pardons, Punishment, Forgiveness, Mercy and Justice." Chambers explores the power of pardon and how this power gives the president (or governor in some cases) the authority, but not the obligation, to exercise spiritual leadership regarding punishment and justice. Chambers concludes his essay saying that although the president does not have the obligation to exercise spiritual leadership, he can be judged poorly for failing to exercise spiritual leadership in this context. In chapter 5, George R. Goethals from the Jepson School of Leadership Studies offers a fascinating piece titled "Reconciliation and Its Failures: Reconstruction to Jim Crow." Goethals writes about forgiveness, reconciliation, and justice in the decades following the Civil War. Abraham Lincoln sought reconciliation with the South and both freedom and justice for former slaves. Achieving both reconciliation and justice proved to be impossible during and after Reconstruction, leading to the Jim Crow era of the early twentieth century. Reconciliation fared better than justice for 100 years. In the last 50 years, a measure of justice has been achieved.

Chapter 6 concludes our section on historical approaches to spiritual leadership. In this chapter, David D. Burhans, chaplain emeritus of the University of Richmond, writes a reflective essay that he aptly calls "The Pursuit of Wonder. Here Burhans offers an institutional and personal model of spiritual leadership in a unique university setting. Burhans provides a 30-year historical account of highlights in the creation and evolution of the University of Richmond Chaplaincy. This chapter recounts details of the personal and professional growth of the university chaplain, "the pastor, preacher and spiritual leader of the University community." Burhans's chapter contains one of our favorite passages in the volume: "Wonder just might be another name for God. The title of this chapter, The Pursuit of Wonder, may be a worthy human goal. But the ultimate truth is, Wonder is in pursuit of us."

The second half of our volume, focusing on contemporary approaches to spiritual leadership. It opens with chapter 7, authored by Elisabeth Rose Gruner, professor of English, and is titled "Leading through Reading in Contemporary Young Adult Fantasy by Philip Pullman and Terry Pratchett." In this stimulating chapter, Gruner analyzes sacred and other texts in the *His Dark Materials* trilogy by Philip Pullman and the Tiffany Aching novels by Terry Pratchett. She argues that reading enables moral and spiritual development—a development that emphasizes storytelling and caregiving. Storytelling and caregiving in fact turn out to be related gifts, elements of a kind of feminist leadership that has its roots in critical reading.

In chapter 8, Jennifer L. Erkulwater, professor of political science, writes a thoughtful piece titled "Engaged Spirituality and Egalitarianism in US Social Welfare Policy." Erkulwater examines, from the lens of American history, the ways in which faith has served as a staging ground for mass movements on behalf of social justice. The contemporary discourse of faith and faith-based organizations, however, buttresses neoliberal policies that risk undermining democratic citizenship and moral outrage at pervasive social and economic inequalities. Erkulwater reviews the emergence of religious neoliberalism in social welfare policy since 1990. Next, chapter 9, authored by Thad Williamson of the Jepson School of Leadership Studies, presents an inspiring essay titled "A Change Is Gonna Come": Spiritual Leadership for Social Change in the United States." In this chapter, Williamson considers the role of religious faith in leadership for social change, with a particular focus on leadership for racial justice in the United States. The chapter shows how religious commitments were integral, not incidental, to the leadership of Harriet Beecher Stowe in the antislavery movement and Martin Luther King Jr. in the civil rights movement. The final section considers the implications of these examples for the current historical era, in which present-day leaders for social change can no longer confidently appeal to widely shared religious beliefs in building coalitions for dramatic social change.

In chapter 10, Craig T. Kocher, the university chaplain at Richmond, writes a stimulating essay titled "Living a Life of Consequence: How Not to Chase a Fake Rabbit." Kocher observes how talented young people in the United States find the process of making meaning and discovering a life path to be confusing and overwhelming. His chapter describes the cultural context in which young people are entering adulthood and then narrates possible ways for them to develop a deeper understanding of themselves, what they are to do professionally, and how they are to live with integrity. The chapter grounds this process in Craig Kocher's own understanding of spiritual leadership. Next, in chapter 11, Scott Allison, professor of psychology, and his student Gwendolyn C. Setterberg write a psychologically interesting piece titled "Suffering and Sacrifice: Individual and Collective Benefits, and Implications for Leadership." Allison and Setterberg review the ways in which suffering and sacrifice provide emotional, behavioral, and spiritual benefits to human beings. They propose six principles of suffering, drawing from both ancient and modern spiritual traditions and a large body of psychological research on the determinants of happiness and mental health. Their conclusion is that suffering is the soil from which exemplary leadership germinates.

Wrapping up our section on contemporary perspectives is chapter 12, written by Richard L. Morrill, Distinguished University Professor of Ethics. Morrill's outstanding essay is titled "Leadership, Spirituality and Values in a Secular Age: Insights from Charles Taylor and James MacGregor Burns." In this chapter, Morrill traces the thought of two eminent scholars concerning the place of values in leadership and in moral experience. Burns, the historian and leadership theorist. places a commanding emphasis on the place of foundational values such as equality and liberty in his concept of transforming leadership, and Taylor, the philosopher and historian of ideas, examines the centrality of moral experience in the human quest for personal and spiritual fullness. Morrill draws on themes from the perspectives of both thinkers in showing the centrality of values in the practice of leadership.

This edited volume concludes with a thoughtful Afterword by Richmond's chancellor, E. Bruce Heilman. We do not exaggerate when we say that none of the editors of this volume, nor any of its contributors, would have found their way to Richmond without the groundbreaking vision and accomplishments of Bruce Heilman. Some of this visionary thinking is described in David D. Burhans's chapter in this volume, but there is much more to Heilman's remarkable stewardship than can be told in a single page, chapter, or book. Heilman's leadership at our university has not just been spiritual; it has been profound and almost mythic in its sweep.

Overall, we hope you enjoy this initial effort of ours to present a rough landscape of spiritual leadership that centers on a number of spiritual principles that are fundamental to effective and inspired leadership. These principles emphasize the values of love, forgiveness, pardon, meaning, purpose, wonder, compassion, humility, trust, sacrifice, courage, justice, caregiving, equality, and liberty. In a world that produces more than its share of disturbed leaders bent on the destructive pursuits of conquest, genocide, and oppression, we pause to rejoice that there are ample gifted and enlightened individuals whose leadership has embodied the most exquisite qualities of humanity. We dedicate this book to all these awakened leaders—past, present, and future.

References

Allison, Scott T., and George R. Goethals. 2011. *Heroes: What They Do and Why We Need Them.* New York: Oxford University Press.

Allison, Scott T., and George R. Goethals. 2013. *Heroic Leadership: An Influence Taxonomy of 100 Exceptional Individuals.* New York: Routledge.

Astrow, Alan, Christina M. Pulchalski, and Daniel Sulmasy. 2001. "Religion, Spirituality, and Health Care: Social, Ethical, and Practical Considerations." *American Journal of Medicine* 110: 283–287.

Benefiel, Margaret. 2005. *Soul at Work: Spiritual Leadership in Organizations.* New York: Seabury Books.

Burns, James MacGregor. 1978. *Leadership.* New York: Harper and Row.

Campbell, Joseph. 1949. *The Hero with a Thousand Faces.* Princeton, NJ: Princeton University Press.

Campbell, Joseph. 1991. *The Power of Myth.* New York: Anchor Books.

Campbell, Joseph. 2013. *Goddesses: Mysteries of the Feminine Divine.* New World Library.

Doohan, Leonard. 2007. *Spiritual Leadership: The Quest for Integrity.* Mahwah, NJ: Paulist Press.

Emmons, Robert A. 2000. "Is Spirituality an Intelligence?" *The International Journal for the Psychology of Religion* 10: 27–34.

Fry, Louis. W., and Melissa Nisiewicz. 2012. *Maximizing the Triple Bottom Line through Spiritual Leadership.* Palo Alto, CA: Stanford Business Books.

Gardner, Howard. 1995. *Leading Minds: An Anatomy of Leadership.* New York: Basic Books.

Goethals, George R., and Scott T. Allison. 2012. "Making Heroes: The Construction of Courage, Competence, and Virtue." *Advances in Experimental Social Psychology* 46: 183–235.

Goethals, George R., and Scott T. Allison. 2014. "Kings and Charisma, Lincoln and Leadership: An Evolutionary Perspective." In George Goethals, Scott Allison, Roderick Kramer, and David Messick, eds., *Conceptions of Leadership: Enduring Ideas and Emerging Insights.* New York: Palgrave Macmillan.

Goethals, George R., and Scott T. Allison. 2016. "Transforming Motives and Mentors: The Heroic Leadership of James MacGregor Burns." Unpublished manuscript.

Haidt, Jonathan. 2003. "Elevation and the Positive Psychology of Morality." In Corey Lee M. Keyes and J. Haidt, eds., *Flourishing: Positive Psychology and the Life Well-Lived.* Washington DC: American Psychological Association.

Kaiser, Leland. 2000. "Spirituality and the Physician Executive: Reconciling the Inner Self and the Business of Health Care." *The Physician Executive* 26(2). March/April.

Love, Patrick, and Donna Talbot. 1999. "Defining Spiritual Development: A Missing Consideration for Student Affairs." *NASPA Journal* 37: 361–376.

Maslow, Abraham H. 1943. "A Theory of Human Motivation." *Psychological Review* 50: 370–396.

Miller, Lisa. J. 2012. *The Oxford Handbood of Psychology and Spirituality.* New York: Oxford University Press.

Mohr, Wanda. 2006. "Spiritual Issues in Psychiatric Care." *Perspectives in Psychiatric Care* 42(3): 174–183.

Paloutzian, Raymond. F., and Crystal Park, eds. 2014. *The Handbook of the Psychology of Religion and Spirituality.* New York: Guilford Press.

Rohr, Richard. 2014. *Eager to Love: The Alternative Way of Francis of Assisi.* Cincinnati, OH: Franciscan Media.

Wigglesworth, Cindy. 2006. "Why Spiritual Intelligence Is Essential to Mature Leadership." *Integral Leadership Review* 6(3).

Zohar, Danah. 1997. *ReWiring the Corporate Brain.* San Francisco, CA: Berrett-Koehler Publishers.

PART I

Historical Exemplars of Spiritual Leadership

CHAPTER ONE

Women's Leadership in the Early Church: Possibilities and Pushbacks

L. STEPHANIE COBB

During the summer of 2010, I studied with 15 other scholars in Tunisia, funded by the National Endowment for the Humanities. We studied two early Christian texts from North Africa: *The Passion of Perpetua and Felicitas* and Augustine's *Confessions*. Although I was excited about traveling to Carthage, I was also nervous. My concerns were partially related to dress. One guidebook gave this advice, "A woman entering a mosque should be covered from her neck to her ankles and wrists; she should also cover her hair and wear a skirt, not trousers, and baggy rather than tight clothes...Women will find that following this dress code on the street will reduce sexual harassment, and make it easier to appeal for support from passers-by if it does occur" (Jacobs 2009, 50). This guidebook underscores the probabilities of sexual harassment by suggesting that female readers learn the Arabic word *shooma* ["shame on you"] so they can shout this at any man making unwanted advances. Another guidebook states succinctly that women "should keep their arms and legs covered" (Hole et al. 2007, 36). Thus the only authoritative voices I had access to before my trip—my guidebooks—suggested that dressing modestly was not enough; women must be covered from head to foot or risk harassment.

African summers are, to state the obvious, hot. But wanting neither to offend nor be harassed, I purchased long-sleeved blouses, long trousers and skirts, and scarves. Imagine my surprise when I arrived and saw Tunisian women in short skirts and tank tops, short-sleeved t-shirts, and short, strapless sundresses. The women of Tunis did not look any different from the women I saw every day in my neighborhood in New York City. In the capital, at least, people were more tolerant of women's sartorial choices than the guidebooks suggested. While there were women who wore traditional dress, it seemed to me that in this case, the guidebooks perpetuated a caricature of Islamic homogeneity. My pre-travel reservations about Tunisia clashed with my personal experiences: what I perceived as authoritative texts (my guidebooks) portrayed women's lives in a homogenous way, while my observations told a different story. There are, of course, caveats to my experience: as an outsider looking in, I had no access to women's motivations for their clothing decisions. But even my superficial experiences told a story very different from that of my guidebooks; it was a story of individuality rather than homogeneity. The discourses were discordant: Are Tunisian women subordinated, even invisible? Or are they independent and autonomous?

Women's legal rights in Tunisia have been heralded as a model of human rights in Africa. In the years immediately following Tunisia's independence from France in 1956, Prime Minister (later President) Habib Bourguiba sought to establish Tunisia as a secularized Muslim state. To this end, he instituted a number of reforms, many of which affected women. Indeed, one of the titles given to Bourguiba was "liberator of women," an epithet so central to his memory that it is engraved on the door of his mausoleum (Bradley 2010, 58). The "Tunisian Code of Personal Status" that took effect on January 1, 1957 abolished polygamy (I.18); instituted court divorce (II.30); raised the marriage age for women from 13 to 15 (I.5; it is now 18, but the average marriage age for women today is 25–29); and established the full legal equality of men and women (Sfeir 1957). The last of these reforms ushered in several related rights for women, including the guarantee of effective birth control options—including abortion (Bradley 2010, 59)—paid maternity leave (DeJong 2012, 254), and free and compulsory education for both boys and girls up to the age of 16 (Yagoubi 2004, 156).

There is, though, another side to this story. I observed many social spaces where women were absent: cafes and bars regularly had only male clientele. According to a 2013 Brookings Institution report, although 60 percent of university graduates are female, they comprise only 27 percent of the workforce (Boughzala 2013, 11). Thus there appears to be resistance to accepting women as an equal part of the labor force. Because so many women are pursuing higher education, they are marrying later, which has led to a decline in birth rates; birth control availability also contributes to this decline. Social concerns about the rising numbers of "spinsters," coupled with the dwindling family size, appear to have revived interest among conservatives in reinstating polygamy (Bouachrine 2014, 104). The sex-segregated cafes, the low employment rate among educated women, and the occasional calls for reinstating polygamy are indicators of continuing social challenges to women and women's roles in Tunisian society. If the full story of Tunisia's women is not told in the guidebooks, neither is it found by rehearsing legal rights. A more comprehensive view of women in Tunisia must account for legal rights and how others—either individuals or communities—push back against those rights, and why.

Thus, I encountered three sources of evidence for women's experiences in Tunisia: first the authoritative texts (e.g., my guidebooks or the Tunisian law codes) that appear to describe women's lives; second, personal, "lived" experiences that may complicate the picture painted by authoritative texts; and third experiences or observations of pushback—understood as either active or passive resistance—against women.

From Tunisia to Ancient Christianity

As women's experience in Tunisia can only be sketched through careful consideration of a constellation of resources—authoritative sources, "rights," lived experiences, and opposition—so also, women's experience in early Christianity must be examined through a variety of lenses. Christian tradition recognizes the New Testament as an authoritative text that, in part, describes ways women participated in the church. Like my Tunisian guidebook, though, its descriptions of women are often conflated and simplified: the New Testament—comprising 27 books, written by 15 or 16 different authors between ca. 50 CE and 120 CE—does not have *one* position on women; it has many, sometimes conflicting, positions. Moreover, the New Testament texts were not the only ones deemed instructive by early Christians. If we widen our search, we find that life "on the ground" in certain communities was vastly different from what some canonical texts suggest. Equally important, our widened search and attentiveness to diverse positions may reveal ways that women's status was (and is) contested.

Two Case Studies: Perpetua and Thecla as Christian Leaders

Women's roles in the early church are often described in stark terms: either there was a golden age of egalitarianism at the beginning that devolved into sex-differentiated roles, or the earliest texts reflect an original misogyny that women have been fighting for 2,000 years (Coon 1997, xix; Cobb 2009, 380–381). The evidence, however, is more nuanced than these polarized positions allow. To highlight the complexity of women's leadership in the early church, my discussion will follow a reverse chronology—from the second and third centuries working back into the first—because our resources are richer in the later centuries and will help illuminate the earlier texts. I begin, then, with two women—Perpetua and Thecla—whose stories illustrate the diverse positions and concerns—the possibilities and pushbacks—regarding women's leadership in the early church.

Perpetua was a Christian in Roman North Africa—perhaps she lived in Carthage itself or perhaps a few kilometers away in Thuburbo Minus. Perpetua was a courageous woman who chose death over apostasy: she was martyred in the year 203 CE and her story is presented as an example for others. We know about her from a text—the *Passion of Perpetua*—that purports to be her prison diary (Cobb 2008, 94–96). According to Augustine, some people accepted this text as authoritative scripture (*De natura et origine animae* I.10.12). In the *Passion,* Perpetua is a leader: she received and interprets visions on behalf of the group, and she intercedes with the authorities on their behalf (4; 16; 18). In one of the visions, for instance, Perpetua sees her deceased pagan brother standing near a fountain, but he is unable to reach the water (7.1–10). Pitying him, she successfully intercedes on his behalf (8.1–4). It is unclear exactly how this is accomplished: Does Perpetua have the power to forgive his sins and, thus, usher him into paradise? (Trumbower 2001, 84) Or, does the water imagery of the vision suggest baptism, which saves him? (Cramer 1993, 83) Either way, the vision evokes Perpetua's power and authority. Similarly, her leadership role within the group is displayed when she rejects the pagans' commands that the Christians be dressed up as priests and priestesses of pagan gods (18.4–6). God speaks to the imprisoned Christians through Perpetua and Perpetua speaks to the persecutors on behalf of her fellow Christians. She is their leader.

The story of Thecla is embedded in the *Acts of Paul*. According to this second-century text, Thecla, a pagan, was engaged. One day, she overheard the apostle Paul preaching a message of strict and uncompromising sexual continence (5–6). Thecla immediately converted, broke her engagement, and became a devotee of Paul (8–10). Thecla was not only a disciple, she was also an apostle: her steadfast faith—even in the midst of persecution—converted others, and Paul sent her out to "teach the word of God" (39, 41). Thecla is cast as an early Christian leader.

Both women, however, experienced familial and social pushback. Perpetua's father begs—even threatens—her to renounce her faith, at one point coming at her "as if to gouge out" her eyes. She endured several bouts of torture before finally dying at the hands of a young gladiator. After Thecla's conversion, she was arrested numerous times and each time, the authorities attempted—unsuccessfully—to execute her: she was to be burned at the stake, but a storm came up suddenly and the rain extinguished the flames (21–22); she was thrown to the beasts, but all the women in the amphitheater—moved by Thecla's beauty— threw their bouquets into the arena, which produced such strong perfumes that the beasts were knocked out and Thecla escaped unharmed (35); in another encounter, a female lion attacked not Thecla but a bear and a male lion, thus saving the Christian (33). In yet another episode, Thecla—as yet unbaptized—was thrown into a pool with killer seals. She took the opportunity to baptize herself and then lightning struck the pool, killing the seals before they could harm her (34). It is this last episode—in which Thecla baptizes herself—that is most closely associated with Thecla's leadership: some in the early church understood her act as setting a precedent for women's clerical roles.

The stories of Perpetua and Thecla are rhetorically effective because they divide the world neatly into "Christian" and "monster." The physical harm that is threatened—and in Perpetua's case, accomplished— against these women comes at the hands of pagans who are stock characters representing irrationality and cruelty. Reading audiences are expected to align with the heroines, not the death-seeking masses. Would we, we are to ask, have the courage to do what Perpetua and Thecla did? Do we believe in anything enough to die for it? In certain circles of the early church, these stories were much beloved, and the cults of Sts. Perpetua and Thecla were important in the church. But both texts also challenged the church. The pushback against Perpetua and Thecla is narratively cast as physical—in the guise of pagan mobs— but it was also subtly and effectively accomplished through the pens of Christianity's theologians.

Thecla was a problem for church leaders who were concerned with women's clerical roles. Tertullian, a third-century North African Christian, was particularly vexed by women who used Thecla to assert their right to baptize. Tertullian writes,

But if certain Acts of Paul, which are falsely so named, claim the example of Thecla for allowing women to teach and to baptize, let men know that in Asia the presbyter who compiled that document, thinking to add of his own to Paul's reputation, was found out, and though he professed he had done it for love of Paul, was deposed from his position. How could we believe that Paul should give a female power to teach and to baptize, when he did not allow a woman even to learn by her own right? "Let them keep silence," he says, "and ask their husbands at home." (*On Baptism* XVII.5; trans. Evans 1964, 36–37)

We will return to these "Pauline" teachings that Tertullian mentions, but his larger point is that women were claiming Thecla as authorizing their own clerical activities. In rejecting this precedent, Tertullian argues that the text itself is a forgery (which it is) and is incompatible with Paul's "true" teachings (which is less certain). Thus the ancient traditions involving Thecla simultaneously attest to women's roles in churches and to pushback against those roles. Thus, Tertullian's position must be recognized as a polemical one; he employs prescriptive language that pushes back against the rights women had asserted in some churches.

Tertullian did not have the last word about Thecla. As her story came to be used, however, he would have little reason to condemn it. Her shrines were centers of Christian asceticism, and her story was read as inspirational literature for Christian ascetics (Davis 2001). Ambrose, bishop of Milan, for example, commended Thecla to his sister as a worthy example to follow (*On Virginity*, II.3). Over time, then, Thecla's leadership position was eclipsed by a form of women's spirituality that the church deemed more appropriate: no longer a precedent for women's clerical roles, she became an exemplar of Christian asceticism.

The literary tradition emerging from the story of Perpetua is equally enlightening. The fifth-century Christian bishop Augustine, for instance, strenuously rejected the idea that Perpetua effected her pagan brother's salvation through intercession with God (*De Anima* I.12 [X]). His opposition is, of course, evidence that certain Christians claimed precisely this. Augustine's sermons on Perpetua also reflect discomfort with Perpetua's behavior toward her father. The *Passion* contains several episodes in which Perpetua refuses to obey her father, as she was legally obligated to do (3.1; 5.2; 6.2, 5; Cobb 2008, 97). Thus, although Perpetua might be a good example of a woman willing to die for her faith, she was a miserable example of an obedient Christian daughter. Augustine worked hard to justify Perpetua's untraditional behavior:

> Saint Perpetua...answered her father with such moderation, that she neither violated the commandment by which honor is owed to parents, nor yielded to the tricks which the real enemy was practicing....She, though, did indeed grieve at the insult offered her aged parent; and while she did not give him her consent, she kept her affection for him undiminished. What she hated in him was his folly, not his nature; his unbelief, not her roots. Thus she earned all the greater glory by resolutely rejecting the bad advice of such a beloved father, considering that she could not see him thrashed without feeling the pain herself. (281.2)

So Augustine reclaims Perpetua by rewriting the original text. He attempts to differentiate appropriate disregard from inappropriate dishonor. The defiant and disrespectful Perpetua of the *Passion* becomes, through Augustine's pen, a discerning woman who recognizes the devil's tricks. Through his creative interpretation, Augustine rejects the Perpetua of the *Passion:* whereas the martyr account describes her autonomy and freedom, Augustine uses her to illustrate ideal Christian gender and family relations. Just as Tertullian pushed back against Thecla, so also Augustine pushed back against Perpetua. Both women—through ensuing theological traditions—were domesticated in an effort to teach particular values to Christian audiences.

Opposition to Perpetua and Thecla is embedded in the narratives—pagans persecute Christians—and in theological reflections on the texts—male Christian leaders rejected these women's leadership roles in the church. But is there further opportunity, I wonder, for pushback: Can modern readers challenge traditions that pit Christian women against family and society? There are troubling aspects to these women's stories that we would be remiss not to acknowledge. Although the stories relate women's piety, there is also a dark side to them: they both depict women rending the nuclear family. While the point is clear—Christianity offers a new, spiritual family that is more meaningful than one's earthly family—this is, nonetheless, a position that has real consequences for those left behind. Thecla's mother is so upset about her daughter's action, which rips apart the social fabric, that she exclaims publicly that her own daughter should be burned at the stake as an example to other young girls (20). Thecla's *mother* initiates the call for execution. It is easy to hear this and think that this is a monstrous woman. But the episode is narratively and contextually complex. The text tells us that Thecla's mother, her fiancé, and the entire household wept and mourned over Thecla's decision (10). These characters are not callous: they love Thecla deeply and are distraught at the prospect of losing her. Imagine, moreover, the vulnerability of the widow whose daughter has abandoned her responsibilities to family. Thecla has tossed her mother aside, leaving her to the mercy of strangers. From this perspective, it is Thecla—not her mother—whose actions seem heartless.

Perpetua's father, in one encounter, responds similarly to Thecla's mother: he comes toward Perpetua as if to gouge out her eyes (3.3). But later, he comes to her in sorrow and begs her to have pity on his old age, on her family, and on her child who cannot live without her (5.3). While these parents react to their daughters' decisions differently, the problem is the same: the family, the foundation of society, is not simply being rejected but utterly demolished. Thecla's mother will be left without any social support, and Perpetua's young son (who is still nursing) will die without her. Neither woman shows concern about the consequences of their actions on those lives. Perhaps the collateral damage depicted in these stories is too quickly dismissed when we marvel at the women's faith.

Physically, pagans, including the women's families, push back. Narratively, later Christians push back. Perhaps modern readers should do some pushback of their own. Do we accept the world-negating, society-crippling message inherent in the texts? Both Thecla and Perpetua are depicted as leaders in their communities, but their leadership comes at significant cost both to themselves and to those who love them. Importantly, the stories of these women are not unique in the early church. Our earliest Christian literature—Pauline epistles—depict women who held positions of authority in their communities and whose authority was challenged.

Women's Leadership in the New Testament

1 Timothy is widely regarded by scholars as written within the Pauline tradition but not by Paul himself (Brown 1997, 662–668). If scholars are right about the authorial attribution, then Tertullian's rejection of the Thecla story as pseudonymous is ironic because the rejection is itself based on a pseudonymous Pauline letter. 1 Timothy's teachings about women differ from Paul's genuine letters. Throughout the undisputed Pauline corpus, women's authority is positively described. In 1 Corinthians 7 Paul argues that continence is the best course for

Christians, but he offers marriage as a concession: "it is better to marry," he famously asserts, "than to burn" (7:9). Sexual abstinence is the highest form of Christian life, Paul asserts; marriage is good but not as good. Scholars suggest that the ascetic movement was particularly beneficial to women since it freed them from the legal constraints and (often emotional and physical) hardships of marriage (Clark 1981). Although Paul's sexual ethic was not part of a feminist agenda, it nevertheless had real consequences for women's positions within the church. Paul, furthermore, argues for the equality of men and women in marriage: the husband has authority over his wife's body, and the wife has authority over her husband's body (1 Cor 7:3–4). This is a sexual ethic concerned with equality not domination. When a married couple commit to continence in order to devote themselves to prayer, they must do so together, willingly, and for only a set period of time (1 Cor 7:5).

After Paul's death, however, the form of Christianity that came to be accepted as "orthodox" largely abandoned Paul's teachings on celibacy, favoring instead marriage and family. The author of 1 Timothy, writing in Paul's name, argues: "Now the Spirit expressly says that in later times some will renounce the faith by paying attention to deceitful spirits and teachings of demons, through the hypocrisy of liars whose consciences are seared with a hot iron. They forbid marriage and demand abstinence from foods..." (1 Tim 4:1–3). Whereas Paul hoped Christians would follow in his footsteps and commit to continence (1 Cor 7:7), the author of 1 Timothy labels "demonic" this very teaching. The differences in sexual ethics between Paul and the later Christian community that claimed his authority, however, extend further. The author of 1 Timothy articulates a unique path to salvation for women: they are saved through childbirth (1 Tim 2:15). The difference is stark: since Paul hoped that women would not marry and, thus, not give birth, he could not logically have tied women's salvation to childbirth. But 1 Timothy does precisely that. Many of the opportunities Paul's sexual ethics made available to women were challenged in post-Pauline churches where women were subordinated, differentiated, and silenced.

It is this later tradition that influences what many Christians think not only about Paul's views of women, but also of the New Testament's position as a whole. And there are good reasons for this belief. Throughout the Pauline corpus, women are praised for their leadership skills, so 1 Corinthians 14:34–36 should strike the attentive reader as peculiar: "As in all the churches of the saints, women should be silent in the churches. For they are not permitted to speak, but should be subordinate, as the law also says. If there is anything they desire to know, let them ask their husbands at home. For it is shameful for a woman to speak in church." On the one hand, Paul writes: "There is no longer male nor female" (Gal 3:28) and "To each is given the manifestation of the Spirit for the common good" (1 Cor 12:7). On the other hand, women must be silent and subordinate to men. How can Paul imply in 1 Corinthians 11:5 that women may be given the gift of prophecy, but in 1 Corinthians 14:34–35 imply they cannot use it (because it requires speaking)? Precisely because it is peculiarly *un*-Pauline, many scholars are convinced that these verses were not originally in this letter and were not, in fact, penned by Paul at all but are, instead, later scribal emendations (Murphy-O'Connor 2009, 266–267). The similarities between 1 Corinthians 14:33b-36 and 1 Timothy 2:11–12—"Let a woman learn in silence with all submissiveness. I permit no woman to teach or to have authority over men; she is to keep silent"—suggest a relationship between these texts: perhaps a scribe wished 1 Corinthians to agree with 1 Timothy and so added these verses to the original letter. Scholars have also observed that 1 Corinthians 14:33b-36 interrupts the flow of the argument: the passage proceeds more logically when these two verses are omitted.

The New Testament injunction for women to be silent in the church is well known, but it is merely one position articulated by the early church, and it had stiff competition. The diversity of opinions regarding women's leadership in Christian tradition necessitates careful reflection on how one appropriates received traditions. Within the Pauline corpus (broadly defined), women are exhorted to use the gifts of the spirit for the benefit of the church, and they are exhorted to be silent; women are taught to value sexual continence, and they are taught that they are saved through childbirth. The positions are irreconcilable; they sit discordantly within the same authoritative text—the New Testament—representing different communities' ideas of right behavior.

Women's Leadership in the New Testament: The Afterlife

There is ample evidence of women's leadership in the early church; there is also ample evidence of pushback against it. But assertions of and challenges to women's leadership in the church are not merely an ancient phenomenon, of course. Modern scholars too have struggled with the spiritual leadership of early Christian women. Indeed, the modern scholarly pushback examined in this section is heir to the long history of obfuscating, rewriting, or outright rejecting women's leadership roles described above. Thus, the cases of Phoebe and Junia—singled out for praise by Paul in Romans 16—illustrate how the erasure of women's leadership from the church's history has influenced modern scholars.

In the conclusion of his Letter to the Romans, Paul sends greetings to a number of individuals. This is not an unusual practice in ancient letter writing, and Paul's letters often contain such final greetings (Weima 2010). What is interesting in Romans 16 is the prominence of women in the list. Ten women are mentioned by name, among them Phoebe and Junia. Paul describes Phoebe with the noun *diakonos* (16:1), translated "servant," "minister," or "deacon." This Greek word occurs often in the New Testament, and before the development of a clerical hierarchy, it referred to someone who served in some capacity. But in terms of the Christian priesthood, *diakonos* is a "deacon." Thus, in 1 Timothy 3 when the author describes the qualities of a male church leader, *diakonos* is consistently translated "deacon" or "office of the deacon." Of greater interest than the translation of the term are the stakes in applying it to a woman. In the King James Version (KJV), when Phoebe is called *diakonos,* the term is translated "servant." But when Paul describes Phoebe as a *diakonos* of God, he invokes a term that is equally applicable to himself. Indeed, when the term is applied to Paul, the KJV consistently translates it as "minister" (1 Cor 3:5; 2 Cor 11:23; Eph 3:7). Whatever translation is preferred, it is, philologically speaking, appropriate for both Paul and Phoebe. In the hands of certain English translators, however, the status of Phoebe in the church—whatever that may have been—seems to have sparked a certain amount of pushback, resulting in a gender-driven translation. Without a robust history of women's positions in the early church, translators have been unable to see the bias of their work. While Paul, Apollos, and other men may be "ministers" or even "deacons," Phoebe is a "servant" (Gaventa 1998). These translation choices are informed by assumptions about women's clerical roles.

Junia has a more complex textual/sexual history. Paul refers to her, alongside Andronicus, as "foremost among the apostles" (16:7). In this case, it is not the title—"apostle"—that has been disputed, but the sex of the individual to whom it is applied. Paul writes the name *Junian,* which can either be a form of the feminine name "Junia" or a form of the masculine name "Junias," depending solely on where one places the accent (Haines-Eitzen 2012, 91; Epp 2005, 23).

For the first 19 centuries of Christian history there was almost unanimous agreement that Paul wrote about a female apostle named Junia.

All of the earliest translations of the New Testament preserve the feminine form of the name (Thorley 1996, 20). The fourth-century archbishop of Constantinople, John Chrysostom, writes this about Junia and
Andronicus: "To be an apostle is something great. But to be outstanding
among the apostles—just think what a wonderful song of praise that is!
They were outstanding on the basis of their works and virtuous actions.
Indeed, how great the wisdom of this woman must have been that she
was even deemed worthy of the title apostle" (*In Ep. Rom.* Hom. 31.2).
The earliest extant commentary on Romans—that by Origen—also
assumes Junia was a woman; so, too, did Jerome and Peter Abelard.

The first time a masculine form of the name was posited appears
to be in the writings of Aegidius of Rome in the fourteenth century
(Brooten 1977, 141). In 1552 Luther, too, opted for the masculine form
in his German translation (Thorley 1996, 18). In English translations,
the tide began to turn against Junia in the late nineteenth century:
the *Revised Version* (1881) made Junia into a man, Junias. The most
decisive shift, however, came in the critical editions of the Greek
New Testament. Both of the most widely used scholarly editions of
the Greek New Testament—Nestle Aland (N/NA) and United Bible
Society (BF/UBS)—had, in their earlier printings, used the feminine
form. But in the 1927 version of the Nestle text (N^{13}), Junia (f) was
moved to a footnote, and Junias (m) was placed in the text as the "most
original" reading. In 1979 (NA^{26}) even the footnote was removed (Epp
2005, 49; Schulz 2008, 270). Thus, a New Testament scholar relying
on the Nestle Aland 1979 critical edition of the Greek New Testament
had no option but to read the masculine form of the name. In spite of
almost 2,000 years of tradition, Junia was now a man.

A similar trajectory can be traced in the other major critical edition
of the Greek New Testament, this one produced by the United Bible
Society. In 1958 (BF^2), it changed the reading from Junia to Junias, but
footnoted the feminine form as an alternative (Epp 2005, 53; Schulz
2008, 271). The editions printed from 1966 to 1993 (UBS^1-UBS^3)
claimed that the masculine form was "virtually certain" (Thorley 1996,
27). Only in 1998 (UBS^4 and NA^{27}) did these two critical editions,
used by virtually all New Testament scholars, reinstate Junia as the
most original reading of Romans 16:7.

The shift from Junia (f) to Junias (m) is more problematic than it
may at first seem because in choosing how to accent the proper noun
all things are not equal. Although Junia is a common Roman name,
Junias is wholly unattested (Epp 2005, xi, 23; Brooten 1977, 142). Thus
the committees who chose the masculine form chose a name that is

unattested in the ancient world. This suggests that the change in the printed form reflects a prejudice about the nature of apostleship: if only men were apostles, then *JUNIAN* must be a masculine name. In some cases, the gender-based assumptions are explicit: F. W. Gingrich, for instance, concedes that, while grammatically possible, the feminine form "seems inherently less probable, partly because the person is referred to as an apostle" (Gingrich 1962, 2:1026–1027). Lientzmann argues that the narrative context rules out the feminine form (Lietzmann 1971, 125). Likewise, the 1988 German edition of the standard New Testament Greek lexicon, Bauer-Aland (6th ed), states that the translation "Junia…is probably ruled out by the context" (Thorley 1996, 27). There is, however, nothing in Romans 16 to confirm or reject the apostle's sex. Thus, Epp argues that the shift from Junia to Junias was ideological: the male apostle Junias was the creation of exegetes who "found it difficult to admit that a woman in earliest Christianity could have been an apostle" (Epp 2006, 125). Brooten states poignantly: "because a woman could not have been an apostle, the woman who is here called apostle could not have been a woman" (Brooten, 1977, 142). While no facts had changed, the social context of the editors had. As was the case with Phoebe, therefore, the example of Junia illustrates an authoritative text that preserves evidence of women's roles, which is met with resistance by modern translators.

But what might it mean for Junia to be called "apostle"? The term, as used by Paul—applied to himself, to James, and apparently to Andronicus and Junia—was not lightly bestowed upon an individual, but neither did it reflect an exclusive and closed membership in "the Twelve." Two things appear to have been requisite of the title "apostle" in Pauline discourse: first, having encountered the resurrected Christ and, second, being given a commission to ministry (Brock 2003, 3; Brooten 1977, 143). Thus, the title in Paul's hands referred not only to the past but also to the present: "it concerned authority in the church of his own day" and was open to any whom Jesus chose in the future (Brooten 1977, 143). It was not a closed group but a dynamic one that could serve the ongoing needs of the Christian movement. And Junia—a woman—was foremost among them.

Junia may be the only woman explicitly given the title "apostle" in the New Testament, but she was not the only woman who fulfilled such a role. Some in the early church referred to Mary Magdalene as the "apostle to the apostles" (Schüssler Fiorenza 1975, 22). That is not the only thing Mary has been called, of course…Of all the women in early Christian tradition, none has fallen victim to the ravages of

rewritten history like Mary Magdalene. The invention of her bad reputation is well established—a combination of conflating New Testament
Marys and creative arguments from silence—but it is not the primary
concern here (Haskins 2005). More relevant is the possibility that
Mary Magdalene and other women were part of a circle of disciples
who followed Jesus during his ministry and who served as apostles
(in deed if not in name) to the early church. The Evangelists agree
that Mary Magdalene was an early follower of Jesus (Mk 15:40–41;
Matt 27:55–56; Lk 8:3; 23:49). Luke notes that Jesus traveled with the
12 and with a group of women—Mary, Joanna, Susanna, and others. These women "served them from out of their belongings" (8:3).
Three aspects of Luke's report are worth noting. First, although he sets
up two parallel groups of followers—men and women—he does not
explicitly subordinate one to the other. Second, he uses the verb *diako-
neo* to describe the women's activities: they are ministering. And third,
there is a textual variant relating to the object of the women's ministry:
Do they serve "them" (*autois;* i.e., Jesus and the disciples) or do they
serve "him" (*autō;* i.e., Jesus alone)? At stake in this textual variant is
the nature of the women's ministry. Many scholars suggest that the
women performed "traditional" chores of hospitality—such as food
service—for the men as they carried out the difficult tasks of itinerant
ministry (Witherington 1979, 247). In a more generous reading, Luke
praises the women as benefactors but not as leaders (Brock 2003, 33).
But Karris, building on the earlier work by Ricci, suggests that this is
a misrepresentation of the women's ministerial role. He translates the
verse in this way: Mary and the others "used their resources in going
on mission for him" (Karris 1994, 9; Ricci 1994). Mary Magdalene and
other women, furthermore, are—in all canonical accounts—the first to
witness the empty tomb and the first to receive an apostolic mission to
relay the resurrection to others (Mk 16:5–7; Mt 28: 1–7; Lk 24: 1–10;
Jn 20:1–2, 14–16). Distinctions between the male and female followers
in Luke 8 and elsewhere may reflect assumptions about the kinds of
service in which women participated in the early church. Indeed, such
assumptions may be traced back to the Evangelists themselves: each of
the canonical Gospels pushes back against the women's contributions to
Jesus's ministry. Mark, for instance, ends his Gospel with the women's
disobedient silence: "they said nothing for they were afraid" (16:8), and
Luke reports that the male disciples thought the women's report about
the resurrection was an "idle tale" (24:11). Importantly, other Gospel
traditions, for example, the *Gospel of Mary* and the *Gospel of Thomas,*
preserve traditions of Mary's exemplary leadership.

For each of the women I have discussed, there are scores of women whose leadership was not remembered, whose stories were never told. Mary, Phoebe, and Junia appear to have been spiritual leaders within their communities; but not all women in all Christian churches shared their experiences. There, are, then, no final conclusions to draw about the realities—or possibilities—for women's leadership in the earliest Christian communities. What is clear, however, is that the questions are more complex than they may at first appear: authoritative texts do not always capture lived experience.

Tunisia's independence from France ushered in new freedoms and rights for women. But as those freedoms and rights were claimed, traditional ways of life were affected. In response, some communities pushed back. Similarly, Jesus's and Paul's apocalyptic teachings anticipated the independence of God's people from Satan's power in the coming Kingdom of God; this apocalyptic expectation suggested—to some, anyway—a new freedom, in which "there is no longer male nor female" (Gal 3:28). As apocalyptic expectations waned, however, traditional gender roles were reasserted and memories of women's leadership were contested. But there never was a homogenous experience for women in the ancient church. Some women taught, evangelized, and held clerical roles. And some women did not. Some individuals and communities— ancient and modern—pushed back against the complex experiences of women in the church in myriad ways: by rewriting the text, through translation choices, by favoring one narrative element over another. The story of women in the early church, therefore, is not merely one of ancient religious history but also of modern historiography. We may be attuned to observe physically violent forms of pushback—persecution and martyrdom, for instance—but no less violent are the diverse forms of narrative pushback, which obstruct our observations of the complex experiences of women in the spiritual leadership of the early church.

References

Bouachrine, Ibtissam. 2014. *Women and Islam: Myths, Apologies, and the Limits of Feminist Critique.* Lanham, MD: Lexington Books.

Boughzala, Mongi. 2013. "Youth Employment and Economic Transition in Tunisia." *Global Economy and Development* Working Paper 57. Accessed August 17, 2014. http://www.brookings.edu/~/media/research/files/papers/2013/1/youth%20employment%20tunisia%20boughzala/01%20youth%20employment%20tunisia%20boughzala.pdf.

Bradley, John R. 2010. *Behind the Veil of Vice: The Business and Culture of Sex in the Middle East.* New York: Macmillan.

Brock, Ann Graham. 2003. *Mary Magdalene: The First Apostle: The Struggle for Authority.* Cambridge, MA: Harvard University Press.

Brooten, Bernadette. 1977. "'Junia…Outstanding among the Apostles' (Romans 16:7)." In Arlene Swidler and Leonard Swidler, eds., *Women Priests: A Catholic Commentary on the Vatican Declaration,* 141–144. New York: Paulist Press.

Brown, Raymond Edward. 1997. *Introduction to the New Testament.* New Haven, CT: Yale University Press.

Clark, Elizabeth A. 1981. "Ascetic Renunciation and Feminine Advancement: A Paradox of Late Ancient Christianity." *Anglican Theological Review* 63: 240–257.

Cobb, L. Stephanie. 2008. *Dying to Be Men: Gender and Language in Early Christian Martyr Texts.* New York: Columbia University Press.

Cobb, L. Stephanie. 2009. "Real Women or Objects of Discourse? The Search for Early Christian Women." *Religion Compass* 3(3): 379–394.

Coon, Lynda L. 1997. *Sacred Fictions: Holy Women and Hagiography in Late Antiquity.* Philadelphia: University of Pennsylvania Press.

Cramer, Peter. 1993. *Baptism and Change in the Early Middle Ages, c. 200–c. 1150.* Cambridge: Cambridge University Press.

Davis, Stephen J. 2001. *The Cult of St. Thecla: A Tradition of Women's Piety in Late Antiquity.* Oxford: Oxford University Press.

DeJong, Jocelyn, Hyam Bashour, and Afamia Kaddour. 2012. "Women's Health: Progress and Unaddressed Issues." In Samer Jabbour and Rouham Yamout, eds., *Public Health in the Arab World,* 249–299. Cambridge: Cambridge University Press.

Epp, Eldon Jay. 2005. *Junia: The First Woman Apostle.* Minneapolis, MN: Augsburg Fortress Press.

Epp, Eldon Jay. 2006. "Minor Textual Variants in Romans 16:7." In Jeff W. Childers and David C. Parker, eds., *Transmission and Reception: New Testament Text-Critical and Exegetical Studies,* 123–141. Piscataway, NJ: Gorgias Press.

Evans, Ernest. 1964. *Tertullian's Homily on Baptism.* London: SPCK.

Gaventa, Beverly Roberts. 1998. "Romans." In Carol A. Newsom and Sharon H. Ringe, eds., *The Women's Bible Commentary,* 403–410. Louisville, KY: Westminster John Knox Press.

Gingrich, Felix Wilbur. 1962. "Junias/Junia." In George A. Buttrick and Keith R. Crim, eds., *Interpreters Dictionary of the Bible,* 2: 1026–1027. Nashville, TN: Abington.

Haines-Eitzen, Kim. 2012. *The Gendered Palimpsest: Women, Writing, and Representation in Early Christianity.* New York: Oxford University Press.

Haskins, Susan. 2005. *Mary Magdalen: Truth and Myth: The Essential History.* London: Pimlico.

Hole, Abigail, Michael Grosberg, and Daniel Robinson. 2007. *Tunisia.* Lonely Planet. Hong Kong: Colorcraft.

Jacobs, Daniel. 2009. *The Rough Guide to Tunisia.* New York: Penguin Books.

Karris, Robert J. 1994. "Women and Discipleship in Luke." *CBQ* 56: 1–20.

Lietzmann, Hans. 1971. *An die Römer.* HNT 8. Tübingen: Mohr.

Murphy-O'Connor, Jerome. 2009. *Keys to First Corinthians: Revisiting the Major Issues.* Oxford: Oxford University Press.

Ricci, Carla. 1994. *Mary Magdalene and Many Others: Women Who Followed Jesus.* Minneapolis, MN: Augsburg Fortress.

Schulz, Ray R. 2008. "Twentieth-Century Corruption of Scripture." *Expository Times* 119: 270–274.

Schüssler Fiorenza, Elisabeth. 1975. "Mary Magdalene, Apostle to the Apostles." *Union Theological Seminary Journal* April: 22–24.

Sfeir, George N. 1957. "The Tunisian Code of Personal Status (Majallat Al-Ahw Al-Shakhsiy Ah)." *Middle East Institute* 11: 309–318.

Thorley, John. 1996. "Junia: A Woman Apostle." *Novum Testamentum* 38: 18–29.

Trumbower, Jeffrey A. 2001. *Rescue for the Dead: The Posthumous Salvation of Non-Christians in Early Christianity.* New York: Oxford University Press.

Weima, Jeffrey A. D. 2010. "Sincerely, Paul: The Significance of the Pauline Letter Closings." In Stanley E. Porter, and Sean A. Adams, eds., *Paul and the Ancient Letter Form*, 307–346. Leiden: Brill.

Witherington, Ben. 1979. "On the Road with Mary Magdalene, Joanna, Susanna, and Other Disciples—Luke 8:1–3." *ZNW* 70: 243–248.

Yagoubi, Mahmoud. 2004. "HRM in Tunisia." In Ken Kamoche, Yaw Debrah, Frank Horwitz, and Gerry Nkombo Muuka, eds., *Managing Human Resources in Africa*, 151–168. London: Routledge.

CHAPTER TWO

Clerical Leadership in Late Antiquity: Augustine on Bishops' Polemical and Pastoral Burdens

PETER IVER KAUFMAN

Augustine returned from Italy to North Africa in 388, apparently elated to have found his calling. The cities he had known, Thagaste and Carthage, and would soon come to know, Hippo Regius, were relatively prosperous, despite taxes collected for the central government, which had been making increasing demands since the time of Emperor Constantine. The funds available for municipal improvements were depleted (*gravement amputés*), Claude Lepelley calculated, siting the African cities in "a history of inexorable decline" from the 380s into the 430s (Lepelley 1979–1981, 1:197, also 1:414). In the coastal city of Hippo, however, Augustine, as bishop, was busy from the late 390s, exchanging ideas and insults with polemicists of various stripes. He had not meant to take a prominent part in African Christianity's bouts with sectarians, secessionists, and pagans. He planned to retire to his family estate in Thagaste with several like-minded friends. He only traveled to Hippo to consult with a man whom he hoped to tempt to join his small company of contemplatives and perhaps to confer with the faithful about the prospects for locating another contemplative collective there. He tells us he disliked traveling. He feared that his reputation for eloquence and insight might tempt the faithful far from his home and friends in Thagaste to waylay him to fill a vacancy. He would be safe in Hippo, he thought; the incumbent, Valerius, was well respected. Yet, at that time (391), Valerius was thinking ahead. He had his parishioners seize Augustine, ordained him, and after several years nominated him as his coadjutor and successor (Augustine, Sermon 355, 2).[1]

Augustine's first biographer, Possidius, bishop of Calama, roughly 30 miles from Hippo, claimed that Valerius's guest-turned-associate-turned-successor consented to serve only after considerable pressure had been applied (*compulsus atque coactus succubuit*), but Augustine was almost certainly the source for that story, which echoed protests, he later expressed, when he seemed fatigued by the business (*negotium*) of being bishop as well as nostalgic for the leisure (*otium*) and learned discourses at Cassiciacum or Thagaste. He insisted that, before the Hippo clergy and laity seized him, he had no interest in leading churches (Weiskotten 1919, 8).

It seems sound to say that socioeconomic factors that drew others to church leadership were irrelevant. Augustine may have been moved by the incumbent's—Valerius's—compelling appeal for help. If so, either he did not tell Possidius or Possidius misremembered the story. Of one thing, we may be fairly sure. Although candidates were often attracted to the episcopacy by fourth-century developments that "open[ed] the church to the world" and that spurred ambition, as Werner Eck argues, Augustine was not (Eck 1978, 568–570, also 576–580). As bishop of Hippo, he doggedly scolded colleagues for chasing promotions. He was austere and expected austerity of colleagues. He emphasized the distinction between the Christians' hopes for eternal reward, which bishops ought to cultivate by preaching the promises in the sacred texts and pillorying desires for temporal gains that appeared to animate pagans' pursuits of name and fame. If we may trust Possidius, even before Augustine became bishop, he urged Christians to turn away from the enticements of this world (*illicebras*) (Augustine, Epistle 209.6; Augustine, Sermon 157.5; Weiskotten 1919, 3).

He admired his faith's martyrs, specifically for that "turn away" and for the virtues he came to identify with the church's leadership and to commend to its laity. Martyrs' perseverance delighted God, Augustine imagined, but heroic deaths were hard to come by, after authorities in government service stopped persecuting most Christians. Suicidal secessionists associated with Donatist Christians, Augustine said, were misguided. Their desire to stage heart-stopping scenes of their suffering by provoking reprisals discredited Christianity (Augustine, *Contra Cresconium* 3.49, 54; Augustine, Epistle 185.12).[2] Presuming to extrapolate from sacred literature what mattered to God, Augustine concluded that it was not how the faithful left this world, how they died (*non qua occasione exeant*), but how they lived in it (Augustine, Epistle 111.6).[3] Yet living in it austerely, living in but not of the world, as he encouraged, did not necessarily preclude political maneuvering. Possidius's biography probably reflected Augustine's notion that the culmination of his career was the outcome of the Council of Carthage (411)—particularly, its proscriptions against Donatists. "All that valuable work," Possidius declared, "was begun and brought to perfection by Augustine" (Weiskotten 1919, 13).[4]

So, despite his reluctance to countenance Christians measuring success in pleasing God in temporal terms, Augustine seems to have placed great value on his concrete policy successes against Donatists who, as it happened, esteemed Christianity's martyrs as much as—if not more than—Augustine and his Catholic colleagues who had welcomed the emperors' agents' material assistance. Ascertainably at the Council of Carthage, but also in the villages and municipalities where bishops served alongside local *curiales* to maintain order, distinctions between bishops and the civil magistracy were "blurry." Bishops and their courts were conspicuous parts of the empire's political infrastructure.[5] In the early fifth century, Emperor Honorius's chancery was unrealistic to assume that the entire clerical community—including the new faith's conspicuous leaders—could devote itself to prayer, freed by imperial decree or law from vexatious concerns related to regional commerce and politics (*Constitutiones Sirmondianae* 425–438, 11; *Codex Theodosiana* 425–438, 16.2, 40).[6]

But bishops became civic patrons in concert with their towns' curiales. To judge from Augustine's correspondence, the best bishops advocated for the poor who were victimized by schemes to maximize tax revenues. To Romulus, whom he had converted to Christianity, the bishop of Hippo wrote indignantly after a plan to extort money from tenants had been exposed. The suffering of those victimized by fraud and intimidation would only last for a time, Augustine pointed out, but Romulus's torment and that of other landlords and tax collectors preying on their neighbors would be everlasting (Augustine, Epistle 247, 1).[7] Of course, the effectiveness of such reprimands would depend on offenders' faith and fears. Hence, Augustine favored the appointment of ombudsmen to cope with commoners' complaints. Perhaps he saw to the appointment of the arbiter or *defensor* who addressed issues related to the liquidation of the Donatist parishes in his diocese—and who heard complaints against the man Augustine designated to preside over such affairs in Fussala. But the evidence is slender and seems contradicted by Augustine's admission that he was unable to place *defensores* in Hippo to defend commoners against the elites in Hippo. Bishops could grieve with afflicted parishioners, as he instructed, yet were powerless to relieve their misery.[8]

The difficulties he was facing may have been related to problems experienced by many cities in the empire that looked to *defensores* to ensure what Robert Frakes's studies of their roles calls "efficient justice." Precisely at the time Augustine articulated the need for respected ombudsmen to umpire civil disputes, the curial "class" was polarized. The affluent preferred a restructuring that gave them greater authority than their less prominent colleagues on the curia and reduced defensores to "minor bureaucratic functionar[ies]." Still, during the fourth century, municipal councils—all curiales—increasingly lost power to representatives of a reorganized and resurgent central government. Augustine and other bishops, "operating in conjunction" with the curiales, with emperors' deputies, and often without defensores, as Claudia Rapp learned, were never fully integrated into the administration of justice.[9]

Even the formidable Bishop Ambrose of Milan was an outsider. The Court used him as an emissary. True, Augustine witnessed his stand-off with Empress Justina, which resulted in an embarrassing setback for Arian Christians at the Court of her son, Valentinian II, in 386. But the rhetoric in correspondence generated by that confrontation is somewhat misleading, as Rita Lizzi reports, insofar as it suggests the parties were *equipollenti*, equally matched. Not so. Indeed, "the torturous process" of negotiations between delegates from the Milanese church and "the state" as well as the outcome were influenced by forces beyond the control of either (Lizzi 1998, 96–97).

Describing the distinct objectives of church and Court, Karl Leo Noethlichs characterizes the partnerships they often contracted as *Konfliktverbindung[en]*, contentious connections. Each partner, protecting its "turf," tried to limit the scope of the other's proclaimed purposes. And the attempt—predictably—limited the extent of their cooperation (Noethlichs 1973, 54). Augustine looks to have been attempting to avoid contention. His overtures to the powerful refrained from pitting his church against *Realpolitik*. He wrote to Tribune Marcellinus, counselling "clemency," as one Christian to another, without insinuating that, as bishop, he possessed a superior perspective or held down a position entitling him to moral outrage (Augustine, Epistle 139.2). And, taking a parishioner's case to civil officials, he reported without recrimination the petty "humiliations" to which he was subjected, kept waiting and made to feel, if not contemptible, insignificant. He only obliquely complained of unlikeable bureaucrats (Augustine, Sermon 302.17).

And he only rarely complained about indifferent or ill-tempered civic officials, although highly placed prelates would have expected some disrespect from African magistrates, many of whom still resented the lost prestige of Rome's old religions. Still, within the churches, bishops were their flock's foremen, their shepherds. They were "in charge," Augustine explained and added that it was nonetheless unworthy of them to exploit their authority to feather their nests. Organizational necessity made bishops bosses, he said, yet they should take neither profit nor pleasure from their prestige and power (Augustine, Sermon 46.2).

Bishops were the apostles' successors. Their leadership, according to Augustine, signaled that the church had not been forsaken when the apostles passed. Replacing Peter, Paul, and other early Christian authorities, bishops comprised—unmistakably, for Augustine—"a new paternity." They were the church's fathers as well as foremen (Augustine, *Enarrationes in Psalmos* 44.32). The necessity they had been appointed to address, at least the most pressing challenge in Africa, where "contrary voices" caused schisms, was organizational unity. Only when fractious church politics ceased, when parishioners were reconciled, and when flocks were fed the truth from the trough of their sacred texts interpreted by right-minded bishops, should the sheep that God entrusted to the apostle Peter and his heirs (John 21:17) expect effective shepherds to emerge from—and to lead—them. Yet, even effective shepherds, Augustine claimed, were burdened with sin. They cleared obstacles to repentance, delivering the laity from captivity, but their "stains" remained. That alone ought to have humbled them and kept them from overreaching when they preached obedience (Augustine, Sermons 46.30; 134.3; 146.1).[10]

Some Christians did overreach. Augustine witnessed them preaching controversial doctrines and demanding obedience to pronouncements bearing on the conduct within—and, more problematically, the importance of separating from—the church. An early sign of such overreaching was insubordination, which tended toward insurrection. Augustine commented angrily on such insolence when he preached on a psalm that scolded defiance. He depicted the bulls mentioned there as sectarians intent on leading cows and calves astray. Bulls, proud and stubborn, proselytized "frivolously," he said, but compellingly. They drew auditors from their more perceptive bishops (*intellegentiores*). Heretical bulls' doctrines tested not only the mettle of the faithful but the competence of the church's leadership. Heresy, Augustine proposed, was a divinely ordained occasion for the intellegentiores to display their abilities to convey the truths of sacred literature and to maintain the unity of their churches. Heresy, moreover, rewarded the best bishops with celebrity and influence. They might have continued in obscurity as humble servants of their churches, avoiding opportunities to exhibit their gifts. But, encountering the insolence and idiocy of their arrogant rivals (*superborum contradictiones*), the church's more erudite yet reluctant and obscure bishops showed themselves, Augustine said, as well as the power of their faith's truths. He acknowledged that there would always be bulls among the herds or wolves to threaten the flocks—yet, extinguishing the errors spawned by their opinions, the better bishops proved their leadership of the Christian community (Augustine, *Enarrationes in Psalmos* 67.39).

Late in his career, Augustine preached a short sermon, airing out his impatience with colleagues who seemed to have had no interest in becoming those "better bishops." It addressed prelates relatively inattentive to their duties and insufficiently serious about the stewardship of their churches. "Let them...work for parishioners rather than offer excuses." They were overseers, ἐπίσκοποί, whose oversight meant disciplining the faithful and answering chronic complainers, Augustine emphasized in that sermon and, in another, suggested that oversight presumed there was something good or creditable as well as discreditable conduct to oversee. The implication was that bishops' reprimands would become intolerable burdens to those who issued them unless they could also attest the uplifting results of their ministries. Augustine apparently hoped that the difficulty of bishops' tasks and especially the parishioners' parts in rewarding their prelates with changes in behavior might not be lost on the faithful (Augustine, Sermon Dolbeau 10.2; Augustine, Sermon 94).[11]

In a sermon delivered in 325, on the anniversary of his ordination, he labored the point. He told parishioners why burdens (*sarcinae*) that bishops carried were heavier than those borne by other Christians. He likely anticipated that the explanation would encourage laity to lighten their load and that of their bishops or, at the very least, to refrain from adding to them. He began with the certainty that parishioners would answer in the hereafter for misbehavior here. God had appointed bishops as overseers yet also watched from a celestial perch the faithful's failures and watched for improvements. Bishops were watched as well. Responsible for the laity's progress, they were in greater trouble should they fall—or fall in with—their fallible flocks. For example, monstrous punishments (*immanissima poena*) awaited those the bishops whose oversight was compromised by their desire for popularity. Augustine's sermon wasted little sympathy on ill-fated bishops; he seemed sure that many eternally condemned could have been spared eternal torment if the church's clerical leaders were more energetic and implacable moral monitors (Augustine, Sermon 339.1–2).

His anniversary sermon exploits the parable in the nineteenth chapter of the Gospel of Luke, which reports a king's displeasure with his deputy who returned only the funds given him on his master's departure. Other stewards invested and increased their sums and were rewarded. The steward who did not even bank the original sum and collect interest was scolded. The lesson Augustine apparently intended to impart was that bishops ought to circulate their faith's truths to collect the souls within their precincts. Prelates' love for parishioners ought to motivate them, he said, particularly because the gospels' promises assured them that the honesty and goodwill they inspired among the faithful would make up for the latter's hypocrisies and indignities. But the alternative, reassuring the faithful-yet-persistently-sinful that God's mercy covered a multitude of sins, was dereliction of duty and a sign that bishops who traded in such assurances had traded probity for popularity. Augustine was scrupulous, stipulating to colleagues and to the laity what bishops could and could not do. They could only—and should tirelessly—pronounce the truths in their sacred texts, truths that set their parishioners free conscientiously to please God. They were not commissioned to condemn but to censure, reiterating what the gospels proscribed, as well as to pronounce God's judgments in advance so that parishioners would knowledgeably recalibrate their courses, or, in the wake of trespasses, bishops were to awaken remorse and spur repentance. No prelate would have elected such onerous duty; Augustine confided that he might have picked another profession, had Jesus's directive ("feed my sheep") not frightened him. To be vexatious and tedious to the laity was not what the church's leaders would have wished for themselves; nonetheless, bishops would be botching their jobs, Augustine said, if they left parishioners to wallow in their possessions—and if they asked to be left to enjoy their own leisure, making no fuss over the immortality of others (Augustine, Sermon 339.2–4).

Augustine later accused the specialists who led the Manichees and whose responsibilities were not unlike those of Christianity's bishops of overvaluing their leisure and failing to monitor their followers' behavior. He spent nearly ten years in North Africa and Italy hearing about—and listening to—that sect's elite. He believed them to be a breed set apart to impart secrets about the origins and conflicts in the cosmos and to liberate Light trapped in matter because they resisted conscientiously the temptations that assailed ordinary men and women. Manichaean specialists and their partisans regarded Mani, a third-century Persian prophet, as their founder, yet many among them also identified as Christians and wrestled with mysteries contained in that faith's sacred texts. From the late 370s into the 380s, Augustine, less impressed than later with truths teased from Christian literature, looked to his Manichaean friends and the sect's itinerant teachers for insights (Augustine, *Confessiones* 3.10, 18).

By the mid-380s, his disappointment in the Manichees' leadership peaked. He regretted his prior credulity. He wrote a series of caustic treatises against the Manichaeism. The first was composed very soon after his baptism. He concentrated on the specialists' interpretations of the Old Testament, but complaints about their lewd behavior sprawled across the pages. And after he became more committed to—and knowledgeable about—Christianity, he appreciated bishops who preached humility and shunned the sort of celebrity (*non amant propatula*) that Manichees' leaders prized. They pretended to be abstemious but were insincere, he charged; the sect's elite were petulant, promiscuous, and duplicitous. Years after he had grown disenchanted with them, Augustine professed that he had never met a member of the Manichaean elite or "elect" whose conduct was above suspicion. He was particularly annoyed at one flimsy excuse lecherous and fatuous teachers offered when they were caught in a compromising position: the offenders explained to other Manichees that Judaism's and Christianity's heroes—from Adam to the apostles—were known to have strayed and to have sinned egregiously, yet were also commemorated as pillars of their faiths (Augustine, *De moribus ecclesiae Catholicae et de moribus Manichaeorum* 2.19, 68–2.19, 72).

Augustine tells us in his *Confessions* that he was expecting to reap considerable profits from his conversations with one Manichaean specialist, Faustus, who had come to Carthage to study classical literature. Faustus assumed that lessons with Augustine would help him make Manichaeism an attractive alternative to Christians. Augustine anticipated that Faustus might make more sense than Christian bishops had of the mysteries and seemingly absurd stories recorded in their sacred texts (Augustine, *Confessiones* 5.7, 12). One could say, notwithstanding the generations of prelates drawing inferences about good, evil, and from biblical passages, that intelligent Christians experienced a crisis of intelligibility in the late fourth century. François Decret exaggerates, although, perhaps, only slightly—when he depicts the expectations that attached to Faustus's coming to Carthage as "messianic."[12]

Before becoming bishop, Augustine recalled his intellectual crisis. He was frustrated, he said; teachers either fended off or failed to answer satisfactorily his questions about the origin of the cosmos, the purposes of human life, and the meaning of "difficult" passages in Christianity's sacred texts. As noted, he found that Faustus was little more than a buffoon. Only snippets from others' philosophies seemed intelligible to him. He could not decide what to profess and what to dismiss as superficial (*quid mihi tenendum, quid dimittendum esset*), until, in Milan, listening to Bishop Ambrose, he rediscovered Christianity. By then, what he came to criticize as Manichaean mystifications, parading as clarifications of sacred literature, lost their power over him. Ambrose showed him how to make sense of the passages in the Hebrews' scriptures that seemed to stretch credulity, stories that were interpreted so absurdly by Manichaean specialists that Augustine and his more sensible friends despised the Pentateuch and the prophets (Augustine, *De utilitate credendi* 8.20). He continued to attack the Manichees, he said, because the not-so-sensible were so easily seduced by them. And, as bishop, he assumed the burden to protect the credulous from the Manichaean elite's "pestiferous" ideas and exegesis, which, he said, would not only leave them in ignorance but lead them to hell (Augustine, *Contra epistulam Manichaei quam vocant Fundamenti* 11.12).

Augustine was sure that the crisis of intelligibility could never be finally resolved for or by the Manichees' leaders who, unlike Christianity's bishops, were convinced that the mysteries of faith might be put on a firm foundation of fact. They were following the lead of their founder, Mani, who, according to Augustine, overlooked human finitude and fallibility. The conceit that a mind could overcome limitations likely mobilized Mani's partisans, yet it could not rally them around a single theme that seemed to Augustine to address conclusively the issues raised by the mysteries of creation and redemption. And, unlike the bishops Augustine came to admire, Mani and his followers forgot that "we are mere men without wisdom" (Augustine, *De moribus ecclesiae Catholicae et de moribus Manichaeorum* 1.7, 11; Augustine, *Contra epistulam Manichaei quam vocant Fundamenti* 13.17; Augustine, *Confessiones* 5.7, 13).

Their misreading of the texture of the Christian faith made their cosmologies untenable. Part of their problem was, as has been noted here—and was repeatedly elaborated by Augustine—the Manichees' conceit. Another reason their specialists, including Faustus, failed to present an impressive and enduring resolution to the crisis of intelligibility was their plurality. Manichaean teachers were at odds with each other. Intense rivalries capsized every effort to reach consensus. Deprived of a basis in fact, which Mani was alleged to have promised, competing Manichaean teachers, not knowing their "unknowing," from Augustine's perspective, in effect, normalized dissent. None could claim "antiquity" for his truths, as could Christianity's bishops, following one another in succession—an apostolic succession—and articulating a consensus handed down from "those most solidly founded sees of the apostles" (Augustine, *Contra Faustum Manichaeum* 11.2).

Generations of Christians had debated whether bishops or sectarian teachers were more reliable sources of truth before Augustine closed ranks with colleagues in the African Christian churches. For example, the *Acta Archelai*, an early anti-Manichaean script circulated 50 years before Faustus and Augustine met. The text records (or stages) two debates between the prophet Mani and Bishop Archelaus of Carchar, a town in Persia, approximately a 100 miles from the Roman garrisons on the frontier. In both confrontations, the bishop prevailed and the prophet fled. Humiliation and flight punctuate an exceptionally unflattering account of Mani's life accusing Mani of having plagiarized his ideas. Just about everything about the Manichees' founder was indefensible—eminently assailable. The *Acta* impugned his aptitude and deportment as well as his originality (Vermes 2001, 26.6). Augustine took a very different tack in his *Confessions* after he reported his disappointment with the widely esteemed Faustus, his admiration for Ambrose, and his intention to profess the Christian faith. He paused to reflect on the years he spent among the Manichees, annoyed with himself for having trusted the sect's elect, for not having ascertained how baseless the specialists' sense of superiority was. He excoriated them for having posed as an aristocracy of virtue as well as an intellectual elite, yet he also pitied them, for they would never find what he had found—a remedy for arrogance in the psalms and in the church (Augustine, *Confessiones* 9.4, 8).

Nor had the Donatists found it. Augustine complained about their sense of superiority, their impatience with prelates who prudently schooled rather than excluded sinners. He most likely exaggerated the secessionists' impatience, increasingly as they failed to cease what he considered provocative behavior, declined chances to confer with him, and refused to listen to reason—to his reasons (Augustine, *Contra Cresconium* 2.1, 1).[13] He welcomed the Donatists who elected to reconcile, practicing what they heard him preach. As bishop, as we learned, he bent every effort to have them repudiate their exclusive sect and join his more inclusive church (Augustine, Epistle 11*.25; Augustine, *Contra Cresconium* 1.3, 4).

Bishops were not only better teachers than were the Manichees' specialists, as Augustine insisted, they were better shepherds than the Donatists' bishops, who complicated the challenges facing the African Catholic Church. One of Augustine's sermons reflected at great length on the duties of his faith's shepherds, stressing the obligation to recall lost sheep. It explicitly accused Donatists of drawing souls ("sheep") from the safety of their church into secessionists' sects in which the misguided were sure to perish for want of charity. Augustine believed so because he considered that secession and unrelenting schism signaled Donatists' uncharitable, intolerant, and intolerable attitude toward others (Augustine, Sermon 46.14). The Donatists appeared to have forgotten the directive in the apostle Paul's first letter to Corinth, positioning charity or love above the other two theological virtues, faith and hope. Donatist bishops boasted of their predecessors' and partisans' eagerness to die for their faith during fourth-century persecutions and to add to Christianity's ample stock of martyrs. But charity superseded all else in Paul's passage, and supersession—in that context—gave Augustine the occasion to explain that suffering and dying for one's faith unaccompanied by love, by one's charitable dispositions, were worthless (Augustine, Sermon 138.2).

Still, Donatist secessionists and separatists had gained ground in the late fourth century. One of their leading bishops allied with an insurgent garrison commander, who shut off supplies to Rome, forcing the emperor to send troops to discipline obstreperous local leaders. Augustine's parishioners panicked, confronting the bishop with another set of responsibilities—only indirectly related to his polemical duties and objectives yet closely associated with a bishop's commitment to commend charity to those hoarding rather than sharing supplies. In a sermon preached at the end of the fourth century, Augustine introduced nautical imagery; churches were ships in rough seas. Without dependable leadership, crews were without direction—without moral compass (Augustine, Sermon 75.5–7).

Subsequently, during crises occasioned by the Goths' invasions of Italy and the steady stream of refugees into Africa, Augustine tried to remain informed when business took him from Hippo, and he relayed instructions on receiving news that the comfortable among his congregation were less than forthcoming with aid. Destitute residents as well as the refugees from Gaul, Spain, and Italy were left "unclothed." Christians were pilgrims, he repeatedly stated; if they anticipated settling in a celestial homeland, he wrote from afar, his parishioners ought to use their surplus to relieve strangers' and neighbors' suffering—particularly when their terrestrial world appeared to be falling apart (Augustine, Epistle 122.2).

Augustine traveled to African church councils, and to his colleagues' dioceses, to hold the church together as the empire disintegrated. He never again crossed the Mediterranean. His first tour in the 380s was his last. Other bishops carried petitions to Rome and Ravenna to importune Emperor Honorius and his deputies at Court. Augustine was in demand closer to home. He was in Milevis, in late 425 or early 426, to ensure the promotion of a candidate whom the recently deceased incumbent, Severus, had nominated. The laity had been overlooked. The incumbent had only consulted his clergy. Augustine appeased the parishioners, but he took no credit for having avoided protracted conflict. He announced that the protests subsided, "by God's will," parishioners resolved to accept the nominee, and the bishop-designate was consecrated (Augustine, Epistle 213.1). But Severus's mistake taught Augustine a valuable lesson. In 426, soon after he returned to Hippo from Milevis, he assembled his clerics and congregation to notify them of his plans for semi-retirement and to present Heraclius, whom he named collaborator and next bishop. He was confident that no objections would be raised. Hippo was acquainted with Heraclius, whose intelligence and modesty, Augustine averred, were widely known. But the conference was organized to test that perception. Augustine wanted confirmation and got it (Augustine, Epistle 213.2).

Scribes recorded the responses, the crowd's cheers (*acclamationes*), which Bishop Augustine predictably took as an endorsement. The document that survives among his letters reads like a transcript of the meeting. It also shows how scrupulous Augustine was to avoid a dual episcopacy. He had been named bishop by Valerius before the latter's death in the 390s, only to learn later that co-episcopacy had been forbidden at the Council of Nicaea earlier that century (Augustine, Epistle 213.4). Possibly, the ongoing rivalries between Donatist and Catholic Christian bishops in some African towns also made Augustine wary of such an arrangement, as did his miscalculation in subdividing his diocese and appointing an obstreperous opportunist, Antoninus, to the new see of Fussala (Augustine, Epistle 20*. 3–4, 8–9, also 18).[14] Yet Augustine was clear that Heraclius would be assigned many of a bishop's daily duties, which—unsurprisingly—included presiding in the diocesan court. For Augustine had never warmed to that part of his job. He had an aversion to the gavel. During previous deliberations, he persuaded parishioners to let him reserve five days each week for study, freeing him from the mind-numbing work plaguing incumbents involved in the laity's worldly affairs and enabling him to provide his colleagues with authoritative exegesis of sacred literature that could counter heretics' claims. But after a short time, everyday business intruded. He was again preoccupied with his parishioners' petty squabbles—cases brought into his "audience" (Augustine, Sermon 137.14; Augustine, *De opera monachorum* 29.37; Augustine, *Enarrationes in Psalmos* 25.2, 13).[15]

From 426 and to the end of his pontificate and life in 430, Heraclius, it seems, presided over the bishop's court in Hippo. Augustine returned to the polemical and exegetical work that bishops, he believed, should pour into their sermons and correspondence. Still, he appeared to be on the defensive. Conceivably, he worried that his parishioners' enthusiasm for Heraclius's appointment might ebb and that the local laity would resent his time for study, seeing it as an objectionable extravagance. But Augustine refused to dignify objections by answering them directly. He had defended his faith's texts against the Manichaean specialists' preposterous interpretations. He marshalled arguments from sacred literature to undermine the Donatists' misreading of the faith's requirements. And he was still summoning passages to counter the excesses of Pelagian exegesis, which minimized the imperfectability of humanity. Bishops' polemical obligations were tightly bound with their pastoral leadership, Augustine insisted, maintaining that leisure was required to comb for, clarify, or correctly construe passages in biblical and extrabiblical texts that could be used against Catholic Christianity's interests. "Leisure" of that sort was a bishop's serious business (Augustine, Epistle 213.6).[16]

Few highly placed prelates today are able to carve out time for leisure, although study is still part of their serious business. Augustine's active career and comments on clerical leadership should serve as a check on any temptations to be too bookish, too far removed, and to pronounce dryly or distantly on issues twenty-first-century church leaders and their parishioners face. What clerical executives (and pastors) might find surprising is the persistence of Augustine's emphasis on humility, which, of course, did not keep him from crusading when he perceived threats to his faith or church. His involvement in confessional controversy and the immodesty characterizing some of his polemics tempt historians to forget his insistence on compassion as well as humility, but that, too, is his legacy. Mulishly opposed to petulance, pretense, and perfectionism, he set a high standard for clerical leadership in his time. In ours, the media make celebrities of the less thoughtful and parade soundbites as wisdom. The spectacles that result would have terribly disappointed Augustine.

Notes

1. References to Augustine's work employ the section divisions used in the *Patrologia Latina*, the most accessible, online edition, http://www.augustinus.it/latino/index.htm. All translations are mine; citations have been checked against Augustine's works in the *Corpus scriptorum ecclesiasticorum Latinorum*.

2. Also see Bernhard Kriegbaum, *Kirche der Traditoren oder Kirche der Martyrer* (Innsbruck: Tyrolia, 1986), 152–154; Kaufman, "Donatism Revisited: Moderates and Militants in Late Antique North Africa," *Journal of Late Antiquity* 2 (2009), 135–139; and, for Donatists' version of "suicide-by-cop," Brent Shaw, *Sacred Violence: African Christians and Sectarian Hatred in the Age of Augustine* (Cambridge: Cambridge University Press, 2011), 762–764. See W. H. C. Frend, *The Donatist Church: A Movement of Protest in Roman North Africa*, reprint edition (Oxford: Clarendon, 1970) for the best account of the secessionists' origins, but also consult Maureen A. Tilley, *The Bible in Christian North Africa: The Donatist World* (Minneapolis, MN: Fortress, 1997), for secessionists' alternatives to armed resistance. To put the persecutions in context, see H. A. Drake, "Intolerance, Religious Violence, and Political Legitimacy in Late Antiquity," *Journal of the American Academy of Religion* 79 (2011), 193–235.

3. Yet bishops' heroism was very much on Augustine's mind after the Vandals invaded North Africa. He urged bishops not to abandon their flocks as the enemy advanced, and Possidius included that long appeal in his biography (*Vita*, 30). Elena Zocca, "La figura santo vescovo in Africa da Ponzio a Possidio," in *Vescovo e pastori in epoca Teodosiana*, vol. 2 (Rome: Institutum Patristicum Augustinianum, 1997), 489–491 suggests Augustine's letter encouraging courage was *raison d'être* for the biographical account.

4. *Coeptum et perfectum est*; also, for correspondences between Augustine's and Possidius's ideals of episcopal service, consult Eva Elm, *Die Macht der Weisheit: Das Bild des Bischofs in der "Vita Augustini" des Possidius und anderen spätantiken und frühmittelalterlichen Bischofsviten* (Leiden: Brill, 2003), 143.

5. For "blurry," see Claudia Rapp, *Holy Bishops in Late Antiquity: The Nature of Christian Leadership in an Age of Transition* (Berkeley: University of California Press, 2005), 172–173.

6. Both accessible at http://droitromain.upmf-grenoble.fr/Codex_Theod.htm.

7. For other "interventions" *de ce genre*, Claude Lepelley, "Le patronat épiscopal aux IVᵉ et Vᵉ siècles continuités et ruptures avec le patronat classique," in *L'Évêque dans la cite du IVᵉ au Vᵉ siècle: Image et autorité*, ed. Éric Rebillard and Claire Sotinel (Rome: École française, 1998), 30–33.

8. Compare Augustine, Epistle 20★.29 (the *defensor* in the diocese) with Augustine, Epistle 22★.2 and 4 (the need for *defensores*). For the former, see Jean-Anatole Sabw Kanyang, *Episcopus et plebs: L'évêque et la communauté ecclésiale dans les conciles africains (345–525)* (Bern: Peter Lang, 2000), 280.

9. See Rapp, *Holy Bishops*, 287–288 and Robert M. Frakes, *"Contra Potentium Iniurias": The "Defensor Civitatis" and Late Roman Justice* (Munich: Beck, 2001), 224–226.

10. Also see Elm, *Die Macht der Weisheit*, 141.

11. *Erogent quod acceperunt, operari magis quam excusare dignentur.*

12. François Decret, *Aspects du Manichéisme dans l'Afrique Romain* (Paris: Etudes augustiniennes, 1970), 58–59. Jason David Beduhn's *Augustine's Manichaean Dilemma: Conversion and Apostasy* (Philadelphia: University of Pennsylvania Press, 2010), 241–243 suggests that a predilection for esotericism initially attracted Augustine to the sect and held his interest until Faustus disappointed him. From then, he doubted the Manichees' leadership and, increasingly, found that insight came with faith and that faith was the threshold to "a gradual conformation to a system as one learns it more thoroughly [from its bishops] and keeps adjusting one's sense of self."

13. *Nolunt nobiscum habere colloquium.*

14. Also consult Serge Lancel's "L'affaire d'Antoninus de Fussala: Pays, choses, et gens de la Numidie d'Hippone saisis dans la durée d'une procedure d'enquête épiscopale," in *Les lettres de Saint Augustin découvertes par Johannes Divjak*, ed. Joahannes Divjak (Paris: Etudes augustiniennes, 1983), 283–284.

15. Also consult Clara Gebbia, "Sant'Agostino e l'Episcopalis Audientia," in *L'Africa Romana*, vol. 2, ed. Attilio Mastino (Sassari: Dipartimento di storia, Università degli studi di Sassari, 1988), 693–694.

16. *Nemo ergo invideat otio meo, quia meum otium magnum habet negotium.*

References

Augustine. *Confessiones.*

———. *Contra Cresconium.*

———. *Contra epistulam Manichaei quam vocant Fundamenti.*

———. *Contra Faustum Manichaeum.*

———. *De moribus ecclesiae Catholicae et de moribus Manichaeorum.*

———. *De opera monachorum.*

———. *De utilitate credendi.*

———. *Enarrationes in Psalmos.*

———. Epistolae.

———. Sermones.

———. Sermones Nuper Reperti, Dolbeau.

Codex Theodosiana. 425–438.

Constitutiones Sirmondianae. 425–438.

Eck, Werner. 1978. "Der Einfluβ der konstantinischen Wende auf die Auswahl der Bischofe im 4. und 5. Jahrhundert." *Ariel* 8.

Lepelley, Claude. 1979–1981. *Les Cités de l'Afrique Romaine au Bas-Empire.* 2 vols. Paris: Etudes Augustiniennes.

Lizzi, Rita. 1998. "I vescovi e i potentes della terra: definizione e limite del ruolo episcopale nelle due partes imperii fra IV e V secolo." L'Évêque dans la cite. Rome: École française de Rome.

Noethlichs, K. L. 1973. "Materialen zum Bischofsbild aus den spätantiken Rechtsquellen." *Jahrbuch für Antike und Christentum* 16.

Vermes, M. J., ed. 2001. *Acta Archelai.* Louvain: Brepols.

Weiskotten, Herbert, ed. 1919. *Sancti Augustini vita.* Princeton, NJ: Princeton University Press.

CHAPTER THREE

The Spiritual Leadership of Madame Guyon and Madame de Maintenon under Louis XIV

SYDNEY WATTS

A woman, born into poverty, suffers childhood neglect, and later, sexual advances of a much older man. In her early adulthood she breaks free of household authority and finds her way independent of a spouse, but still subject to the rule of men. Fearlessly, she steps out into the world and becomes a woman of prominence. Other women see her rise as evidence of a certain social magnetism and hard-won, self-determination; to her, it is a response to what she has gained from her past suffering, and, perhaps, it leads her to what her heart desires: greater spiritual intimacy and honesty. Living in a world that affords her financial security and educational opportunity, she develops an acute intellect. The public recognizes her beauty—what is seen as charm and grace, while she regards it with caution (an inner-conflict?) for its powerful effect on others. She reaches a point in her life when her conscience is awakened. Faith in a loving god, which was nurtured when young, now becomes a source of strength and a voice that calls her to lead other women, to teach them to see themselves as a spiritual force.

This biographical narrative could belong to any influential woman whose rise to leadership is marked by adversity. A woman, for example, like Oprah Winfrey, who came from humble beginnings, later became prominent in the media through pure charisma and an unrelenting drive for greatness. Her celebrity status is humanized through a personal faith of self-help known as "the secret," whose popularity relies on the tale of hardships of the past redeemed by material successes of the present. Kathryn Lofton names it the "gospel of an icon" (Lofton 2011). Her study of Oprah Winfrey suggests a unique vantage point for scholars to see how one of the wealthiest, self-made African Americans in America has become an embodied spiritual force to a vast public. Oprah's power emanates from the visible hand of the "Oprah-Effect" on product placement, the strategically produced self-image of the "O" brand, the spiritually infused affect and effect of Oprah's soul-bearing interviews and public confessions, the appetite for self-fulfillment by a sisterhood of redeemed women, and the immense fortune put to good works in her name.

In a very public way, Oprah offers a purposeful self-narrative that reconciles the material disadvantages and sexual abuse of her past with the self-determined faith in her future. She vanquishes hardship, wins favor, gains the blessings of wealth and influence, and more recently, has established her legacy with the "Oprah Winfrey Leadership Academy for Girls" in Henley-on-Kilp, South Africa. The school offers a "fresh start" to a young generation of "liberated" post-Apartheid girls who have lost so many of their fathers, mothers, and siblings to AIDS. The school's mission (as listed on its Web site as of December 2014) is marked by a tale of redemption more characteristic of Oprah's own life than what we know of the girls in South Africa. Oprah's legacy fosters female leadership through spiritual resilience. It lionizes her exercise of power through an act of gendered patronage, by a woman, for women.

Oprah's contemporary model of female leadership is far different from the tacit example of elite women of the early modern age who demonstrated their leadership with a much greater degree of self-effacement. This chapter focuses on the spiritual leadership of two women of seventeenth-century France, whose inner search generated highly critical notions of self. Yet, in overcoming their own obstacles, they turned to a holy purpose that resembles Oprah's mission: a girls' school for impoverished families. In this case, the secular school for the French aristocracy at Saint-Cyr, founded as a royal household in 1686, highlights the obligations of noble privilege—what was considered the Christian duties of virtuous leaders—while it drew on the enlightened view of women's education that provided women with a broader understanding of themselves and their role in the world. The conditions that led these French noblewomen into a world where women had no place leading and the result of their work that inspired generations of women who followed them is the subject of this chapter.

Both Madame de Maintenon (1635–1719) and Jeanne Guyon (1648–1717) lived precarious lives, not uncommon given the social and political uncertainties of the period in which they lived, but remarkable considering what they were able to achieve. Their childhoods and early adulthoods were marked by emotional and physical suffering in addition to the economic hardship that stood in sharp contrast to the incredible wealth and power of the established elites who surrounded them. Their roles as teachers and mentors to other women and their children brought them close to the upper ranks of a highly stratified society. Both rose to become spiritual leaders to other noblewomen in distinct ways. One born a commoner, another a noblewoman, their paths crossed at the court of Louis XIV, a place beyond luxury for any French person, yet not without its snares. On the one hand, these two women navigated the winds of the king's will and the narrow confines of Roman Catholic Orthodoxy to arrive and secure positions at the most illustrious court of Europe. On the other hand, their upbringing and marriages that offered them entry to Versailles were contingent upon cultural conditions, many of which put strict limitations on women's freedom. For this was a world that treated daughters as moveable property, that minimized schooling to the point of functional literacy, and that circumscribed their religious lives in the secular world under an authoritarian, male priesthood. Their spiritual fortitude, which focused on bringing piety to the palace, gave one of the ladies access to the royal apartments, leading her into a private, holy union with the aging monarch. The other lady pursued a heartfelt devotion to God through unorthodox spiritual practices, which attracted other pious noblewomen to her initially. Later, these practices (and her spiritual instructions surrounding them) would be labeled "Quietism"—a heresy in the eyes of the Catholic Church and a capital crime against the state. These and other events in their lives, revealed in their private letters and diaries, recount moments of adversity and spiritual growth that shaped the aspirations that they held for women of their era.

Two Female Narratives of Adversity

Madame de Maintenon, born as Françoise d'Aubigné, lived most of her childhood on the margins of French society. Her family origins would be widely acknowledged as socially inferior, if not recognized as highly

disadvantaged. Françoise's childhood, similar to Oprah's, began in relative poverty and was also socially disadvantaged: one, a rural Mississippi
born African American woman with a single mother and no known
father, the other, born a commoner of Protestant lineage, of a father
who was disowned because of various crimes he committed, including abduction, treason, murdering his wife, and counterfeiting money.
Francoise's father, Constant d'Aubigné, was in prison when he met her
mother, the daughter of the prison warden. Upon his release, the two
married and left for Martinique with their new baby Françoise, Constant
intending to re-establish himself as ruling governor overseas (Conley
2002, 2–4). Françoise's mother soon found herself deceived and left destitute in the West Indies. In addition to this shattered beginning, the
time spent abroad inflicted the racial slur "jeunne indienne" upon the
girl. It isn't clear if Françoise ever knew her father. Her mother, finding
passage back to France, was reduced to begging in the streets, and placed
Françoise in the care of a relative, before leaving Françoise an orphan.
In one of her earliest memories, Françoise on her return to France falls
ill and nearly dies. The preparations were already being made for committing her body to the deep, when her mother realized there were still
signs of life. After retelling the story to the Bishop of Metz many years
later, Françoise was reminded, "Ah Madame, one does not come back
from that for nothing." (d'Aumale 1901–2, 16). Clearly, what she had
survived in her childhood—retold as an adult—had a profound effect
on her commitment to achieving something of worth.

   Bloodline and religious identity, while far from the racial divide of
America's long history of slavery and discrimination, distinguished
noble privilege in this period of the French Reformation. Because of
their commoner status, Madame de Maintenon's family maintained a
lesser rank that put them apart and cut off from noble ties of patronage.
The d'Aubignés came from a highly placed family of Huguenots, that
is, French Protestants, who served under "reformed" princes against an
"ultra" Catholic league of princes. In the prior century, wars between
these two groups cost thousands of lives; many Protestant noble families lost their titles and property to Catholics. Françoise's grandfather,
Théodore Agrippa d'Aubigné, was a distinguished general in these
religious wars that persisted for nearly two generations, first under
Condé (a Prince of the Blood) and, finally, under Henry of Navarre
(later Henry IV of France). The tightly controlled peace that ended
the Wars of Religion, the Edict of Nantes (1598), aimed at protecting Protestants, known as those of the "supposed reformed religion."
In effect, the Edict established a state within a state for this religious

sect. By the mid-seventeenth century, the increasingly diminishing Protestant minority had lost many of their "separate and unequal" legal protections (Holt 1995). Louis XIV, who as many biographers have conjectured, was under the moral suasion of Madame de Maintenon and her pious party at court, revoked the Edict in 1685, a year after their marriage. This ruling, which established "One King, One Law, and One Faith," forced Protestants to convert or emigrate, leaving little tolerance for religious pluralism of any kind.

Early biographers of Madame de Maintenon (Danielou 1946 and Langlois 1932), looking to find any evidence of her direct influence over the king's crushing blows against religious pluralism, would point to the early Protestant influences of her paternal aunt (her "real mother") and her "first conversion" to the Catholic faith at age 14 while boarding at a Ursuline convent in Paris. For Françoise, these and later conversions would be less doctrinal than personal in nature, explained in terms of shaping her own moral character. In a confessional conversation with Madame Glapion, Madame de Maintenon writes of her own battles with seeking her favored reputation out of self-love, saying "that was my idol, from it I would be then punished by the excesses of favor" (Maintenon 1810, 252). Because of her lowly status, she could never presume the blue-blooded virtue of a noble, it had to be proven and witnessed by others. Françoise's relationship with the king would develop slowly, first as governess to his bastard children, later as a secret love, admired for her virtue. By the time the queen had died and Louis had entered into the "religious" phase of his reign, he would entitle her Marquise de Maintenon and make her his spouse, but never the Queen of France. As her writings attest, her greatest triumph was the king's turn toward God and against the threat of schism posed by religious sects; her most highly valued legacy was the establishment of a secular school for girls at Saint-Cyr.

The rise of Madame de Maintenon is remarkable in many ways, but not unlike many ambitious families who saw the greatest opportunity for social advancement in marriage. As unmarried and attractive young women, Françoise d'Aubigné and Jeanne de la Mothe (later Jeanne Guyon) followed the path of many successful families who sought an early marriage for their daughters to build cultural capital among elites as well as moneyed assets to assure their futures. Françoise married at age 16 to poet Paul Scarron, an infirm man of 41, who introduced her to the highly privileged, intellectual world of the French salon. Jeanne's father arranged for her to marry at 15 a man more than 20 years her senior, and only after having met him two days before the wedding! Even as Françoise's marriage of eight years to an impotent, bed-ridden man could hardly have been happy, it did afford her an education in literature and languages. By contrast, it would be over a decade before Jeanne found herself free from the psychological strains inflicted by a domineering husband and an intrusive mother-in-law who chastised and limited her fervent daily devotions. Her marriage to Jacques Guyon du Chesnoy, a nobleman of enormous fortune, would decide much of her future as it provided her the means to establish a household that afforded hospitality to and intimate friendship of other women, most notably the Duchess of Charost, the wife of the disgraced finance minister Fouquet, who introduced her to the mystical teachings of the time, and other spiritual directors who would further her learning.

These marriages at the advent of puberty also forced Jeanne and Françoise into early adulthood with much older spouses. It seems doubtful that their education prepared them for sexual activity. But to speak of these relations as abusive (as our currently sensibilities might signal) would deny the fact that they entered marriage knowing that wives submitted to the demands of their husbands and that maintaining their virtue within marriage was paramount. Marital abuse is never implied in their life narratives. Why would it be? The confessions of these women focused on their own sins of pride, the abuse of other women or siblings, never seeing the power men held over them as unjustified or oppressive. Yet it seems clear that their relatively early widowhood comes as blessing to both. In each case, their husbands' deaths released them from the boundaries of the home, providing them with capital of various kinds to build their future careers. Widowhood also furthered their spiritual growth, cultivating the virtues of a quiet, interior life, one that humbly submits to a heavenly father.

Jeanne Guyon may not have faced the same type of precarious upbringing as Françoise. She never risked any transatlantic voyages at a young age, nor was she orphaned and then abandoned by her relatives. But Jeanne's early life was beset by her own fragile health and maternal neglect, which fostered a sense of isolation in her and urged her to seek divine love through prayer. Her mother's indifference was reinforced by her second marriage to a nobleman who had little interest in keeping his stepdaughter. Both favored Jeanne's brother in ways that forcibly demeaned her. Jeanne, like Madame de Maintenon, was sent off to a convent to be boarded and minimally schooled, in this case, at the fragile age of two-and-a-half. Jeanne's memoirs speak of her mother's overt favoritism toward her brother, who stole her food, burned her, and threw her from a carriage trying to kill her, all under the uncaring eyes of her mother (Guyon 2001, 126–128). The brunt of Jeanne's criticism fell upon "the harm that ensues when parents neglect the conduct of their children." Having been left to fend for herself and seemingly forgotten by the sisters who were supposed to be her caregivers, Jeanne sought affirmation through other channels, in this case, through reading the scriptures and the lives of saints. Jeanne's life narrative, written as a spiritual autobiography, speaks of her bodily suffering and worldly abandonment as the impetus to seek God's pure love. The confessional character of her memoirs elicit a new interior awareness of God that focused on intense introspection to deepen her spiritual experience. Encouraged by devout noblewomen around her, she sought to serve the church by converting Protestants in Calvinist strongholds. Once widowed, she realized the dream, leaving her children in the care of her mother-in-law to go to Geneva on mission. Her independent life as a spiritual leader had begun.

Once freed from her household, Jeanne Guyon began writing about her spiritual experiences and methods of prayer, putting her in touch with leading theologians and bishops François Fénelon and Jacques-Bénigne Bossuet, who served as the pious leaders at court. Winning the favor of these men and Madame de Maintenon, Madame Guyon began teaching at the newly formed school for girls at Saint-Cyr. During this time, she introduced unorthodox contemplative practices that spread throughout the school and raised rancor among orthodox church leaders because of their neglect of sacramental traditions. Guyon's own teachings on spirit-led prayer, closely associated with other "heretical" authors, were condemned by the church as Quietist, although she would continually deny the association. Madame Guyon was first put under "house arrest" at the Visitation convent outside Paris, and then released after Madame de Maintenon pressured the bishops of France to review her case. In November 1689, four years after the Revocation of the Edict of Nantes, Guyon's works were placed on the Papal Index of forbidden books. By the end of 1695, she was charged with heresy and imprisoned, first at the Chateau de Vincennes, then transferred to the Bastille in 1698. Her close companion and spiritual director, Father La Combe, would die in prison. Over the course of five years, after numerous appeals from loyal friends and by Jeanne herself, she was released from the Bastille a cripple, carried out on a stretcher.

French Nobility: Power and Sociability at Court

Jeanne Guyon and Madame de Maintenon experienced periods of hardship early in their lives, not unlike other women of their era. What is remarkable is how they overcame such oppressive and marginalized conditions to become women of significance whose influence was felt in the highest echelons of society. It would be wrong, however, to characterize their acts of defiance and pursuit of reform that set them apart from other women simply as a series of adroit maneuvers that they alone orchestrated, for both women had to acquire and maintain their elevated status through the favor of a chimerical and often heartless social elite. The world of nobility in the seventeenth century was highly refined, far from the "warrior caste" of the Middle Ages, but one that still "jousted" with words of wit and ridicule in the drawing rooms of the powerful. A woman's noble bloodline served as an enormous asset for commoners to enter into the ranks of the nobility, especially for wealthy bankers and merchants like Jacques Guyon, whose marriage to Jeanne assured their offspring would climb further into the upper aristocracy. Madame de Maintenon's service to the king's bastard children would be noted and her discretion would allow her greater access to the king. They had to win favor and be well placed to prove theselves in ways that others would notice.

The court culture at Versailles, while domesticating the nobility, also changed the ways in which elites participated in learned society. For noblewomen, participation meant the social intercourse of ideas exchanged in the formal atmosphere of Versailles and, increasingly, in the informal salons of their urban estates. Madame de Maintenon's own early marriage to poet Paul Scarron afforded her plenty of interaction with noble elites, many of whom noted her sharp mind and graceful demeanor, which served her well later at court. A fellow noblewoman, Madame de Sévigné (1626–1696), noted her cultivated intellect in a letter to her daughter:

> I have supper every evening with Mme Scarron. She has an agreeable and a marvelously sensible mind. It is a pleasure to hear her discussing the horrible disturbances of a region she knows well [such as love].... The most envied of them all [Madame de Montespan, Louis XIV's official mistress] is not always free from them.... This discussion sometimes takes us far and wide, from one moral to another, sometimes Christian, sometimes political. (1982, 116)

Female Elites and the Gallican Church under Renewal

While the growth of social intercourse among the nobility and the upper bourgeoisie drew attention to the intellectual capacities of women and called for greater educational opportunities for them, the Church in

France under Louis XIV provided a much greater institutional force, whose impact on female learning reached far beyond the capital and the upper social strata. Known as the "Gallican Church," with a political head governed by the "most Christian King" of France, the body of the church remained Roman Catholic in practice, while decidedly French in its administrative structure. Catholic reform that began at the Council of Trent (1543–1563) was carried out by French bishops throughout the late sixteenth and early seventeenth centuries under Louis XIV's command: "one faith, one law, one king." Reform codified pastoral instruction and church liturgy, change eventually making its way down to local priests in hundreds of parishes, bolstered by generations of the newly trained Jesuit leaders on mission to the local parishes throughout France. The renewal of the pastoral vocation through the education of male spiritual leaders benefited many women as it drew them into a greater concern for spiritual formation and good works. Many leaders of Catholic renewal – bishops, priests, and laypeople among them – directed their efforts to engage women in new forms of religious devotion, founding new female orders aimed to serve the poor, the sick, and the orphaned.

The most famous among the leaders of this conventual life was Jeanne de Chantal, who, along with Francis de Sales, founded the Sisters of Visitation. A daughter of a French noble magistrate in the Parlement of Burgundy, she turned from the role of manager of her late husband's estates to fulfill her dream as a bride of Christ under a new female order for young girls and widows that followed more relaxed rules without the austerities of long fasts and mortifications. When de Sales died in 1622, there were 13 convents; by the end of Jeanne de Chantal's life nearly 20 years later, there were over 80 that she inspired, if not had a hand in directing.

Inasmuch as the seventeenth century provided avenues for women, like Jeanne de Chantal and Jeanne Guyon, to flourish spiritually and intellectually in more public ways, the Gallican Church subjected these women (like all French people) to its repressive hand. Even as large numbers of women flocked to join the teaching order of the Ursulines, or to seek the spiritual purity of Jansenism behind the walls of Port-Royal, or to find a much freer atmosphere of intellectual conversation in the salons and, to a more limited extent, at court, the king censored theological literature and brutally policed challengers of orthodoxy as the church and all its satellite institutions fell under civil authority. Within this patriarchal system there was little room for female leadership in the church; female orders led by independently minded women were regarded with suspicion. Given these limitations, Jeanne Guyon's

own publication of *A Short and Easy Method of Prayer* appears as note-
worthy. The fact that her book inspired a generation of women to
follow her, even more so. But the widespread appeal of this work only
came when she had made herself independent of her family and reached
the inner female circles at Versailles, and as we shall see, introduced the
unorthodox practice to the girls at Saint-Cyr.

Patriarchal authority over women extended beyond the king, pope
and bishops into the household where fathers, like Jeanne Guyon's
own, did not always see the life religious with its vow of lifelong chas-
tity working in soup kitchens and hospitals as a satisfactory choice for
their daughters. Rather, most families of rank sought convent schools
as relatively inexpensive shelters to maintain female virtue until girls
were of marriageable age. Ursuline convent schools, like many other
new female orders, were dedicated to the secular vocations of teaching, but within the confines of conventual life. The Ursulines remained
the largest in France, with no less than 320 convents in various parts
of the country, the most prominent of which was Saint-Denis, north
of Paris, that took in 4,000 pupils between 1628 and 1657 (Rousselet
1883, I:322–24). Many of these convent schools sustained themselves by
boarding girls of the wealthier classes, while others, such as the school at
Saint-Denis, accepted day students, an option much more accessible to
the poor. Jeanne Guyon's two sisters, both Ursuline nuns, played a key
role in her early education and exposure to devotional literature. For
Madame de Maintenon, her tutelage under the Ursulines of Niort and
Paris gave her some Latin and shaped her literary skills, while it revealed
the institution's narrow focus on empty religious exercises and rote
learning. By the end of the seventeenth century, as religious renewal and
enlightened sociability among laywomen increased, the convents' traditional form of education appeared outdated, locked within the bounds
of monastic discipline. Talk of reform in female education at this time
came from noblewomen of the salon and liberal-minded church leaders, who sought to foster the intellectual acuity of young, privileged
women through stages of learning. Their developmental pedagogy also
captured the spiritual longing of laywomen, directing them toward an
authentic faith necessary for girls' moral upbringing.

Female Discipleship and Modern Devotion

The growing popularity of a vast devotional literature written for
women in the seventeenth century led many to seek a more meaningful

connection with God. The most popular work that reached a wide audience from young women in convent schools to elderly widows in society was the *Introduction à la Vie dévote* by Francis de Sales. The publication ran through 40 editions between 1608 when it first appeared and 1622, the year of the author's death. More popularly known as *La Philothée*, the guide was directed to women of means. It borrowed the name from the martyred saint of Athens, Philothée, who was forced to marry at age 12 to a cruel and violent man and was "delivered" by her death three years later. Noblewomen of the household, like Philothée, would endure suffering and be purified by it through their devotion to God. Piety was the premier noble quality that a woman would want to pursue, if not evince, through a desire to glorify her reputation.

While piety may have been the focus of a modern devotional movement, the structure of traditional convent schools focused on the preparation of girls as future brides of Christ, not future brides of men. The curriculum of these convent schools addressed a young girl's religious training, which followed the nuns' own daily exercises: mass, confession, communion, prayers, and prescribed silences. Their practical education was limited to learning basic arithmetic and giving girls a functional literacy that focused on transcribing devotional literature. There was little teaching that would help them fulfill the duties of motherhood. Rather, life lessons focused on the rules of precedence (highly useful at court), an ability to dance, to scrawl a badly written and worse spelt letter of compliment, to move gracefully in and out of rooms, and to parrot the gossip of society (Lewis 1997, 243). Even as these schools sought to bring a life of holy devotion into the world, the focus of their spiritual formation remained on the ordered life behind the convent walls.

Traditional convent teaching saw the education of women as secondary to providing strict habits of spiritual discipline. Even with ten years as a boarder in a Visitation convent, the young Jeanne de la Mothe was barely literate. Her ability to read and write was largely self-taught with some help from her half-sisters and her son's tutor. Because of her frequent convalescence, she often found herself in the company of a book. In her early teenage years, she discovered a penchant for novels and devotional literature, including Francis de Sales's works. She also spent a great deal of time reading the Bible. Her biblical literacy served her well later in life when her theological principles of God's love were challenged by theologians and church officials, but more often, it was a source of inspiration and reverie.

By contrast, Françoise was well schooled, but had little respect for what female education offered young women of the upper classes.

She was sent to the Ursulines in Niort and later to another convent at Faubourg Saint Jacques in Paris. While the nuns taught her reading, writing, spelling, and arithmetic, she held them in low regard for their lack of attention to moral upbringing. She was skeptical of the claim that a governess guaranteed a better education, as Madame de Maintenon herself was the one who taught her own governess how to read and write. In an instruction to one of Saint-Cyr's youngest students she writes,

> What would have happened to you if you had not come to Saint-Cyr? Your mother would have had at most two femmes de chamber, one of whom would have been your governess. What sort of education do you think such a woman would give you? As a rule they are peasants or at best *petites bourgeoises*, who know nothing beyond making you stand straight, and lace your corsets properly, or showing you how to curtsey well... The greatest fault according to them, is to upset the ink on the cloth; that is a crime worthy of the cane, because the governess has the trouble of washing and ironing it; but it doesn't matter if you tell lies as much as you like, because that does not necessitate any ironing or mending. (Maintenon 1861, II: 16–17)

The Women at Saint-Cyr, Its Educational and Spiritual Direction

Both Madame de Maintenon and Madame Guyon, who would lead noblewomen under a new vision for female education at Saint-Cyr, would speak of the inefficiencies and cruelties they experienced with Ursuline nuns. While the girls forged close friendships during their time at school, the nuns regarded any particular friendship as dangerous in that the pleasures of sisterly affection might lead to sinful behavior. Women, including Madame de Maintenon and Madame Guyon, were taught according to the Ursuline rules "that the contempt of the world and its vanities is one of the essentials of the Christian life" (Ursuline rules). The mistresses of these schools regarded it their duty to sanctify themselves through the strict education of girls, and in some extreme cases, to inflict severe rules of penance with the understanding that harsh discipline was morally beneficial. The work of Madame Guyon and Madame de Maintenon to institute a new school for girls at Saint-Cyr was in many ways a reaction to this treatment. As much as they sought their own virtues and noble glory blossom through forms of piety that were part of their own spiritual growth, the two also saw a need for moral education to temper the desire for religious vocation and spiritual intimacy. Their turn to moral foundations of female education was fostered by their relationship with François Fénelon.

Fénelon, the intellectually inspired archbishop of Cambrai, had gained his reputation a leading pedagogue with his publication *On the Education of Girls* in 1687, which advocated a holistic formation of the spirit, intellect, and character of young women so that they may be well prepared for their future responsibilities. His work, endorsed by Madame de Maintenon even before it was published, shifted the focus of education away from rote memorization and strict discipline. Fénelon directed his reform, like many other leading Catholics at this time, to raise the level of respect toward women, positing them as spiritual and moral leaders of their households. Just as François Fénelon called on parents to consider their daughters as sources of religious revival, Louis Bourdeloue, the most popular Jesuit preacher of the age, addressed women sitting in the pews of Versailles and Paris: "It is for you, mesdames, and on you who depends the sanctity and reform of Christianity; and if you were as Christian as you should be, the world by the good will will become Christian" (1750, 104). This attention to the spiritual formation of women brought Fénelon into aristocratic circles at Versailles, first as the tutor to the daughter of the Duchess of Beauvilliers and later as the royal tutor of Louis XIV's grandson, the Duc de Bourgogne.

Madame de Maintenon may have been influenced by Fénelon's approach to female education, but the making of the school at Saint-Cyr was entirely her own. Commissioned by the king, but clearly under her direction, the school took over a nearby estate and expanded it to include rooms to board (initially) over a 100 students. Like the many military academies the king established for the sons of noble military officers, Saint-Cyr was to serve girls of poor noble families, many of whom had lost their fathers in the numerous wars Louis fought in Europe and abroad. Louis's yearly endowment of 120,000 livres was to support the education of up to 250 demoiselles to the age of 20, whereupon each graduate was to be given a dowry of 3,000 livres whether she wished to marry or to enter a convent. Each applicant to Saint-Cyr not only had to establish her four degrees of noble lineage, but also her family's service to the king.

To be sure, the royal commissioning of Saint-Cyr elevated its reputation, but it was Madame de Maintenon's wide-reaching, holistic vision of education that gained the school long-lasting respect from the elite. Following her own enlightened salon background, Maintenon's school focused first and foremost on developing a lady's "capacity for reason." Yet the school went much further to exercise the virtuous character of women through spiritual exercises. As Madame de Maintenon wrote to her teachers: "Stir up their hearts, lift their spirit, tear down their bad inclinations, in a word, make them know and love virtue, as one always needs to work on it" (Maintenon 1885, 4–5). Her aim was to develop a girl who has learned to think and to see things as they are, who is well-read but was no pedant; she, according to Madame de Maintenon, was truly a thing of virtue. As headmistress of the school, she wanted to instill in her "demoiselles" the visible demonstrations of piety: a love of the catechism and a conviction that nothing is so important as the reception of the Sacraments. At the same time, she encouraged the performance of sacred music and theatrical productions, including the staging of the biblical heroine, Queen Esther. Chroniclers at court had commented on the "delightfulness" (Sévigné 1982) of Racine's play. The girls of Saint-Cyr were emboldened by it, seeing this singular royal figure who hides her Jewish identity and, with her dazzling beauty and deference, wins the favour of the king. More than simply an example of someone whose female attraction helped her rise to power, Esther embodied a virtuous role model for future queens, using her moral suasion to unveil a plot to annihilate her people. Esther, guided by God's sovereign hand, also posited a secular message of courageous female leadership that dazzled (and troubled) audiences, especially seeing the number of male suitors in attendance. They, along with other courtiers who were curious to visit Saint-Cyr (less than five miles from Versailles), came to observe what Madame de Maintenon's obsession was all about. Saint-Cyr, now far from the cloistered tradition, had become not only forward-thinking, but fashionable.

Perhaps the greatest innovation in Saint-Cyr's formation of young women to modern pedagogues came in the structure of classes that embraced developmental learning in a nurturing environment, at least one more open to conversation. Madame de Maintenon herself composed a number of dialogues that girls at the lowest level recited and put to memory with the intent of learning to speak properly and to the point. In numerous letters to the schoolteachers, the Dames de Saint-Cyr, Madame de Maintenon advised that they go softly with their pupils and be humble and docile with their religious instruction. The emphasis was on modeling behavior rather than forcing obedience and demanding acts of penance. Scholars have noted her pragmatic virtue and a "salonnière's concern with the style, not only the content, of ethical conduct" (Conley 2002, 137). She was well aware of indiscretion, if not self-possessed about the dangers of excessive piety. Temperance herself speaks in the dialogue, *On the Cardinal Virtues,* that her students recited:

> I calm the religious zeal that is too combative, too angry, too aggressive. I have to help religious faith conduct itself in a way that avoids excess. I moderate the desire to give alms as well as the desire to keep them. I limit the time for prayer, penances, retreat, silence, good works. I abbreviate a sermon. I shorten a session of spiritual direction or an examination of conscience. Finally, I have to soften even the flames of religious fervor. (Maintenon 2004, 35)

During the tumultuous "Quietist Affair," Saint-Cyr became "infected" with a highly unorthodox method of prayer. Not long before, Madame Guyon had been invited to Versailles and had established a friendship with Fénelon, who had sought the mystic for her spiritual counsel, helping him to escape "a dryness of soul" (James 2007, 14). In her method, others found a way to attune one's soul through the conduit of spirit-led prayer. It was Fénelon who introduced Madame Guyon to the court and to Madame de Maintenon. Together, the three formed the core of the devout party, praying regularly for God's hand to gently nudge the king to a more holy place. The personal piety of other grandees of the French court, dukes among them, also participated in this faction, leading many to identify them as "le court cenacle" or "Convent of the Court" with Fénelon at the center. While many women were initially drawn to the teachings of Guyon, her downfall (precipitated by another bishop, Bossuet, Fénelon's rival) would sever the relationship she had built with Madame de Maintenon at Saint-Cyr.

The Legacy of Saint-Cyr under Madame de Maintenon and Madame Guyon

During the seventeenth- and early eighteenth-centuries, religious identity among female elites was often caught between the political and ecclesiastic tensions under absolutism and the personal demands put upon women as forms of movable property as much as ossified vessels of female virtue. As the Counter-Reformation brought with it a place for women to engage their intellectual faculties in the salon, many sought new ways to cultivate their spiritual lives by focusing on questions of religious piety and morals. Madame de Maintenon's contribution to this significant shift in women's education is visible in the letters and chronicles of the life of Saint-Cyr. Founded upon religious and moral principles, this school sought to remain a center for women's education, particularly through religious conversation, throughout its life until the French Revolution. Even after the school's reform and its turn toward stricter conventual life, the intentions of female instructors remained fixed on developing the interior life of these women to make them great citizens, good mothers, and virtuous wives. Their formation was in keeping with Mme de Maintenon's religious leanings that aimed to build a Christian character through blessed living, one centered on a personal piety lived out in family and marriage.

The legacy of this education persists in the generations that followed Madame de Maintenon, particularly the eulogistic biography of her by her former students, the Dames de Saint-Cyr. This was a school whose mission was clearly imprinted in the minds of its graduates, evidenced in the memoires of Henriette Victoire de Bombelles, who spoke of the importance of modesty, piety, kindness, gentleness, a disciplined life, the fear of God and his divine love and faithfulness in all realms of life—virtues taken directly from the school's own statutes (Cuirot 2002, 169). For Jeanne Guyon, whose final years were spent in self-imposed isolation having escaped execution for accusations of heresy, her mystical union with God and method of prayer inspired generations of religious reformers and continue to do so today.

In aspiring to foster a sense of holiness for elite women, who were more often attuned to skills of deception and artifice, Madame Guyon and Madame de Maintenon dedicated their lives to the kind of upbringing they never received. They sought to instill in young women a desire for virtue and pure love—spiritual goals that eclipsed the subordinate place women held under patriarchal authority. Knowing how feminine beauty or, at the very least, a desire for social status directed false attention to them, how their own pride and vanity misled them, they sought to carve out a sanctuary for women, a site where the formation of moral character would provide the governing beliefs that women needed in order to thrive.

References

Aumale, Madamoiselle d'. 1901–02. *Souvenirs sur Madame de Maintenon: Memoire et lettres inédit de Madamoiselle d'Aumale*, vol. 1. Paris: Editions Haussonville.

Barnard, H. C. 1934. *Madame de Maintenon and Saint-Cyr*. London: A. C. Black.

Bourdeloue, Louis. 1750. "Sermon sur l'impureté, 1682" in *Sermons du père Bourdeloue pour l'Avent*. Paris: Au depens de la Compagnie.

Conley, John J. 2002. *The Suspicion of Virtue: Women Philosophers in Neoclassical France*. Ithaca, NY: Cornell University Press.

Conlin, Michelle, Lauren Gard, and Jessie Hempel. "The Top Givers." *Bloomberg Businessweek*, November 28, 2004.

Cuirot, Marie. 2002. "Henriette Victoire de Bombelles: Une jeune fille issue de Saint-Cyr se marie au siècle des lumières (1773–1775)." *Histoire, économie et société* 21(2): 161–172.

Dames de Saint-Cyr. 1846. *Memoires sur Madame de Maintenon*. Paris: Olivier-Fulgence.

Danielou, Madeleine. 1946. *Madame de Maintenon, Educatrice*. Paris: Editions Bloud & Gay.

Dubu, Jean. 1999. *Les Demoiselles de Saint-Cyr: Maison royale d'éducation, 1686–1793*. Versailles: Archives départementales des Yvelines.

Faguet, Émile. 1885. *Madame de Maintenon, Institutrice: Extraits de ses lettres, avis entretiens, conversations et proverbs sur l'éducation*. Paris: Librairie Classique H. Oudin.

Fénelon, François de Salignac de La Mothe. 1883. *Traité de l'éducation des filles*. Paris: Ch. Delagrave.

Goodman, Dena. 1998. "Women and the Enlightenment." In Renate Bridenthal, Susan Mosher Stuard, and Merry Wiesner, eds., *Becoming Visible: Women in European History*, 233–262. Boston: Houghton-Mifflin Co.

Guyon, Jeanne-Marie. 2001. *La vie par elle-même et autres écrits biographiques*. Edited by Dominique Tronc. Paris: Honoré Champion.

Guyon, Jeanne. 2012. *Selected Writings*. Translated, edited and introduced by Dianne Genin-Lelle and Ronney Mourad. New York: Paulist Press.

Guyon, Madame Jeanne de la Mothe. 2012. *Bastille Witness: The Prison Autobiography of Madame Guyon (1648–1717)*. Edited by Nancy Carol James. Translated by Sharon D. Voros. Lanham, MD: University Press of America.

Holt, Mack P. 1995. *The French Wars of Religion, 1562–1629*. Cambridge: Cambridge University Press.

James, Nancy. 2007. *The Pure Love of Madame Guyon: The Great Conflict in King Louis XIV's Court*. Lanham, MD: University Press of America, Inc.

Langlois, Marcel. 1932. *Madame de Maintenon*. Paris: Plon.

Lewis, W. H. (1953) 1997. *The Splendid Century: Life in the France of Louis XIV*. Long Grove, IL: Waveland Press, Inc.

Lofton, Kathryn. 2011. *Oprah: The Gospel of an Icon*. Berkeley: University of California Press.

Maintenon, Françoise d'Aubigné. 1810. *Madame de Maintenon par elle-même*. Paris: Maradan.

Maintenon, Madame de. 1756. *Lettres de Madame de Maintenon*. 7 vols. Troisième edition. Glasgow: aux dépens des libraires associés.

Maintenon, Madame de. 2004. *Dialogues and Addresses*. Edited and translated by John J. Conley. Chicago: University of Chicago Press.

Oprah Winfrey Leadership Academy for Girls. 2014. "OWLAG Promo" Accessed December 15. http://www.owla.co.za/leadership.html#.

Prevot, Jacques. 1981. *La premiere institutrice de France, Madame de Maintenon*. Paris; Belin.

Rousselot, Paul. (1888) 1971. *Histoire de l'éducation des femmes en France*. 2 vols. New York: B. Franklin.

Sévigné, Madame de. 1982. *Selected Letters*. Translated by Leonard Tancock. New York: Penguin Books.

Steinbrügge, Lieselotte. 1992. *The Moral Sex: Woman's Nature in the French Enlightenment*. Translated by Pamela E. Selwyn. New York: Oxford University Press.

Timmermans, Linda. 1993. *L'acces des femmes à la culture (1598–1715): Un débat d'idées de Saint François de Sales à la Marquise de Lambert*. Paris: Champion.

Ward, Patricia. 2005. "Madame Guyon (1648–1717)." In Carter Lindberg, ed., *The Pietist Theologians*, 161–174. Oxford: Blackwell Publishing.

CHAPTER FOUR

The President as Spiritual Leader: Pardons, Punishment, Forgiveness, Mercy, and Justice

HENRY L. CHAMBERS, JR.

A pardon is an act of grace....
—*United States v. Wilson*, 32 U.S. 150, 160 (1833)

A pardon in our days is not a private act of grace from an individual happening to possess power.
—*Biddle v. Perovich*, 274 U.S. 480, 486 (1927)

Introduction

The Constitution of the United States empowers the president of the United States to curtail or eliminate punishment for actual or possible federal criminal wrongdoing by issuing pardons.[1] As the quotes that begin this chapter suggest, the nature of a presidential pardon is subject to dispute. A pardon can be thought to be an act of grace or an extension of the president's executive power to administer the criminal justice system, or something in between.[2] This chapter does not resolve the issue, but considers the nature of the pardon power while considering whether or how the president can or should exercise spiritual leadership through the use of the pardon power.[3] The pardon power, with its focus on punishment, provides the president the opportunity to exercise spiritual leadership where law, punishment, forgiveness, mercy, and justice meet.

For the purposes of this chapter, spiritual leadership is defined as values-based leadership that focuses on the humanity and humanness of those who will be affected by a decision rather than on primarily seeking to identify the best or most administratively sound decision that could be made.[4] In the context of pardoning, spiritual leadership does not entail ignoring the proper administration of the law and should be exercised with due respect for the law.[5] Nonetheless, spiritual leadership grounds the administration of the criminal justice system in the service of goals such as justice and compassion rather than merely in the service of just punishment as defined by the sentence the law authorizes a defendant to receive.[6] Spiritual leadership may be informed by religion, but it need not be religion based.[7] It is fundamentally moral leadership that may or may not lean toward religion. The definition of spiritual leadership this chapter adopts could be refined, but need not be. The line between spiritual and nonspiritual leadership will never be crystal clear. The key is not whether one agrees with precisely how spiritual leadership is defined, but whether one agrees with the considerations that this chapter suggests can and, at times, arguably should underlie the president's use of the pardon power.

Considering whether the president ought to exercise spiritual leadership may seem nonsensical. The president is the political leader of the United States and the chief executive of the federal government. The president exercises leadership, but may need to exercise spiritual leadership no more than the chief executive of any large or significant organization.[8] More important, the president need not be trained in any way that would prepare him to provide spiritual leadership. Wisdom might suggest that the president seek spiritual guidance from others while leaving spiritual leadership to others as well. However, when President Abraham Lincoln summoned the better angels of our nature and spoke of malice toward none and charity toward all during his inaugural addresses, he spoke as more than just the president. A century later, when President Lyndon Johnson called for equal civil rights, equal voting rights, and a war on poverty, he spoke not only as the president, but as the nation's conscience. As the leader of an ostensibly peaceful nation that has used armed force when it thought necessary, the president of the United States ought to understand and reflect the nation's spiritual and moral core.[9]

As the leader of the United States, the president could be considered the most appropriate person in the country to provide spiritual leadership to the country. The Declaration of Independence and the Constitution are two of the United States' foundational documents.

Both documents have spiritual roots. The Declaration notes that the point of government is to facilitate the exercise of the rights that the Creator has given the people. The Preamble to the Constitution notes that the Constitution was established to "in order to form a more perfect union, establish justice, ensure domestic tranquility, provide for the common defence, promote the general welfare and secure the blessings of liberty to ourselves and our posterity[.]" The head of the government created by the Constitution should be able to exercise secular spiritual leadership when performing the functions of government, even if he is not a spiritual leader.[10] In matters of punishment and pardon, war and peace, and life and death, spiritual decision making is appropriate if not necessary. Situations may arise where the president may wish to call on religious or spiritual leaders prior to making a decision. Not only may the president be required to call upon his own spirituality or morality in the course of performing his regular duties, he may be expected to justify his decisions in terms that suggest a recognition of the spiritual or moral dimension of a problem.[11] At the least, the president ought to have the capacity to demonstrate spiritual leadership when necessary.

This chapter considers the president's constitutional pardon power and what opportunities that power creates for the president to demonstrate spiritual leadership. This chapter first outlines presidential power and the parameters of the pardon power. Then, it discusses how pardons relate to punishment and forgiveness. Last, it considers how the president can use the pardon power to demonstrate spiritual leadership.

The Presidency

The powers of the president of the United States are not structured to guarantee or forestall spiritual leadership. The Constitution vests the executive power of the United States in the president, but does not define what executive power is.[12] The president takes an oath of office requiring that he swear or affirm that he "will faithfully execute the Office of President of the United States" and "will preserve, protect and defend the Constitution of the United States," but the Constitution does not explain how the president is supposed to do that.[13] Though the president is the chief executive of the federal government, the presidency requires no special training or skills. Natural born citizens who are at least 35 years old and have been residents of the United States for 14 years are eligible to serve as president.[14] The dearth of textual constraints on the president's exercise of power suggests that the president is generally free to style the presidency as the president wishes. That provides the president significant latitude to exercise spiritual leadership in using the powers of the presidency or not.

Specific Powers of the Presidency

In addition to assigning the president the executive power of the United States, the Constitution provides the president specific powers and responsibilities that help illuminate the breadth and content of the president's function. For example, the president is directed to take care that the laws of the United States are faithfully executed,[15] serves as the commander-in-chief of the armed forces, and may veto legislation subject to the possibility of a congressional override of the veto.[16] However, the Constitution does not explain how those powers and responsibilities should be exercised, save in the service of preserving, protecting, and defending the Constitution. As with the general executive power, the president is not much constrained by textual limitations on the aforementioned powers. The Supreme Court may divine constitutional limits to presidential power, but such limits tend to be based on the interpretation of structural constitutional limits rather than on explicit textual commands.[17]

The "take care" power is related to the executive power, but its contours are unclear.[18] The take-care power necessarily provides the president the latitude to interpret statutes and determine how best to implement legislation; it does not tell the president how to interpret laws for the purpose of executing them. The president may not interpret laws so aggressively as to functionally legislate, as the legislative power of the United States has been granted to Congress.[19] Other than that, textual limits on the president's take-care power are few. As important, the Constitution does not tell the president whether he should take care that the laws be faithfully executed for the spiritual or moral good of the country or for other reasons.

Though the contours of the commander-in-chief power seem clearer than the contours of the take-care power, that clarity may be illusory. Whether the commander-in-chief provision merely guarantees civilian control of the military or demands that the president have day-to-day control over the military is unclear from the Constitution's text. Similarly, the commander-in-chief clause appears to provide the president broad powers to administer the armed forces and to prosecute war, but does not tell the president how to do so.[20] Though the commander-in-chief power has a moral dimension in times of war, the power arguably can be exercised strictly administratively or amorally in times of peace.

The Constitution gives the president the power to veto legislation, but does not explain why the president has the veto power or how it should be exercised.[21] The president can veto legislation that the president believes is unconstitutional or that the president does not think is good for the country or that the president does not like. However, those reasons are not equally justifiable. The president may have a moral obligation to veto legislation the president believes to be unconstitutional if the president's oath to preserve, protect, and defend the Constitution is to have meaning. If the president believes legislation is bad for the country, consistent with the president's obligation to serve the country, the president arguably has a responsibility to veto the legislation. The president has the power to veto legislation based on mere personal dislike for the legislation though the president believes the legislation to be good for the country, but has relatively little justification for doing so. The Constitution appears to allow the president to exercise veto power whenever and however the president wants, in service of higher purposes or lower purposes.

The Constitution does not explain how the president should take care that the laws are faithfully executed or how the president should discharge his commander-in-chief responsibilities or when the president should veto legislation. It does not indicate whether the president should exercise spiritual leadership when discharging those duties. The lack of detail suggests that these powers need not be exercised in any particular fashion, leaving the president to decide whether to exercise them consistent with administrative efficiency or spiritual leadership or both. The same appears to apply to the pardon power. However, the pardon power may implicate morality and spirituality more directly than the presidential powers mentioned above. That may suggest that a president's decision to consider or decline to consider spiritual leadership when exercising the pardon power may itself have a moral dimension.

The Pardon Power

The Constitution empowers the president "to grant reprieves and pardons for offences against the United States, except in cases of impeachment."[22] This allows the president broad power to eliminate the possibility of punishment for criminal offenses against the United States and to commute and nullify sentences for convictions for criminal offenses against the United States.[23] A pardon can be thought to be an exercise of preemptive or post-hoc prosecutorial discretion that is consistent with the use of executive power to administer the criminal justice system or the pardon power can be thought to operate in derogation of law.[24] That the pardon power is largely unfettered and unchecked and is exercised solely by the president does not clarify its nature.[25] Various eighteenth-century political thinkers, including some of the Constitution's framers, worried about the nature of pardoning.[26] Concern that the presidential pardon power may be antidemocratic and monarchical[27] is unsurprising given that, though pardoning is an ancient practice, the Constitution's pardon power is drawn from the royal prerogative of English monarchs.[28] Nonetheless, the presidential pardon power must be exercised consistent with democratic principles and with the Constitution's recognition that the citizenry, not the president, is the sovereign.[29]

The pardon power can be exercised in five ways.[30] The president can issue a full pardon that reverses a conviction or forestalls the possibility of prosecution. For example, President Ford's pardon of President Nixon eliminated the possibility of Nixon's prosecution.[31] The president can truncate punishment by commuting a sentence. The president can reverse fines and forfeitures. The president can grant a reprieve to postpone punishment to allow the justice system to reconsider its decision or for other reasons. Finally, the president can grant amnesty, which typically focuses on a group and is aimed at not prosecuting a particular crime rather than a particular person. The Civil War and post–Civil War pardons of Confederates amounted to an amnesty.[32] The use of the pardon power in the various manners mentioned above, as a way of regulating the criminal justice system, makes it a legitimate part of the democratic republic rather than a monarchical power held over from the colonial era.[33]

Pardoning can serve many different functions. A pardon can be an act of grace limited only by the executive's standard of mercy that is exercised for the benefit of the pardoned.[34] A compassionate pardon that allows release so a prisoner can die at home might qualify as an act of grace. A pardon can be a discretionary act by the executive limiting punishment to guarantee that punishment carried out in the name of the citizenry is fair and proportional rather than too harsh and unjust. A pardon can be a purely administrative act when the justice system needs to be corrected by its ultimate administrator, for example, when a wrongfully convicted prisoner is pardoned. A pardon can be given to end the specter of prosecution when such prosecution is thought to be potentially bad for the country. Why the president issues a pardon is left to the president, as is whether the president exercises spiritual leadership when issuing a pardon.

The next section of this chapter considers how pardons relate to punishment and forgiveness as a prelude to considering whether and how the president can or should use the pardon power to demonstrate spiritual leadership.

Punishment, Forgiveness, and Pardon

Punishment, forgiveness, and pardon are often connected, and all can be related to spiritual leadership. Forgiveness can be a central justification for lessening a punishment or it can be tangential to punishment. A pardon often relates to ending or negating punishment, but may also be granted after punishment—in the form of a criminal sentence—has been fully served. How punishment, forgiveness, and pardon are related is important. Their interrelatedness allows the president to demonstrate spiritual leadership when exercising the pardon power. In this context, spiritual leadership may require that the president recognize that an offender is not merely an abstraction to be punished or acted on, but that the offender should be treated with humanity and dignity even though his or her actions were criminal.

Punishment and Mercy

Criminal punishment is the state-sanctioned negative treatment of an individual in response to criminal wrongdoing. It reflects society's moral outrage in response to the crime. The harsher the crime the more serious the outrage and the harsher the punishment given.[35] Punishment can take several forms, including death, incarceration, probation, and fine.[36] Punishment can be justified by retribution, ostensibly because the criminal deserves the punishment, or it can be justified by utilitarian reasons, such as incapacitation, deterrence, or rehabilitation.[37] Even when authorized by the criminal justice system, punishment can be considered a wrong that must be justified.[38] The punishment ought to be justified when the sentence is announced and as the sentence is served.

Mercy is a grant of leniency for the punishment that the law allows or requires that the criminal receive, such as a mandatory minimum sentence for a particular crime, or deems the criminal to deserve.[39] Justifications for mercy are varied. The circumstances surrounding a particular crime, including the reasons the wrongdoer may have had for commiting the crime, may be such that an appropriate punishment would appear to be less punishment than the law requires. Mercy might seem appropriate at sentencing, even though mercy may be prohibited at sentencing. In addition, as a prisoner serves a sentence, circumstances may arise or factors may be uncovered that would appear to make continued punishment unnecessary though continued punishment is authorized or mandated by law. Under those circumstances, mercy may be sensible though it is never required.

Forgiveness

Forgiveness can be related to, but is more complex than, punishment or mercy. It has multiple meanings.[40] For example, forgiveness can entail foregoing what is owed, such as forgiving a debt, or it can focus on how a victim processes the harm a transgressor has caused.[41] This chapter focuses on the latter conception. Though precision may obscure as much as clarify, a working definition of forgiveness is useful.[42] Forgiveness is the abandonment of the ill will or ill feelings that a victim may reasonably feel toward a transgressor as a result of being harmed.[43]

The nature of forgiveness is tricky. Though some suggest that forgiveness is supposed to involve getting past or getting over a harm, forgiveness is not about forgetting or ignoring the harm.[44] Forgiveness is as much about remembering with a purpose as it is about forgetting.[45] Rather than focusing merely on pushing through the harm a transgressor has caused, forgiveness is about recognizing the harm that has been caused while understanding that the past should not imprison the victim.[46] Forgiveness requires remembering, but without rancor or resentment.[47]

Forgiveness has not always been a commonplace practice and it is not a timeless concept. Indeed, it was not considered a classical virtue.[48] The modern concept of forgiveness may not have been invented by Jesus of Nazareth, but it has been given significant life through his teachings.[49] However, forgiveness need not be religious.[50] Though some may suggest that forgiveness is more easily understood when it has a religious basis, religiosity need not be a precursor to or justification for forgiveness.[51] Secular forgiveness can be as important as religious forgiveness, particularly if religious forgiveness is considered too automatic and reflexive to be useful as an incentive for transgressors to correct their behavior.[52]

What forgiveness requires and, consequently, how easily forgiveness can occur is subject to debate. Forgiveness may be quite limited if it requires that a transgressor seek forgiveness from a victim for a harm inflicted. The transgressor may not feel the need to be forgiven if the transgressor does not believe he acted wrongfully.[53] The transgressor may not be remorseful even if he knows he committed the wrong. Lastly, even if the transgressor is remorseful and knows he was the wrongdoer, he may not wish to request forgiveness. Though limiting forgiveness to situations in which the transgressor requests forgiveness may seem sensible, if forgiveness focuses on the injured person foregoing rancor and resentment regarding a past wrong, whether the transgressor seeks forgiveness may be irrelevant.[54] Forgiveness without a request for forgiveness may not serve to reconcile a wrong in any meaningful way; it may merely allow the victim to move on. Of course, forgiveness need not always lead to reconciliation. Though feelings of resentment dissipate when forgiveness is given, that alone does not ensure that the transgressor and victim will reconcile. Rather, they may merely no longer be openly hostile.[55]

A limitation on who can forgive may limit how often forgiveness occurs. Though an interpersonal vision of forgiveness that requires that the injured be willing to forgive and that the transgressor be willing to ask for forgiveness may appear to be the most traditional or authentic form of forgiveness, it is also quite limiting.[56] The victim appears to be the only person who can forgive the harm. Such a limitation may be problematic if forgiveness is to be the first step in encouraging a change in the transgressor.

Though the power to forgive may be limited to victims, a transgression may have multiple victims yielding multiple avenues for forgiveness. The transgressor's immediate victim can forgive. In addition, a form of forgiveness may come from someone who has been harmed by the transgression, but was not the primary victim of the harm. These secondary victims can forgive the transgressor for the harm that was done to them. For example, a transgressor who harms my spouse has harmed me as well. I can forgive the wrongdoer for the hurt he caused me by harming my spouse.[57] This forgiveness is not complete, but may begin a process of change in the transgressor.

The secondary victim may not be able to forgive the wrongdoer for the harm he did to the primary victim because the secondary victim may not have the authority to do so.[58] Allowing such third-party forgiveness on behalf of another is controversial and problematic. Nonetheless, some have argued that such forgiveness is appropriate when some form of authority to forgive has been passed to the third party by the victim or could be reasonably assumed by the third party.[59] The circumstances under which that would be sensible appear few and very specific.[60] In the absence of such circumstances, third-party forgiveness would appear to be just words spoken by someone without the authority to forgive, even if the circumstances were such that forgiveness should have been given.[61] Conversely, some argue that not only can third parties forgive, but that groups can forgive.[62] As noted below, who has the authority to forgive and what may be forgiven has important implications for forgiveness through presidential pardon.

Forgiveness and Punishment

Forgiveness does not preclude punishment. Forgiveness relates to the victim's feelings toward the transgressor and the transgression and may depend on whether the transgressor has requested forgiveness. Punishment focuses on whether the transgressor should suffer a negative outcome because of the transgression. When punishment is based on retribution or just desert, the factors that may trigger forgiveness may be unrelated to the factors that trigger punishment.[63] When punishment is based on utilitarian reasons, remorse and acceptance of wrongdoing by the transgressor that may precede a request for forgiveness may be relevant to the amount of punishment an offender should face.[64]

Mercy entails foregoing punishment that is authorized or deserved. Forgiveness and mercy are related, but forgiveness does not guarantee mercy. An offender can be forgiven, but be punished without mercy precisely because punishment is deserved.[65] Conversely, one can be given mercy, with punishment foregone, but not be forgiven for the wrongdoing that triggered the punishment. This is clear when the forgiver and the punisher are different people or entities, such as, when a victim is the forgiver and the government is the punisher. However, even in an interpersonal relationship, such as a parent-child relationship, where the parent may have the power to both punish and forgive, the forgiver need not be merciful. The parent's forgiveness does not always preclude the need for punishment, particularly if other children will be influenced by the lack of punishment.[66]

Pardon and Punishment

Punishment and pardon are inextricably linked. A pardon can end or eliminate the possibility of punishment; the refusal to grant a pardon may extend punishment. Punishment is a wrong—consider the death penalty or imprisonment—though it can be beneficial, necessary, or justifiable.[67] Given that punishment is a wrong, it should be re-justified or re-justifiable each day that a wrongdoer is punished. An official's decision to eliminate punishment or possible punishment may have a spiritual dimension, one that focuses on the offender's humanity, if the official takes seriously the obligation to justify punishment each day it is given. Releasing a prisoner from serving the remainder of a sentence that has been lawfully authorized may have a spiritual dimension. Barring new information about the crime, the discretionary decision to curtail a sentence usually should be based on the prisoner's transformation in response to punishment or some reason that suggests that a pardon would be for the good of the country or the judicial system.

Refusing to pardon a prisoner and continuing to allow the prisoner to be punished may also have a moral or spiritual dimension. When punishment is provided for retributive purposes, that is, because the offender deserves to be punished, enforcing the punishment may carry a moral dimension. When the punishment is deserved, society may have an obligation to punish the offender fully.[68] Requiring that punishment be inflicted may affirm the victim's humanity by indicating that harm to the victim is worthy of the offender's continued punishment. Conversely, when punishment is provided for purely utilitarian purposes, whether an offender's punishment should or should not continue may become primarily an administrative matter. If society, through the legislature, has determined that punishment of a certain length will be given because punishment of that length will serve a penal purpose, forcing the prisoner to continue serving his sentence may not be a matter of spirituality or morality as much as a matter of confirming the certainty of punishment and wresting any additional utilitarian value from the punishment that may exist.

Pardon and Forgiveness

A pardon need not be premised on forgiveness, though it may be.[69] A president can pardon in circumstances that do not suggest forgiveness. For example, President Ford's pardon of President Nixon did not suggest forgiveness. It merely suggested that the country would not be well served by the prosecution of a former president.[70] The same can be said of some amnesties. The Civil War–era amnesty of former Confederates could be justified by a desire for the country to reconcile and move on after the war, but it may have been unrelated to forgiveness.[71]

Grounding pardons on forgiveness appears difficult because of problems related to third-party forgiveness. A pardon will often appear to entail third-party forgiveness. Indeed, even if a pardon is grounded on beliefs regarding the changed nature of the prisoner's soul, the pardon would not seem to be based on traditional first-party, interpersonal forgiveness.[72] A presidential pardon and forgiveness would seem hopelessly separate. The president could encourage the victim to forgive, but could not forgive on the victim's behalf.

However, a pardon may reflect a type of forgiveness that echoes interpersonal forgiveness. A crime that has a victim is both an attack on the victim and an attack on the sovereign, both the jurisdiction and its people.[73] Indeed, given that presidential pardons apply to federal crimes or offenses against the United States,[74] the president may be able to forgive on behalf of the country for the harm the country suffered from the commission of the crime.[75] Indeed, arguably, no one other than the president is in the position to forgive a crime in a representative capacity, in the same way that no one other than the victim is in the position to forgive the harm to the victim. The president cannot forgive for the harm a victim has suffered because of the act, but the president may be able to forgive for the harm that the country has suffered because of the crime.

The style of forgiveness the president can give can be likened to political forgiveness discussed by Peter E. Digeser in his book *Political Forgiveness*. Political forgiveness focuses on what can be forgiven, by whom, and what that might mean for reconnecting a transgressor with the state. Political forgiveness bridges the concept of mere administrative pardon and pardon that entails interpersonal forgiveness. Political forgiveness allows a president to pardon and give real forgiveness from the state's perspective, but would not necessarily allow for the interpersonal forgiveness that the state lacks the standing to provide. Though political forgiveness is not interpersonal forgiveness, political forgiveness may encourage interpersonal forgiveness.[76] The president could justify political forgiveness with reference to spiritual forgiveness, but need not do so.

The president has the power to pardon. That power arguably comes with the power to provide political forgiveness for the harm that criminal activity caused to the nation. That power could help reconcile the transgressor with the polity. The power to pardon does not come with the power to provide interpersonal forgiveness on behalf of the victim of a crime, but it does come with the power to make a statement about punishment and demonstrate spiritual leadership. The last part of this chapter considers whether and how the president should use the pardon power to exercise secular spiritual leadership.

The President, Pardon, and Spiritual Leadership

The president can demonstrate spiritual leadership focused on the humanness and humanity of offenders through the use of the pardon power. As the head of the federal criminal justice system, the president has ultimate responsibility for punishment meted out by that system. Though recent presidents have used pardons sparingly and somewhat poorly, the president has the explicit power to cancel punishment and to attempt to reconcile offenders with society through the pardon power.[77] As important, the president has the implicit power—through the Attorney General and the Department of Justice—to defer criminal prosecutions and effectively provide pre-emptive pardons without using the pardon power. Those tools allow the president to manage the punishment provided by the criminal justice system in a purely administrative fashion or to comment on how and why we punish, while demonstrating spiritual leadership in the process.

When a pardon is used to block punishment for an offender's criminal activity or to provide amnesty to a group of people for committing a particular crime in a particular way, the president may signal that the prosecution of such cases is unjust as a matter of principle. The president must enforce the laws of the nation. However, when the enforcement of a particular law in a particular way may lead to an unjust result, pardon or amnesty may be appropriate.[78] For example, some may consider prosecution for the use of medical marijuana under federal drug laws to be an unjust attempt to deny medicine to people. Prosecution of such cases would unquestionably be lawful, but may not be consistent with justice.[79] When the enforcement of a law may lead to an unjust result, punishment may be legally justified but undeserved. A refusal to allow punishment for such a violation of the law through use of the pardon power is a commentary on what the president believes is right and wrong, just and unjust. That some crimes need not be punished, even when the criminal justice system allows an offender to be punished, can be a powerful comment on why the government does or does not punish.

The president can use the pardon power, in the form of a reprieve, to delay punishment. Delaying punishment is fundamentally different than cancelling the punishment. Nonetheless, when a reprieve is given to allow the justice system an additional opportunity to reconsider before punishment is rendered, the reprieve may serve the ends of justice, even if the punishment is reaffirmed and ultimately enforced. A reprieve may serve as a reminder that the United States does not punish until it is sure the punishment is deserved.

Even when punishment is justified, the president can use the pardon power to commute sentences when the president believes that an offender has been punished sufficiently. The use of the power to reverse fines and forfeitures can be justified in similar fashion. The president may determine that a sentence that was authorized by law and justified when given may not continue to be justifiable if continued punishment does not serve an appropriate penal purpose. When the prime justification for continued punishment is that the law authorized such punishment at some point in the past, the president could deem the use of the commutation power appropriate to end the punishment. That could be an important comment by the president that punishment ought to be justified or justifiable every day that the sentence is carried out and that punishment must stop once it can no longer be justified, because an offender continues to be a human rather than an entity to be acted upon.

How the president explains the use of the pardon power—which the president ought to do—may determine whether the president exercises spiritual leadership through its use.[80] The president can use the pardon power, in any of its manifestations, to call for societal reconciliation with offenders.[81] Such reconciliation with the polity could be facilitated regardless of the posture the pardoned offender may occupy—an offender who has served a full sentence or an offender who has yet to complete his sentence or an offender who has received amnesty.[82] In circumstances where a conviction has led to the loss of political or civic rights, a pardon could be the first step toward the restoration of rights that might trigger reconciliation. Such a restoration would call for treating those who have been sufficiently punished for their wrongdoing as full citizens again.[83] Eventually, that may lead to the public treating reengaged offenders in a way that might suggest forgiveness. That may be an exercise of spiritual leadership.

The pardon power can be used to encourage interpersonal forgiveness by victims or to request forgiveness on behalf of the federal government. A well-reasoned pardon can suggest that extracting punishment may be secondary to the process of forgiveness and possible reconciliation. Though the pardon may, at best, provide for political reconciliation, it can encourage citizens to reexamine their own actions. A pardon may have no effect on the hearts or minds of the public, but it can send a bold message of spiritual and political leadership. Conversely, the president can use the pardon power to ask for forgiveness for the federal prosecution of criminal activity when prosecuting such activity was patently unjust, though technically authorized by the United States.[84] Such a pardon could act as an apology or a nonmonetary form of reparation. A governmental request for forgiveness for engaging in actions that were authorized by law would be an act of spiritual leadership.

Broadly, the president can use pardons, whether supported by forgiveness or mercy or not, to begin or sustain a national conversation about why we punish and how much we punish. Our traditional bases for punishment, particularly retribution, necessarily consider the spiritual and the individual. Even if the goal of the justice system is to provide an administrative structure that attempts to provide equal punishment for equal crimes, individualized justice may require consideration of spiritual issues. The president can note that spiritual considerations are relevant to how much punishment the offender deserves and how much punishment an offender needs to endure for society to have done its job of enforcing justice. Those issues can be spoken about in spiritual terms and those issues are at the core of how the president executes the pardon power that we the people as the sovereign in the United States have given to the office.

Conclusion

The president is the leader of the United States of America in whom many powers have been vested. Spiritual leadership is about recognizing the humanity in everyone—offender and victim—and using power to honor that humanity. As the chief administrator of a criminal justice system who wields the power to pardon, the president can and should demonstrate spiritual leadership when using the pardon power. The pardon power authorizes acts of grace and acts of justice through which a president can demonstrate spiritual leadership.[85] A president may use the pardon power rarely, believing that the power should be used sparingly. Nonetheless, when the president uses the power, the president should do so with due concern for the power's high purpose.

The president ought to use the pardon power not only in a purely administrative fashion when necessary to correct errors in the judicial system, but also to demonstrate spiritual leadership to begin a discussion of the role of punishment in the federal criminal justice system.[86] Pardons can illuminate what conduct the federal law criminalizes and how much the system punishes such conduct. In addition, the pardon power provides an opportunity to consider the treatment of individual offenders who have served an appropriate sentence by questioning whether offenders should be forgiven for their crimes and in what manner they should be reconciled with society. All of these issues allow serious discussion of how to consider the humanity of offenders when punishing them, an issue at the heart of spiritual leadership.

Though the president can choose whether or not to demonstrate spiritual leadership, he should recognize that failure to use the pardon power may be an abdication of duty for which he could rightly be judged.[87] The president has been given the pardon power in the shadow of a presumably well-functioning judicial system. The president's responsibility is to do right, as defined by the Constitution, for the benefit of the country using all of the tools at his disposal. Consequently, the president arguably has an obligation to use the pardon power for the good of the country in ways that suggest spiritual leadership. Unfortunately, if the last several presidents are guides, presidents will not exercise such leadership through use of pardon power. If the citizenry wants the president to demonstrate secular spiritual leadership in this area, the citizenry may have to push the president in that direction. Of course, if the president decides to demonstrate serious spiritual leadership that tends toward maximum forgiveness, the citizenry should realize that such spiritual leadership may take the country past where it has historically been willing to go in forgiving offenders and their criminal actions.

Notes

1. U.S. Const. art. 2 sec. 2.
2. *Biddle v. Perovich*, 274 U.S. 480, 486 (1927) ("When granted [a pardon] is the determination of the ultimate authority that the public welfare will be better served by inflicting less than what the judgment fixed.").
3. Some of this chapter's analysis is transferable to state governors who can exercise pardon power at the state level. Moore, *Pardons*, 5–6 (discussing presidential and gubernatorial pardons). For a discussion of the shared features of federal and state pardons, see Love, "Reinvigorating the Federal Pardon Process," 730.
4. Fairholm, *Perspectives on Leadership*, 119 (noting that spirituality distinguishes humans from other animals by allowing humans to contemplate more than biological needs).
5. See 18 U.S.C. sec. 3553 (noting the principles that should undergird criminal sentences given in the federal criminal justice system).
6. See Fairholm, *Real Leadership*, xx (distinguishing leadership and management).
7. See Fairholm, *Perspectives on Leadership*, 119.
8. See Fairholm, *Perspectives on Leadership*, xxiii (noting that spirituality is values-based).
9. The Constitution demands space for religious plurality and bars religious tests for federal office. See U.S. Const. art. 6. sec 3. Nonetheless, religion is discussed in the public square

and can inform public decision making. See Hicks, *With God on All Sides*, 8 (discussing religion in the public sphere).

10. Hicks, *With God on All Sides*, 7.
11. See Fairholm, *Perspectives on Leadership*, 118 (suggesting that spirituality can trigger good leadership).
12. See U.S. Const. art. 2, sec 1.
13. U.S. Const. art. 2, sec 1.
14. U.S. Const. art. 2. sec 1.
15. U.S. Const. art. 2. sec 3.
16. U.S. Const. art. 1, sec 7.
17. For example, see *Youngstown Sheet & Tube Co. v. Sawyer*, 343 U.S. 579 (1952) (discussing limitations on presidential power under the "take care" clause).
18. Chambers, "Lincoln, The Emancipation Proclamation, and Executive Power," 121–124 (discussing Court's spare approach to the "take care" clause).
19. U.S. Const. art. 1. sec 1.
20. War is declared by Congress. U.S. Const. art. 1. sec. 8. However, the president has much latitude to manage a war once declared. See Chambers, "Lincoln, The Emancipation Proclamation, and Executive Power," 100–103.
21. That arguably makes the president a part of the legislative process. See U.S. Const. art. 1. sec. 7 (lodging veto power in Article I where legislative power and Congress are discussed).
22. U.S. Const. art. 2. sec. 2.
23. However, a pardon cannot stop an impeachment and cannot be granted for crimes that have not yet been committed. See Crouch, *The Presidential Pardon Power*, 9.
24. See Palacios, "Faith in Fantasy," 331.
25. See Morison, "Presidential Pardons and Immigration Law," 278–288 (noting that the pardoning authority may have broad limits even though individual pardons are largely unreviewable); Sarat and Hussain, "On Lawful Lawlessness," 1312 (noting strict limits on reviewing pardons); Alexander Hamilton, Federalist No. 74, in *The Federalist Papers*, ed. Clinton Rossiter (New York: NAL Penguin, 1961), 447 (noting that the pardon power should be largely unencumbered).
26. See, for example, Alexander Hamilton, Federalist No. 69 & 74, in *The Federalist Papers*, ed. Clinton Rossiter (New York: NAL Penguin, 1961), 415–423, 447–449; Morison, "Presidential Pardons and Immigration Law," 280–281 (discussing eighteenth-century views of the pardon power).
27. See Crouch, *The Presidential Pardon Power*, 13 (discussing Blackstone's views on the pardon and democracy).
28. Moore, *Pardons*, 15; Sarat, *Mercy on Trial*, 145.
29. See Alexander Hamilton, Federalist No. 69, in *The Federalist Papers*, ed. Clinton Rossiter (New York: NAL Penguin, 1961), 417–419 (discussing the antecedent monarchical pardon, but explaining the president's pardon power in the context of the Constitution); Sarat, *Mercy on Trial*, 145–146.
30. See Crouch, *The Presidential Pardon Power*, 20; Moore, *Pardons*, 5; Kobil, "The Quality of Mercy Strained," 575–576.
31. Crouch, *The Presidential Pardon Power*, 1; Moore, *Pardons*, 4.
32. Crouch, *The Presidential Pardon Power*, 40–49; Moore, *Pardons*, 163.
33. Moore, *Pardons*, 7 (suggesting that with abolition of parole, pardon may be one of few ways to individualize a sentence after it is given).
34. Some courts and commentators have seen pardons as acts of grace while other have not. See *Biddle v. Perovich*, 247 U.S. 480, 486 (1927)(suggesting that a pardon is not an act of grace); Palacios, "Faith in Fantasy," 336 (noting that Supreme Court has described a pardon as an act of grace); Morison, "Presidential Pardons and Immigration Law," 290 (noting that Supreme Court has suggested that a pardon is not an act of grace).

35. *Gregg v. Georgia*, 428 U.S. 153 (1976) ("In part, capital punishment is an expression of society's moral outrage at particularly offensive conduct.").
36. See 18 U.S.C. §3553 (listing reasons to impose criminal sentence at federal level).
37. See *Kennedy v. Louisiana*, 554 U.S. 407, 420 (2008) ("punishment is justified under one or more of three principal rationales: rehabilitation, deterrence, and retribution").
38. Brudner, *Punishment and Freedom*, 37–38 (discussion on punishment as a wrong); Matravers, *Justice and Punishment*, 2–3 (noting that punishment is fundamentally about making wrong-doer suffer); Murphy and Hampton, *Forgiveness and Mercy*, 126–127 (discussing essential nature of punishment); Zaibert, *Punishment and Retribution*, 25 (noting that one element of the "standard case" of punishment requires "pain or other consequences normally considered unpleasant). Such harm requires justification.
39. See Murphy, *Punishment and the Moral Emotions*, 7 (discussing mercy); Haber, *Forgiveness*, 65.
40. Griswold, *Forgiveness*, 213 (noting that forgiveness of debt, political pardon, judicial pardon, or clemency are in the same family of forgiveness and political apology, but are all quite separate).
41. Blustein, *Forgiveness and Remembrance*, 1; Haber, *Forgiveness*, 11.
42. Murphy, *Punishment and the Moral Emotions*, 5.
43. Holmgren, *Forgiveness and Retribution*, 32.
44. Hawkins, "A Man Had Two Sons," 158 (forgiveness is not forgetting).
45. Griswold, *Forgiveness*, xv (discussing the notion that forgiveness is and is not about forgetting); Holmgren, *Forgiveness and Retribution*, 40–41 (forgiving is not about forgetting, but is about not remembering vindictively).
46. Griswold, *Forgiveness*, xiv (forgiveness entails more than merely getting past harm).
47. Logan, *Good Punishment?* 161–166 (forgiveness is not forgetting; it is remembering with a purpose and with understanding). That can be extremely difficult. Konstan, *Before Forgiveness*, 157 (discussing possible difficulty in seeing transgressor in new light that would justify forgiveness).
48. Griswold, *Forgiveness*, 2 (noting that the ancients did not consider forgiveness to be a classical virtue); Haber, *Forgiveness*, 3 (noting that Aristotle did not list forgiveness as a virtue); Konstan, *Before Forgiveness*, ix (arguing generally that the ancients and even the early Christians did not have a modern conception of interpersonal forgiveness).
49. Indeed, Bishop Butler's influential sermons on Christian forgiveness have been instrumental in applying Jesus's message of forgiveness. See Griswold, *Forgiveness*, 19–37 (noting Bishop Butler's account of forgiveness); Murphy *Punishment and the Moral Emotions*, 6 (discussing Bishop Butler's definition of forgiveness). However, there is debate regarding the genesis of modern forgiveness. Griswold, Preface, in *Ancient Forgiveness*, xii (discussing whether Jesus was progenitor of modern concept of forgiveness); Haber, *Forgiveness*, 3 (noting Jesus's role in elevating the concept of forgiveness).
50. Griswold, *Forgiveness*, xv (treating forgiveness as a secular, rather than a religious, virtue); Haber, *Forgiveness*, 3 (noting that while some may tie forgiveness to religion, it can be a fully secular issue).
51. Logan, *Good Punishment?* 165 (placing forgiveness in the context of Christianity).
52. See Murphy, *Punishment and the Moral Emotions*, 10–12 (discussing problems that may accompany quick forgiveness).
53. Holmgren, *Forgiveness and Retribution*, 34 (no need to forgive true accident that causes harm).
54. Haber, *Forgiveness*, 11 (suggesting that forgiveness need not involve the transgressor); Murphy, *Punishment and the Moral Emotions*, 15 (repentance by injurer can pave the way to forgiveness, but it may not be necessary for forgiveness).
55. Govier, *Forgiveness and Revenge,* 77 (distinguishing forgiveness and reconciliation); Murphy, *Punishment and the Moral Emotions*, 8 (noting that there can be forgiveness without reconciliation and reconciliation without forgiveness).

56. Konstan, *Before Forgiveness*, 7 (suggesting that forgiveness is a two-way street that requires action by forgiver and forgiven); Griswold, *Forgiveness*, xvi (suggesting that forgiveness must affect forgiver and forgiven); Morton "What Is Forgiveness?" 6 (suggesting that forgiveness requires participation by forgiver and forgiven).

57. Griswold, *Forgiveness*, 117–118.

58. Holmgren, *Forgiveness and Retribution*, 36–37 (third-party forgiveness cannot occur because the act of forgiveness is personal); Konstan, *Before Forgiveness*, 15 (noting problems with forgiveness that is anything other than interpersonal, such as group forgiveness or third-party forgiveness given on behalf of others); Griswold, *Forgiveness*, 117–118 (discussing and noting problems with third-party forgiveness).

59. Some argue that the right to forgive can be lost if it is withheld for insufficient reasons. Digeser, *Political Forgiveness*, 94–95 (it may be possible for the victim to lose the right to forgive through an unwillingness to forgive and to have forgiveness provided by some other means).

60. Digeser, *Political Forgiveness*, 106 (discussing limited circumstances under which vicarious forgiveness might be acceptable); Griswold, *Forgiveness*, 119 (suggests that third-party forgiveness might be possible if the forgiver had standing to forgive on victim's behalf based on being in a position of care for the injured and knowing of the victim's proclivities respecting forgiveness in this situation).

61. Holmgren, *Forgiveness and Retribution*, 47–49 (arguing that the principles of forgiveness can apply to forgiveness on behalf of a group even though forgiveness is personal and cannot actually be given on behalf of a group).

62. Govier, *Forgiveness and Revenge*, 99.

63. Holmgren, *Forgiveness and Retribution*, 5 (noting that punishment is justified differently under retributive regimen than under forgiveness-based regime); Murphy, *Character, Liberty, and Law*, 69–70 (when retribution is concerned with the act, repentance makes little difference; when retribution is concerned with the morality of the person, repentance may matter). Some have argued that why the state punishes based on morality is unclear. Murphy, *Character, Liberty, and Law*, 67.

64. Retributive and utilitarian reasons can support a federal sentence. See 18 U.S.C. §3553.

65. Murphy, *Punishment and the Moral Emotions*, 7–8 (punishment may be appropriate even if forgiveness has occurred; there may be good reasons to punish wrongdoer even if victim has forgiven).

66. Logan, *Good Punishment?*, 165–166 (discussing Hauerwas and legitimacy of punishment).

67. Murphy and Hampton, *Forgiveness and Mercy*, 126 (describing punishment as infliction of suffering against the person punished).

68. Moore, *Pardons*, 29 (discussing Kantian view of retribution).

69. Pardons may be unrelated to forgiveness. Griswold, *Forgiveness*, xviii–xix (noting that legal pardons do not necessarily entail forgiveness of criminal wrongdoing); Haber, *Forgiveness*, 60; Konstan, *Before Forgiveness*, 2 (noting that a pardon by governor or president may not involve forgiveness, as in situations where clemency comes when executive believes that the prisoner was wrongfully convicted).

70. Morton, "What Is Forgiveness?," 7 (noting that presidential pardons need not be related to forgiveness or reconciliation).

71. Digeser, *Political Forgiveness*, 124 (pardoning is not the same as political forgiveness); Konstan, *Before Forgiveness*, 14 (noting possibility of clemency as generosity rather than as forgiveness); Morton, "What Is Forgiveness?" 10 (noting that a pardon may involve forgiveness, but may be nothing more than a technical lifting of punishment, with no remorse by offender or change of position by state).

72. Haber, *Forgiveness*, 61 (suggesting that pardons are public while forgiveness is personal); Murphy, *Punishment and the Moral Emotions*, 7 (noting that mercy can be given by official, but does not necessarily trigger forgiveness by the victim).

73. Digeser, *Political Forgiveness*, 120.
74. U.S. Const. art. 2. sec. 2.
75. Digeser, *Political Forgiveness*, 120 (discussing crime as harm to sovereign [and to individual victim] that provides opportunity for political forgiveness).
76. Haber, *Forgiveness*, 62 (suggesting that in pardoning, an official expresses some of the same sentiments as individuals do when they forgive).
77. See Kobil, "Compelling Mercy," 698–699 (noting the sparing use of pardons by Presidents George W. Bush and Barack Obama). The same appears true of governors. See Sarat and Hussain, "On Lawful Lawlessness," 1309 (noting limited use of pardons by governors in death penalty cases). A bigger concern may be that the pardon power is not used or explicitly disavowed in death penalty cases. See Lain, "Passive-Aggressive Executive Power," 228–232 (arguing that some governors address or decline to address death penalty issues by passive-aggressive refusal to sign death warrants).
78. See Alexander Hamilton, Federalist No. 74, in *The Federalist Papers*, ed. Clinton Rossiter (New York: NAL Penguin, 1961), 447 (suggesting that criminal codes may allow punishment when justice might suggest pardon).
79. President Obama's decision to decline to fully enforce the federal drug laws that might apply to medicinal and other marijuana sales might qualify as pre-emptive prosecutorial discretion that would make a pardon unnecessary.
80. Sarat, *Mercy on Trial*, 146–147 (noting that executives often explain their clemency practices, albeit possibly self-servingly).
81. Digeser, *Political Forgiveness*, 121 (pardon as form of forgiveness that helps reconcile offender with society).
82. Digeser, *Political Forgiveness*, 20–21 (noting that a pardon effectively gives, or should give, the transgressor a new start).
83. Digeser, *Political Forgiveness*, 122.
84. Consider prosecutions related to World War II Japanese American internment camps.
85. Moore, *Pardons*, 8–9.
86. The president may have an obligation to pardon when the judicial system has erred, as in the case of a wrongful conviction.
87. Moore, *Pardons*, 9 (viewing pardon as duty of justice).

References

Biddle v. Perovich. 274 U.S. 480, 486 (1927).
Blustein, Jeffrey M. 2014. *Forgiveness and Remembrance: Remembering Wrongdoing in Personal and Public Life.* New York, NY: Oxford University Press.
Brudner, Alan. 2009. *Punishment and Freedom: A Liberal Theory of Penal Justice.* New York, NY: Oxford University Press.
Burkhardt, M. 1989. "Spirituality: An Analysis of the Concept." *Holistic Nursing Practice* 3: 69–77.
Chambers Jr., Henry L. 2013. "Lincoln, The Emancipation Proclamation, and Executive Power." *Maryland Law Review* 73: 100–132.
Crouch, Jeffrey. 2009. *The Presidential Pardon Power.* Lawrence: University Press of Kansas.
Digeser, P. E. 2001. *Political Forgiveness.* Ithaca, NY: Cornell University Press.
Fairholm, Gilbert W. 2011. *Real Leadership: How Spiritual Values Give Leadership Meaning.* Santa Barbara, CA: Praeger.
Fairholm, Gilbert W. 1998. *Perspectives on Leadership: From the Science of Management to Its Spiritual Heart.* Westport, CT: Quorum.
Govier, Trudy. 2002. *Forgiveness and Revenge.* London: Routledge.

Gregg v. Georgia. 428 U.S. 153 (1976).

Griswold, Charles L. 2007. *Forgiveness: A Philosophical Exploration.* New York, NY: Cambridge University Press.

Griswold, Charles L., and David Konstan, ed. 2012. *Ancient Forgiveness.* New York: Cambridge University Press.

Haber, Joram Graf. 1991. *Forgiveness.* Lanham, MD: Rowman & Littlefield.

Hawkins, Peter S. 2012. "A Man Had Two Sons: The Question of Forgiveness in Luke 15." In Charles L. Griswold and David Konstan, eds., *Ancient Forgiveness,* 158–175. New York, NY: Cambridge University Press.

Hicks, Douglas A. 2009. *With God on All Sides: Leadership in a Devout and Diverse America.* New York, NY: Oxford University Press.

Holmgren, Margaret R. 2012. *Forgiveness and Retribution: Responding to Wrongdoing.* New York, NY: Cambridge University Press.

Kennedy v. Louisiana. 554 U.S. 407 (2008).

Kobil, Daniel T. 1991. "The Quality of Mercy Strained: Wresting the Pardoning Power from the King." *Texas Law Review* 69: 569–639.

Kobil, Daniel T. 2012. "Compelling Mercy: Judicial Review and the Clemency Power." *University of Saint Thomas Law Journal* 9: 698–729.

Konstan, David. 2010. *Before Forgiveness: The Origins of a Moral Idea.* New York, NY: Cambridge University Press.

Lain, Corinna Barrett. 2013. "Passive-Aggressive Executive Power." *Maryland Law Review* 73: 227–246.

Logan, James Samuel. 2013. *Good Punishment? Christian Moral Practice and U.S. Imprisonment.* Grand Rapids, MI: Eerdmans.

Love, Margaret Colgate. 2012. "Reinvigorating the Federal Pardon Process: What the President Can Learn from the States." *University of St. Thomas Law Journal* 9: 730–756.

Matravers, Matt. 2000. *Justice and Punishment: The Rationale of Coercion.* New York, NY: Oxford University Press.

Moore, Kathleen Dean. 1989. *Pardons: Justice, Mercy and the Public Interest.* New York, NY: Oxford University Press.

Morison, Samuel T. 2010. "Presidential Pardons and Immigration Law." *Stanford Journal of Civil Rights and Civil Liberties* 6: 253–342.

Morton, Adam, 2012. "What Is Forgiveness?" In Charles L. Griswold and David Konstan, eds., *Ancient Forgiveness,* 3–14. New York, NY: Cambridge University Press.

Murphy, Jeffrie G. 1998. *Character, Liberty, and Law: Kantian Essays in Theory and Practice.* Dordrecht, Netherlands: Kluwer.

Murphy, Jeffrie G. 2012. *Punishment and the Moral Emotions.* New York, NY: Oxford University Press.

Murphy, Jeffrie G., and Jean Hampton. 1988. *Forgiveness and Mercy.* New York, NY: Cambridge University Press.

Palacios, Victoria J. 1996. "Faith in Fantasy: The Supreme Court's Reliance on Commutation to Ensure Justice in Death Penalty Cases." *Vanderbilt Law Review* 49: 311–372.

Rossiter, Clinton, ed. 1961. *The Federalist Papers.* New York: NAL Penguin.

Sarat, Austin. 2005. *Mercy on Trial.* Princeton, NJ: Princeton University Press.

Sarat, Austin and Nasser Hussain. 2004. "On Lawful Lawlessness: George Ryan, Executive Clemency, and the Rhetoric of Sparing Life." *Stanford Law Review* 56: 1307–1344.

Youngstown Sheet & Tube Co. v. Sawyer. 343 U.S. 579 (1952).

Zaibert, Leo. 2006. *Punishment and Retribution.* Burlington, VT: Ashgate.

CHAPTER FIVE

Reconciliation and Its Failures: Reconstruction to Jim Crow

GEORGE R. GOETHALS

As Abraham Lincoln and the federal government groped their way toward the end of the Civil War in early 1865, the shape of the postwar nation challenged and divided America's leaders. Under what terms would the seceding states be brought back into their "practical relation with the Union?" (McPherson 1988, 770). Would the former leaders of those states be allowed a role in governing them once they had been returned to the Union? Would the Constitution be amended to remove its implicit but unequivocal protections of slavery? If emancipated, what would become of former enslaved persons now known as "freedmen"? Would they have equal citizenship? Would they be educated? Could they own land? Could they serve on juries? Could they vote? What laws and regulations would govern their labor?

These questions challenged the leadership capacities of even Abraham Lincoln, arguably our greatest president. Among those gifts were the patience and magnanimity that has been emphasized by many historians. These qualities and Lincoln's general approach to such difficult issues is revealed in the memorable last paragraph of his second inaugural address, delivered on March 4, 1865, six weeks before he was assassinated: "With malice toward none; with charity for all; with firmness in the right, as God gives us to see the right, let us strive on to finish the work we are in; to bind up the nation's wounds; to care for him who shall have borne the battle and for his widow, and his orphan; to do all which may achieve and cherish a just, and a lasting peace, among ourselves, and with all nations" (Fehrenbacher 1989, 686–687). But exactly how would the nation's wounds be bound up, and what defined a just peace? Binding up the nation's wounds seemed to point toward reconciliation between North and South, as did the overall tone of the address, as did Lincoln's advice to the commander of the Union forces occupying Richmond ten days before John Wilkes Booth shot him: "let 'em up easy." But could a just peace, including the "new birth of freedom" for African Americans, which Lincoln at Gettysburg so eloquently identified as central to "the great task remaining before us," be achieved along with harmony between warring white people in the two sections of the country (Fehrenbacher 1989, 536)?

A short answer is that while an uneasy reconciliation between the sections was established in just over a generation, a just peace was not achieved until much later. It took another century, until the Civil Rights and Voting Rights Acts were signed into law in 1964 and 1965, before anything resembling a just peace took shape. The history of efforts to reconcile North and South, and to combine that reconciliation with justice for African Americans, is one of the subjects of this essay. Another is how things might have been different. More specifically, could Lincoln—had he lived—or any other American president after Lincoln have brought about racial harmony and justice before the 1960s, or were the dynamics leading to disenfranchisement, segregation, and lynching, for example, beyond the reach of anyone's political leadership in America between 1865 and the beginning of the civil rights initiatives of the 1940s? Was a nation "with liberty and justice for all," including white Northerners, white Southerners, and African Americans, possible at some point in time after Lincoln's death but before the mid-twentieth century? More broadly, can the spirit of reconciliation, so eloquently articulated by Abraham Lincoln, be inclusive enough to embrace all the parties to complex conflicts? We know from research in psychology that relations among three parties with different degrees of power can be contentious, and that coalitions form quite readily. In many cases a coalition arises between the two more powerful parties, to the detriment of the weakest. In some ways, efforts toward reconciliation between the white North and the white South against African Americans followed the "conservative coalition" script quite exactly. It took many years to undo that coalition and replace it with a coalition between the white North and African Americans, which overturned Jim Crow rule in the South. With better leadership, could that outcome have been accomplished sooner?

We start by considering some of the leadership capacities of Abraham Lincoln, to more fully appreciate what was lost when he was assassinated. First, Lincoln exemplified what seems to me to be spiritual leadership. Using biblical language, Lincoln often and eloquently pointed the way toward peace, harmony, humility, generosity, freedom, reconciliation, and justice, and he consistently asked for divine blessing. Just a few phrases make the point: in his first inaugural address, "the better angels of our nature"; in his December 1862 annual message to Congress, "the way is plain, peaceful, generous, just—a way which if followed, the world will forever applaud, and God must forever bless"; in the Emancipation Proclamation, "upon this act, sincerely believed to be an act of justice,... I invoke the considerate judgment of mankind and the gracious favor of Almighty God"; and, in the second inaugural, "but let us judge not, that we be not judged... The Almighty has His own purposes."

Second, Lincoln had an uncanny sense of the people's will, and its importance. In one of his 1858 debates with Stephen Douglas, Lincoln argued "public sentiment is everything. With it, nothing can fail; against it, nothing can succeed." On numerous occasions the president demonstrated his skill in garnering public support for politically fraught actions. As Edward Ayers observed, Lincoln "worked at the very edge of public opinion, repeatedly testing its boundaries and its strength" (Ayers 2010, 27). Two examples are helpful in illustrating this point. Faced during his first day as president with deciding what to do about Confederate demands that the United States surrender Fort Sumter in Charleston Harbor, Lincoln received conflicting advice from his cabinet. He eventually wrote the governor of South Carolina explaining that he was sending humanitarian but not military aid to the soldiers stranded in the fort. Confederate president Jefferson Davis ordered rebel forces to fire on the fort and demand its surrender. By doing this Lincoln put the onus of starting the war on the Confederates and rallied Union support to put down the rebellion. A second example occurred a year and a half later. Having decided to issue the preliminary Emancipation Proclamation, Lincoln waited until the Union had achieved an important military victory, at Antietam, before announcing the new policy. He believed that public support for this radical departure would be stronger if it was announced from a position of relative strength. Lincoln was particularly sensitive to opinion in the crucial border states of Missouri, Kentucky, and Maryland. He is reputed to have replied to the claim that God was on his side, by remarking "I hope to have God on my side, but I must have Kentucky" (Astor 2011). The substance as well as the timing of the preliminary Emancipation Proclamation was responsive to border state sentiment. It did not threaten emancipation in states that were loyal to the Union.

Part of Lincoln's strategy to maintain broad public support for his conduct of the war was to maintain a broad spectrum of political views within his cabinet, within what Doris Kearns Goodwin has called his "team of rivals" (Goodwin 2005). Lincoln struggled with considerable success to keep the good offices and political support of both more radical, abolitionist-leaning cabinet members such as Secretary of State William Seward and Treasury Secretary Salmon Chase, as well as the more conservative Attorney General Edward Bates and Postmaster General Montgomery Blair. His adept balancing of the sometimes rancorous dynamics of his cabinet attests to his deft leadership touch in dealing with individuals personally.

Of special relevance here is Lincoln's subtle understanding of the relationship between the military and the political. His views of those contingencies is seen in his Fort Sumter actions described earlier and, most importantly, in his justification for the Emancipation Proclamation, which he claimed was "warranted by the Constitution upon military necessity." In the months following that proclamation, and the political act of freeing slaves, Lincoln repeatedly defended emancipation as a military necessity. For example, in a famous April 1864 letter, Lincoln referred to emancipation as an "indispensable necessity" for military victory numerous times, echoing the memorable words of the Proclamation itself (Fehrenbacher 1989, 585–586). Lincoln returned to the military-political linkage once again in an early portion of his March 4, 1865, second inaugural when he noted "the progress of our arms, upon which all else chiefly depends." Understanding how the military and political moved forward in concert was an essential element of Lincoln's leadership genius.

In this regard, understanding what did happen from 1865 going forward starts with considering two important developments on the military side, occurring shortly before Lincoln's death, that had far-reaching implications for the political prospects for a just peace on the one hand and sectional reconciliation on the other. The first, known as Field Order No. 15, involved Lincoln's Secretary of War Edwin Stanton and Union General William Tecumseh Sherman. In December of 1864, Sherman wrote a jaunty telegram to the president, saying that he wished "to present to you, as a Christmas gift, the city of Savannah" (Sherman 1875, 592). Sherman had completed his famous "march to the sea" from Atlanta and had peaceably occupied Savannah. But several difficulties were entailed in administering that captured city and the areas around it. One was the fate of large numbers of former slaves who were following Sherman's army, and who had been following it for two months. They were in a wretched condition, and in a strained relationship with the army that was good for neither party. Sherman and Stanton met with a group of African American leaders to hear their views about how best to resolve the situation.

That such a meeting took place, between black leaders and a member of the president's cabinet and a high-ranking military officer was extraordinary in itself. As their discussions evolved, Sherman and Stanton were persuaded by the group's African American spokesman, Garrison Frazier, a former preacher, that the freed people needed land, so that they could work it themselves and earn an independent living. In consultation with Stanton, Sherman issued something called Special Field Order, No. 15. It provided that islands and land stretching from near Charleston, South Carolina, to near Jacksonville, Florida, going about "thirty miles back from the sea," be divided into 40-acre plots and given to freed refugees from Georgia and South Carolina (Sherman 1865). The refugees also came to expect that they might be given surplus Army mules to help till the soil. Thus the phrase "40 acres and a mule" came to signify in the broader context what former slaves expected would be provided by the federal government, enabling them to live with a degree of autonomy and dignity scarcely imagined just months earlier. As we shall see, the promise of Field Order No. 15 was overtaken by political events after Lincoln's assassination. Still, it illustrates one early attempt to define a framework for a just peace. It suggested that steps would be taken to make freedom meaningful for emancipated slaves.

A second important military development in April of 1865 ended with promising steps toward reconciliation between North and South, or at least between Union and Confederate armies. After a siege of nine months, Robert E. Lee led the withering Army of Northern Virginia out of the trenches around Petersburg, Virginia, in an attempt to join a second Confederate army in North Carolina under the leadership of General Joseph E. Johnston. Although Lee's army had a head start over Union forces under Ulysses S. Grant, Grant's army caught up with Lee and forced his army to negotiate a surrender on Palm Sunday, April 9, 1865. In their famous meeting at the home of Wilmer McLean in Appomattox Court House that afternoon, Lee and Grant carefully arranged a surrender that would point toward reconciliation between North and South. First, Grant did not take Lee or any of his soldiers prisoner. Rather, they were paroled, that is, sent home, "not to take up arms against the government of the United States." Even more importantly, Grant wrote that these men were "not to be disturbed by United States authority so long as they observe their paroles" (Grant 1886, 493). This last statement actually exceeded Grant's authority because it touched on political policy after the war. It was however, consistent with Lincoln's general directive "to bind up the nation's wounds" and to "let 'em up easy."

Grant went even further by offering Lee's starving men plentiful rations and in allowing officers to keep their side arms and their horses for spring plowing. Lee commented that this last gesture would "be very gratifying and will do much toward conciliating our people." Thus Grant and Lee, through one's magnanimity and the other's gracious appreciation, provided a model, very broadly followed, for Confederate military leaders to surrender to their Union counterparts. When Joseph Johnston surrendered to Sherman a few weeks later, they treated each other with the mutual respect modeled by Lee and Grant. Years later, Johnston served as honorary pall bearer at Sherman's funeral. And in early May, Union General Edward Canby shared a generous supply of champagne with Confederate General Richard Taylor (son of former US president Zachary Taylor) when the latter surrendered in Alabama. Taylor recalled the opening of the bottles as "the first agreeable explosive sounds I had heard in years" (Winik 2001, 320). Thus, while Sherman's Field Order No. 15 pointed the way toward justice for former slaves, and perhaps even reconciliation between freedmen and former masters, Grant and Lee pointed the way toward reconciliation between former Union and Confederate soldiers.

The assassination of Lincoln changed everything. Now there was a new president, Andrew Johnson, who lacked most of his predecessor's leadership qualities. From humble origins, he had become successful in Tennessee politics and had remained loyal to the Union when his state seceded. Lincoln made him his vice presidential candidate in 1864 to broaden the sectional appeal of what was then called the Union Party. Stubborn and insular, Johnson resented the planter class that had dominated Southern politics prior to the war. While his seeming hatred of the planters, and his more punitive approach to Confederate military leaders, including Robert E. Lee, initially pleased Republican radicals, who believed that Lincoln was too generous and lenient in his post-war plans, his deep-seated racism quickly ended any romance between Johnson and the radical wing of the GOP. Unfortunately for African Americans, Johnson's racist attitudes and policies went relatively unchallenged during his first eight or nine months in office. The Congress elected in 1864, overwhelmingly Republican, would not take office until early December of 1865. Thus Johnson was free to initiate what has been called "Presidential Reconstruction." Most Southern political leaders were granted full citizenship, even if they had been involved in the rebellion, and Johnson adopted a states' rights stance toward the treatment of blacks, opposing any federal support for African Americans. Among other things, Field Order, No. 15 was revoked, and land confiscated from Southern whites was returned to them. Very few blacks were permitted to own land. Here was a large step toward reconciliation between northern and southern whites, and a giant leap backward for African Americans. The peace was shaping up as anything but just.

For African Americans, there was at least some resistance within the Johnson administration to the new president's course. Both Secretary of War Stanton and army chief Ulysses S. Grant did what they could to solidify the gains of the just-ended rebellion. Grant was sent by the president on a tour of the South in November of 1865 and reported that while the region was largely peaceful, it would be necessary to leave federal troops there, and to maintain the Freedmen's Bureau established toward the end of Lincoln's presidency. Johnson was therefore unable to get Grant's endorsement for withdrawing federal support for African Americans in the South. Also, in January, 1866, Grant, working with Stanton, issued orders authorizing occupying troops to use federal courts to protect black rights when state courts declined.

Most promising for a "just peace" was the action of the 39th Congress when it finally convened at the end of 1865. The so-called radical branch of the Republican Party, led by Thaddeus Stevens, steered a civil rights bill through Congress, a bill that was startlingly similar to the 1964 Civil Rights act passed nearly a century later. In March of 1866, President Johnson vetoed the bill, but it was passed over his veto and made, for a time, the law of the land. Then Stevens and his colleagues went further and rallied both moderate and radical Republicans to pass the landmark Fourteenth Amendment to the Constitution of the United States, guaranteeing equal protection of the laws and due process in disputes with state governments. The amendment passed both houses of Congress by the required two-thirds margins in June 1866. It did take, however, two years, until 1868, for it to be ratified by the states.

By the time of the mid-term elections of November 1866, most Americans, at least in the North, had reacted so strongly against

Johnson's apparent efforts to oppose the most basic black rights that an even more radical Congress was elected. The 40th Congress opened in late 1867 with a Republican margin of 45–8 in the Senate and a 140–45 margin in the House of Representatives. That Congress impeached President Johnson in 1868 in an effort to maintain Congressional control of Reconstruction. The president was acquitted, by one vote, in May, 1868, but his political power was essentially over for the time being. The 40th Congress also passed the Fifteenth Amendment to the Constitution in a February 1869 lame-duck session. Ratified in early 1870, that amendment prohibited denying citizens the right to vote on the basis of race or color.

While Congress had wrested control of the federal Reconstruction policy from President Johnson and had strongly supported rights for African Americans, blacks on the ground in the South faced a dismal reality. While many Southerners accepted the new status of blacks, extreme groups took violent steps to suppress civil rights and political rights for blacks. Their tools were both economic coercion and extra-legal practices of violence and intimidation. Congress had been unable to keep the Johnson administration and the states from returning land confiscated from planters at the end of the war. Complex labor contracts were negotiated, which severely limited blacks' rights to leave plantations, and allowed them barely a subsistence standard of living. A so-called sharecropping system was devised whereby blacks worked cotton fields, much as they did under slavery, and kept a certain portion or share of what they cultivated for bartering or for cash. Black assertions of their rights to vote, legal in some Southern states after the war, was suppressed by violence, including lynching. By the end of Johnson's presidency the size of the army, really the only tool available to the federal government, if it were so inclined to use it, to protect black rights, had been severely reduced, and in some cases withdrawn from the South for service in the West to protect against Indian attacks.

Making the challenge of combining sectional reconciliation with justice for African Americans even more difficult was an evolving narrative of white Southern virtue that almost completely erased the aspirations of blacks. This so-called Lost Cause storyline took shape soon after the end of war. In fact, the day after Robert E. Lee surrendered at Appomattox, he wrote an eloquent farewell document to his troops, thanking them for their "arduous service, marked by unsurpassed courage and fortitude" and assuring them that they had only been "compelled to yield to overwhelming numbers and resources." He proclaimed his "unceasing admiration of your constancy and devotion to your country." David Blight argues that those words contain "virtually all the ingredients that would form the Lost Cause" (Blight 2001, 37–38). That narrative, according to Gary Gallagher, "offered a loose group of arguments that cast the South's experiment in nation-building as an admirable struggle against hopeless odds, played down the importance of slavery in bringing secession and war, and ascribed to Confederates constitutional high-mindedness and gallantry on the battlefield" (Gallagher 2008, 2). This narrative of valor and virtue, embodied in increasingly heroic portrayals of Lee, and of harmony between slaves and their masters, appealed to both North and South. It encouraged both reconciliation and a sense of Southern correctness that increased resistance to pressures for change benefitting African Americans.

It was in this context that the presidential election of 1868 unfolded. There was little doubt that the Republican nominee would be Ulysses S. Grant, clearly the most popular figure in the nation. Grant had won the war for the North, and had meaningfully modeled reconciliation toward the South. However, he had evolved from having little interest in politics to a quite radical devotion to Lincoln's desire to protect African Americans and to a strong working relationship with Secretary of War Edwin Stanton. This made those who favored white control of labor, land, and politics in the South uneasy. The Democrats nominated New York governor Horatio Seymour and Francis Blair, brother of Lincoln's former Postmaster General Montgomery Blair, as their ticket. The Democrats campaigned in large part on race issues, asserting that they were the party of the white man, and that the "Black Republicans" would encourage black domination and "mongrelizing" of the races. While race prejudice had been, and still is, a staple of American society, the blatant racist nature of the 1868 Democratic campaign is stunning. Grant won a clear victory in the Electoral College, but his 5 percent margin of victory in the popular vote revealed considerable unease, North and South, with radical Republican Reconstruction policy. It is likely that Grant lost the white vote, and only won the overall popular vote by roughly 300,000 thanks to approximately 400,000 black votes.

Grant had campaigned on the slogan "Let us have peace." He very much wanted reconciliation, but he would not abandon efforts to protect African Americans and to promote racial equality in politics and before the law. In his inaugural address he spoke of settling questions facing the nation "calmly, without prejudice, hate, or sectional pride" but also argued for ratification of the recently passed Fifteenth Amendment so that "a portion of the citizens of the nation" not be excluded from voting (Grant 2012). With significant lobbying by Grant, the states, as noted earlier, ratified the amendment within a year of Grant taking office.

Fully describing Grant's leadership during Reconstruction is far beyond the scope of this chapter. I believe a fair summary is that Grant consistently supported the rights of African Americans, that he used military force to protect them on numerous occasions, that some of his actions provoked considerable backlash in the North as well as the South, and that he became increasingly reluctant to use Federal troops—his only real leverage—when he considered the political costs to Republican leadership of continuing to do so to be too high. He feared that black interests would be damaged considerably if those costs included Democratic control of Congress and/or the presidency.

With strong Congressional support during the first six years of his presidency Grant was able to enact several important pieces of legislation, including "Enforcement Acts" to back up the Fifteenth Amendment, and, in 1875, a Civil Rights Act, passed with the vigorous support of Senator Charles Sumner of Massachusetts and Congressman John R. Lynch, an African American from Mississippi. However, the mid-term election of Grant's second administration in 1874 gave Democrats a strong majority in the US House of Representatives and effectively ended Congressional efforts on behalf of African Americans. Another 20 years passed before the Republicans gained firm control of both houses of Congress, and by that time Republican politics focused on issues other than racial justice. Grant biographer Jean Edward Smith wrote that "from 1874 onward, the Republican party became the party of economic conservatism" and that "a commercial, pro-capitalist stance replaced emancipation as the party's raison d'etre" (Smith 2001, 682). Furthermore, during the last years of the Grant administration (1875–1877), the US Supreme Court made rulings overturning the Enforcement Acts and narrowly interpreted the Fourteenth Amendment, declaring that while the federal government could prohibit *states* from denying citizens equal rights, it could not prosecute *individuals* for denying other citizens their rights. Dealing with individuals was a state responsibility. These decisions essentially left blacks at the mercy of state courts in the South, exactly what Edwin Stanton and Grant had tried to prevent in early 1866 during the Andrew Johnson years.

Could Grant have led more effectively on behalf of African Americans? Despite charges of corruption and Southern and Democratic opposition to his use of federal military force on behalf of African Americans during his first term, Grant won re-election in 1872 by a large margin, nearly 12 percent. He had a great deal of political capital. However, the resistance to black rights had coalesced in the white South by 1873. Northern Radicals had overplayed their hand. The total transformation of the South, and American society, envisioned by men such as Thaddeus Stevens and Charles Sumner, and to a lesser extent, Grant, was opposed by legal and extra-legal means that were probably insurmountable. Edward Ayers has argued that "white people could not imagine that black Americans deserved freedom and equality." Consistent with well-established principles of cognitive dissonance theory in social psychology, Ayers continues, "Moreover, because white Americans denied black Americans what they deserved, white Americans felt obligated to denigrate and abuse black people for generations to come" (Ayers 2005, 154). One might still ask whether a more effective leader than Grant, say, one with Lincoln's rhetorical abilities, could have persuaded the South to go along with civil rights and justice for African Americans. While it is difficult to say, the forces of reaction against Executive action on behalf of blacks were deeply embedded in the Congress of the United States, the Supreme Court of the United States, and much of the public, North and South.

The outcome of the presidential election of 1876 is considered the end of Reconstruction. The Democratic candidate, New York governor Samuel J. Tilden won a clear majority of the popular votes but lost the election when a special commission appointed by Congress awarded all 20 disputed electoral votes to Republican Rutherford B. Hayes, the nineteenth president of the United States. Democrats acquiesced to this "compromise" in return for the final withdrawal of federal troops from the South. From then on, African Americans in the South were pretty much on their own. One early twentieth-century historian, critical of Reconstruction efforts on behalf of African Americans, wrote that with Grant "there was no peace; with Hayes peace came" (Dunning 1907, 341). But it was not Lincoln's just peace. Hayes employed a rhetoric of unity, which he hoped, and to some extent believed, could include African Americans. However, he underestimated Southern racist sentiment and the South's readiness to act on that sentiment (Slagell 2008). Hayes himself had an abolitionist background and had supported radical Reconstruction in Congress, but was unable to exert leadership on behalf of African Americans. The terms of the "compromise of 1877," Democratic majorities in the House of Representatives—and after the mid-term elections, the Senate—Hayes's reluctance to use Executive power, and lack of much political capital made it nearly impossible for him to take action toward a just peace. The one exception is that Hayes vetoed a number of bills passed by the Democrats designed to weaken protections for black voting rights.

Another opportunity for Republican leadership on behalf of African Americans came with the narrow election of President James A. Garfield over Democrat Winfield Scott Hancock in 1880. General Hancock was a Union Civil War hero, who, despite his anti-secessionist credentials, supported Southern states' rights policies and their opposition to Reconstruction. Garfield, in contrast, had been an abolitionist as well as Union general in the Civil War. In his inaugural address he spoke eloquently on behalf of African Americans. Referring to "the emancipated race," Garfield proclaimed, "With unquestioning devotion to the Union, with a patience and gentleness not born of fear, they have 'followed the light as God gave them to see the light'.... They deserve the generous encouragement of all good men. So far as my authority can lawfully extend they shall enjoy the full and equal protection of the Constitution and the laws" (Millard 2011, 79). How much difference Garfield might have made is unknowable. Like Hayes he had few means with which to combat racial intimidation and coercion in the South. In any event, Garfield was shot by a deranged assassin four months into his term and died two months later. His successor, Chester A. Arthur, was nowhere near as passionate about African American rights, and after the mid-term elections of 1882 faced a solidly Democratic House of Representatives. Furthermore, during Arthur's presidency the Supreme Court, in 1883, ruled the Civil Rights Act of 1875 unconstitutional.

Thus by the mid-1880s, opposition from Congress and the Supreme Court, narratives of unity and of the Lost Cause, the lack of much Executive will or power, and strong white Southern resistance to African American equality fairly doomed hopes for a just peace. The election in 1884 of Democratic president Grover Cleveland and a heavily Democratic House of Representatives did even more to put issues of racial justice aside. Then, in July of 1885, Cleveland's first year in office, the death of Ulysses S. Grant quite perversely served to further strengthen the growing emphasis on reconciliation. A huge funeral in New York City, the largest by far that the nation had ever seen, united former Union and Confederate foes as pallbearers. Grant's actions on behalf of blacks were eclipsed in media accounts of his steps toward harmony at Appomattox. Grant biographer Joan Waugh considers that Grant's death and funeral "became a vehicle for a religiously tinged emotional and political reconciliation of North and South," or a "Romance of Reunion" (Waugh 2009, 218).

The last notable presidential effort toward justice for African Americans in the nineteenth century came with the election of Benjamin Harrison as the twenty-third president of the United States in 1888. Harrison, like Grant, Hayes, and Garfield, had been a Union general during the Civil War. His dedication to African American justice was unequivocal. However, Harrison took office at nearly the same time that Southern states began to re-write their constitutions to disenfranchise black voters. Early in his term, efforts by Republican senator George F. Hoar and Representative Henry Cabot Lodge, both of Massachusetts, to enact a voting rights bill that would counteract these disenfranchisement efforts nearly succeeded. Kirt Wilson notes, however, that Republicans in the Senate "were either unwilling or unable to overcome a Democratic filibuster" (Wilson 2008, 267–288; 284). Harrison was unable to give it the push it needed to pass. Although Harrison was a skilled speaker, and gave hundreds of addresses advocating equality, Wilson maintains that his rhetoric was too abstract and logical, and therefore failed to overcome competing racist narratives and to challenge "a public memory that excluded African Americans," a memory of harmony between white Northerners and Southerners (Wilson 2008, 285).

Starting with the end of the Harrison presidency, things went from bad to worse for African Americans. In addition to the increased use of literacy tests, poll taxes, and white primaries to suppress black voting, in 1896, the United States Supreme Court delivered its 7–1 decision in *Plessy v. Ferguson*, and made the principle of "separate but equal" the law of the land. In 1892, Homer Plessy, a man considered nonwhite in New Orleans, bought a railway ticket to sit in a white-only first class car. He was arrested for violating a state law requiring separate seating for whites and "colored" travelers. His case moved through a long legal odyssey and ended up in the US Supreme Court. Through somewhat tortuous reasoning the court declared that Louisiana's state law did not violate the equal protection of the laws sections of the Fourteenth Amendment and that the principle of "separate but equal" withstood Constitutional scrutiny. (The separate but equal principle did not meet its final demise until *Brown v. Board of Education* in 1954.)

Shortly after the Plessy ruling, in 1897, Republican William McKinley became president of the United States. McKinley, an Ohionan, had served in the Union army during the Civil War and was the last veteran of that conflict who became president. African Americans had hopes that another Republican administration, with strong GOP majorities in both houses of Congress, would advance their interests and protect them from increasing racial violence. Their expectations were raised even further when they served courageously and effectively during the Spanish-American War in 1898. Indeed, black "Buffalo Soldiers" played a crucial role in Theodore Roosevelt's highly publicized charge up San Juan Hill. United States Colored Troops had also made major contributions to Union victory in the Civil War and their actions greatly strengthened Lincoln's defense of his emancipation policies. In a widely circulated letter to a group of Illinois supporters who nevertheless opposed emancipation, Lincoln's eloquent defense of the proclamation included the lines "You say you will not fight to free negroes. Some of them seem willing to fight for you; but, no matter," and "there will be some black men who can remember that, with silent tongue, and clenched teeth, and steady eye, and well-poised bayonet, they have helped mankind" achieve a peace "worth the keeping in all future time" (Fehrenbacher 1989, 498–499). Since black soldiers' contributions to Union victory enhanced their status in some eyes, for some period of time, African Americans hoped that their combat role in Cuba would likewise lead to some acknowledgments of their basic rights. Ironically, the Spanish-American War did more to accomplish the goal of reconciliation than of justice. Former Union and Confederate veterans fought together. Their collaboration was celebrated. The equally important role of African Americans was ignored.

The Spanish-American War produced another result that significantly undermined the welfare of African Americans, and the strong relationship that had existed between blacks and the "Party of Lincoln" since the very founding of the GOP. In his classic book *The Strange Career of Jim Crow,* C. Vann Woodward entitles his chapter considering the 1890s "Capitulation to Racism" (Woodward 2002). Woodward notes that the Spanish-American War advanced American imperialism, and that it brought under American dominion "some eight million people of the colored races, 'a varied assortment of inferior races,' as the *Nation* described them, 'which of course could not be allowed to vote'" (Woodward 2002, 72). Woodward goes on to note that Northern newspapers and magazines expressed sentiments that were as racist as Southern publications: *The New York Times,* he reports, editorialized that "Northern men...no longer denounce the suppression of the Negro vote [in the South] as it used to be denounced in the reconstruction days. The necessity of it under the supreme law of self-preservation is candidly recognized" (Woodward 2002, 73).

A third consequence of the Spanish-American War was the elevation to the presidency of Theodore Roosevelt. His role in that conflict, and his canny ability to publicize that role, had made him a war hero. He was elected governor of New York in 1898, and then became a somewhat reluctant vice presidential candidate when William McKinley ran for re-election, and won, in 1900. The New York Republican establishment was happy to have the boisterous and independent Roosevelt out of state politics and had helped arrange his elevation to the national ticket. When McKinley was assassinated in September of 1901, Theodore Roosevelt became president. Though African Americans had reasonable hope that Roosevelt would protect their interests, the prospects for those hopes were complicated.

In his earliest writings about the War of 1812, Roosevelt expressed "a nascent imperialism in his depiction of white settlers filling empty lands and subduing backward races" (Cooper 1993, 13). He shared a "white man's burden" view of governing the Philippines after it was annexed by the United States in 1898. In his view, white people were a superior race. Furthermore, with the tacit acquiescence of Northerners, by 1901, blacks in the South had been effectively disenfranchised. Since there were few Southern black votes, Republicans began courting white ones. Still, the GOP was the party of Lincoln, and perhaps TR would be a friend to African Americans, as James Garfield and Benjamin Harrison had been. The early signs were promising. As vice president, Theodore Roosevelt had made arrangements to visit Booker T. Washington's Tuskegee Institute in Alabama in the fall of 1901. Washington had done a brilliant job of advancing black education and entrepreneurship in South, though critics such as W. E. B. DuBois perceived him to be too deferential to whites. (Of course, DuBois had not been enslaved in the South in his youth.) In fact, as president, William McKinley had visited Tuskegee (on the same trip where he wore a gray patch in speaking to the Georgia legislature, to honor Confederate veterans and point toward sectional reconciliation). If Washington could establish a relationship with the new president, perhaps he would help counter some of the reverses that African Americans had suffered in the previous decade. When Roosevelt became president, he invited Washington to the White House. The meeting seemed a propitious moment for African Americans.

As events played out, Booker T. Washington's 1901 visit to the White House provoked a Southern backlash that caught Roosevelt by surprise. The Southern press excoriated Roosevelt for having a black man in the White House, especially for a dinner where he might touch thighs with Mrs. Roosevelt. Newspapers used the "n-word" liberally for the first time in decades, and stories were circulated about Roosevelt's daughter

Alice marrying a black man. For Booker T. Washington, this was run of the mill. But Theodore Roosevelt was unused to such criticism, and now that he was president it was even more upsetting. The president never met publicly with Washington in the White House again.

The Booker T. Washington affair began Theodore Roosevelt's retreat from standing up for African Americans. The low point during his presidency occurred five years later when he summarily issued dishonorable discharges to 167 black soldiers after an incident of racial tension in Brownsville, Texas, led to the shooting of a white man. Booker T. Washington, among others, urged the president to review the facts of the case more carefully, but Roosevelt simply dug in. In subsequent years he defended all-white Southern delegations to his new Progressive Party convention and even wrote a letter endorsing the work of eugeneticist Charles Davenport, stating "we have no business to permit the perpetuation of citizens of the wrong type" (Roosevelt 1913).

The Republican Party continued backing away from prioritizing African Americans rights and strengthened its embrace of sectional reconciliation with the election of President William Howard Taft in 1908. In his inaugural address Taft endorsed constitutional laws that would "exclude from voting both negroes and whites not having education or other qualifications thought to be necessary for a proper electorate," that is, the literacy test laws the South used to disenfranchise blacks (Taft 1909). Not surprisingly, several prominent black leaders, including W. E. B. DuBois, supported the election of a Democrat, Woodrow Wilson, in 1912. But as it turned out, Wilson's election made the prospects of a just peace even worse. University of Richmond scholar Eric Yellen's book, *Racism in the Nation's Service: Government Workers and the Color Line in Woodrow Wilson's America*, details the segregation of Federal offices that took place in Wilson's two terms, from 1913 to 1921, strengthening already well-entrenched Jim Crow laws from the 1890s and beyond.

In short, both major political parties had effectively abandoned African Americans during the first decades of the twentieth century. In contrast, sectional reconciliation still captured the nation's attention. In 1913 white Northern and white Southern veterans of the Civil War observed the fiftieth anniversary of the Battle of Gettysburg with smiles and handshakes. No United States Colored Troops, or USCTs, participated. However, 25 years later, in 1938, change was evident at Gettysburg. President Franklin Roosevelt dedicated the battlefield peace memorial inscribed with the words "Peace Eternal in a Nation United." On leaving the ceremony, the president spoke to the oldest veteran present, 112-year-old William Barnes of the USCT.

The change from the dismal state of Lincoln's "a just, and a lasting, peace" in the 1920s to the emerging of civil rights initiatives in subsequent decades was slow but steady. African American leaders such as A. Philip Randolph played a central role in pressing Democratic presidents Franklin Roosevelt and Harry Truman to support civil rights during the 1940s, and in the 1960s Martin Luther King Jr. and others likewise pressed Democratic presidents John F. Kennedy and Lyndon B. Johnson. The rhetoric of both Kennedy and Johnson had elements of spiritual leadership heard earlier in the words of Abraham Lincoln, and, to a lesser extent, Grant, Garfield, and Harrison. In pressing for civil rights legislation in 1963, Kennedy argued, "We are confronted primarily with a moral issue. It is as old as the scriptures and is as clear as the American Constitution" (Kennedy 1963). By then African Americans had bid, in the words of Nancy Weiss's book, *Farewell to the Party of Lincoln* (Weiss 1983). An entirely different political dynamic has led to the present day. Both sectional reconciliation and justice for African Americans have been achieved in significant measure. The nation has elected an African American president. But America has also seen the rolling back of important sections of the 1965 Voting Rights Act, and Lincoln's Republican Party now seems hostile to black citizens. Time will tell whether the just peace of today, such as it is, is also a lasting one.

References

Astor, Aaron. 2011. "Bluegrass Blues and Grays." *New York Times,* May 7. http://opinionator. blogs.nytimes.com/2011/05/07/bluegrass-blues-and-grays/?_r=0

Ayers, Edward L. 2010. "What Lincoln Was Up Against: The Context of Leadership." In George R. Goethals and Gary L. McDowell, eds., *Lincoln's Legacy of Leadership,* 27. New York: Palgrave Macmillan.

Ayers, Edward L. 2005. *What Caused the Civil War? Reflections on the South and Southern History.* New York: Norton.

Blight, David W. 2001. *Race and Reunion: The Civil War in American Memory.* Cambridge, MA: Harvard University Press.

Cooper, John M. 1993. *The Warrior and the Priest: Woodrow Wilson and Theodore Roosevelt.* Cambridge, MA: Harvard University Press.

Dunning, William A. 1907. *Reconstruction: Political and Economic.* New York: Harper and Brothers.

Fehrenbacher, Don E. 1989. *Abraham Lincoln: Speeches and Writings 1859–1865.* New York: The Library of America.

Gallagher, Gary W. 2008. *Causes Won, Lost & Forgotten: How Hollywood and Popular Art Shape What We Know about the Civil War.* Chapel Hill: University of North Carolina Press.

Goodwin, Doris K. 2005. *Team of Rivals: The Political Genius of Abraham Lincoln.* New York: Simon & Schuster.

Grant, Ulysses S. 2012. "First Inaugural Address, March 4, 1869." In *U.S. Presidential Inaugural Addresses*. Ebook. Start Publishing.

———.1886. *Personal Memoirs of U.S. Grant, Volume 2*. New York: Charles L. Webster.

Kennedy, John F. 1963. "Report to the American People on Civil Rights, 11 June." http://www.jfklibrary.org/Asset-Viewer/LH8F_0Mzv0e6Ro1yEm74Ng.aspx.

McPherson, James M. 1988. *Battle Cry of Freedom: The Civil War Era*. New York: Oxford.

Millard, Candice. 2011. *Destiny of the Republic: A Tale of Madness, Medicine and the Murder of a President*. New York: Doubleday.

Roosevelt, Theodore. 1913. Letter to Charles B. Davenport, January 3. http://www.dnalc.org/view/11219-T-Roosevelt-letter-to-C-Davenport-about-degenerates-reproducing-.html.

Sherman, William T. 1875. *Memoirs of General W. T. Sherman*. New York: Appleton.

———. Field Order, #15. 1865. http://www.blackpast.org/primary/special-field-orders-no-15.

Slagell, Amy R. 2008. "The Challenges of Reunification: Rutherford B. Hayes on the Close Race and the Racial Divide." In Martin J. Medhurst, ed., *Before the Rhetorical Presidency*, 243–266. College Station: Texas A & M University Press.

Smith, Jean E. 2001. *Grant*. New York: Simon & Schuster.

Taft, William H. 1909. "Inaugural Address, March 4." http://www.bartleby.com/124/pres43.html.

Waugh, Joan. 2009. *U. S. Grant: American Hero, American Myth*. Chapel Hill: University of North Carolina Press.

Weiss, Nancy J. 1983. *Farewell to the Party of Lincoln: Black Politics in the Age of FDR*. Princeton, NJ: Princeton University Press.

Wilson, Kirt H. 2008. "The Problem of Public Memory: Benjamin Harrison Confronts the 'Southern Question.'" In Martin J. Medhurst, ed., *Before the Rhetorical Presidency*, 267–288. College Station: Texas A & M University Press.

Winik, Jay. 2001. *April 1865, The Month That Saved America*. New York: Harper Collins, 2001.

Woodward, C. V. 2002. *The Strange Career of Jim Crow*. Third Edition. New York: Oxford University Press.

CHAPTER SIX

The Pursuit of Wonder

DAVID D. BURHANS

Figure 6.1 Cannon Memorial Chapel on the University of Richmond campus.

American poet Mary Oliver (2004), in her poem *Mindful* said, "It was what I was born for—to look, to listen..." (35). Rabbi Abraham

Joshua Heschel (1983) said, "Never once in my life did I ask God for success,....I asked for wonder and he gave it to me" (47). Looking back over more than seven decades, *mindfulness* and *wonder* capture the essence of my spiritual and professional journey. Though having been a minister/pastor of three churches, the transition to ministry on a university campus became an exercise in looking, listening, and instruction—applying personal interests, I developed skills and theological education to an intergenerational community of people (students, faculty, staff, administration) with diverse social, economic, and religious or nonreligious backgrounds and perspectives. Following is a 30-year historical account of highlights in the establishment and evolution of the University of Richmond Chaplaincy and how my role as chaplain informed and broadened my understanding of spiritual leadership.

In 1971, Dr. E. Bruce Heilman became the fifth president of the University of Richmond. Within his first three years he created a new position titled *Chaplain to the University,* historically marking his vision and initiative as an example of bold spiritual leadership. In the earliest years of Bruce Heilman's presidency, he began to reflect on what kind of spiritual/religious leadership would be effective and become integral to the mission and purpose of the university, a university that aspired to become one of the finest, small universities in the country. He wrote,

> I decided that I wanted to find somebody who would be interested in providing spiritual leadership, a kind of pastor to the University community, someone who could minister and proclaim through personal influence and thoughtful persuasion something of his/her own moral and spiritual commitments and do so comfortably within a community of fellow-believers, persons from different religious traditions, non-believers, and persons uninterested in religious/spiritual issues. This would of necessity be someone who would appreciate the opportunity and relish the challenge of being a faith and values advocate in an educational community. This person would serve as a member of the President's administrative team (University Vice Presidents, Athletic Director, etc.) and would be a close advisor to the President. (Heilman, 2008, 78)

During the summer of 1974, President Heilman extended an invitation to me to become the first minister to hold this position describing the role of chaplain as "pastor, preacher and spiritual leader for the University community." Serving at the time as a Baptist parish minister in Huntsville, Alabama, I accepted the position and arrived on the University of Richmond campus with my wife, Ellen, and our four children—Ann, David, Emily, and Will—in September, 1974. We were graciously welcomed by the university community and by Dr. Linwood Horne, the university's director of Church Relations, who helped nurture the university's relationship with the Baptists of Virginia (affiliated with the Virginia Baptist General Association).

This personal journey began with a profound sense of awe and wonder prompting a fresh consideration of three great spiritual questions I had contemplated through college and graduate school. Who am I? Why am I here? What difference can I make? Essentially it was about the human search for meaning and purpose. These questions became a major focus for the newly created University Chaplaincy—questions any well-educated person is expected to consider. Furthermore, there was hope that the Chaplaincy would contribute to an atmosphere of openness and acceptance in the community and become a place at the heart of the campus that would encourage a free exchange of ideas, become a safe place to ask questions, and help initiate faith in "seekers" of purpose and meaning. It would also be a place to retreat to discuss personal issues, share experiences of grief, celebrate joy and achievement, and a place to examine and strengthen one's own faith perspective. The vision was a Chaplaincy that would help articulate the University of Richmond narrative, become integral to the academy's purpose, and be personally meaningful to people who represented the varied constituencies of the University of Richmond.

Somewhere along this journey of discernment and transition, I became aware that deep within me there had been growing this profound spiritual truth, which I strongly embraced, namely, *Life is gift: handle this journey with gratitude, with compassion, with humility—gifts of Divine Grace.* This insight and motivating spirit was what I was hoping I could bring to the academy and to the relationships that developed. I felt strongly that I was on an educational pilgrimage with the students, on a professional journey of personal growth with faculty, staff, and administrators, on a daily, demanding sojourn with university families like my own, who welcomed support and encouragement.

Years earlier in graduate study, I had been intrigued by the work of the influential American psychologist Carl Rogers and his theory of personality. My ideas resonated with and embraced what Rogers described, through his work as a clinical psychologist and his subsequent writings, as three essential qualities of an effective therapist (counselor) and the basis of a healthy person–centered therapy. These qualities were *congruence, empathy,* and *respect.* Rogers described *congruence* as being genuine and honest with the client. *Empathy* was the ability to feel something of what the client feels. And *respect* was an unconditional, positive regard for the client. These qualities immediately identified for me spiritual leadership at its best. They would be clearly adaptable, I thought, and meaningful in creating trust and respect between people. It would be valuable not only in a therapist-client relationship, but also creative and affirming in pastor and parishioner interactions, personal friendships, in clergy and other professional contacts, and also in one's expanded service to committees, boards, and community organizations.

First, congruence would reflect a leader's sincerity, integrity, and authenticity. I recall one person who happily complimented her minister when she said of him, "His life and work is within a stone's throw of his pronouncements and proclamations." Second, there is no substitute for empathic understanding. We are all drawn to those people who not only feel something of what we feel—those individuals who know loss, heartache, pain, and failure but can also share with us moments of joy, love, and laughter. And, third, respect is acceptance, valuing the individuality of another. Life and work on a university campus is a distinct challenge and an opportunity to move beyond one's comfort zone. Spiritual leadership requires an unequivocal conviction that race, ethnicity, gender, sexual orientation, and religious faith and affiliation are natural, vital characteristics of who we are as children of God and are deserving of acceptance, affirmation, and respect. Again the admonition, *Life is gift: handle this journey with gratitude, with compassion, with humility—gifts of Divine Grace.*

These qualities outlined by Rogers came to serve as guiding principles for ministry on the university campus and became worthy goals for this writer's personal and professional development. What a wonderfull opportunity this was to be able to give shape to this new university position. Having been reared in a home that embraced the Christian faith and a family that was actively, happily involved with a church community, I came to a point of confession and a public declaration of faith and trust in the Living God. From that moment forward there were experiences of what I can describe only as divine encounters or intimations of the Holy—moments of profound gratitude, insight, guidance, wonder upon wonder, and ultimately a compelling desire to proclaim the Love of God. Adopting as my own the Early Christian Church's Confession of Faith, "Jesus is Lord!" there grew within me an overriding conviction that this Man's life and teachings, His way of thinking, living, loving, and relating was a distinctly worthy investment of one's mental, emotional, physical, and spiritual energy and somehow could become a divine force for goodwill, for trust, and for compassionate service in this university community. "And what does the Lord require of you but to do justice, to love kindness and to walk humbly with your God" (Micah 6: 6–8).

A Ministry of Presence—The first order of business was to initiate what became popularly known in Chaplaincy circles around the country as "the Ministry of Presence." A major task for the Chaplaincy was a thorough exploration of the university landscape, wanting to discover the many facets of university life, which had four distinct schools at the time: the School of Arts and Sciences, the E. Clairborne Robins School of Business, the School of Professional and Continuing Studies, and the T. C. Williams Law School (the Jepson School of Leadership Studies was established in 1990). In addition, there were the various academic disciplines, campus-wide lectures, Richmond College and Westhampton College student life programs including student leadership opportunities, student, faculty, and staff social and athletic events to experience.

Given the university's historic relationship with the Baptists of Virginia and consistent with such basic Baptist tenets as religious liberty, soul competency, and local church autonomy (a free church in a free society), it seemed that a worthy Chaplaincy and its programming could complement the academy and become a contributing, shaping presence in the physical, mental, emotional, and spiritual development of the individual. The presence of the University Chaplaincy at the heart of the campus raised two questions: (1) How does one with integrity encourage spiritual growth, broaden one's faith perspective, and address ethical issues in an academic community without being sectarian? The academic community in which one lives out his/her own faith commitments must of necessity be expanded, become flexible, less rigid, require fresh thinking of old truths and broader, more accurate translations, interpretations of sacred texts. (2) How does one authentically advocate the human integration of body, mind, and spirit so as to counter the fragmentation of knowledge, learning, and human development? This happens, we believe, in the way God often comes to us by conjoining the love of God and the love of learning in the flesh, in the human flesh of persons—persons in the Chaplaincy, persons in the faculty and staff, and persons among the student body. A worthy Chaplaincy helps celebrate and energize the life of the mind, nourishes and expands and enriches that life, and connects it with the great traditions of faith and service to God and our fellow humans.

Other major tasks for Chaplaincy presence involved making new friends, developing relationships, discovering kindred spirits, and looking for connections with the university's many constituencies. This inevitably led to the heightened role of pastoral care. Personal counseling, hospital visitations, pre-marriage counseling, presiding over weddings, leading funerals or memorial services, while providing grief support, were offered on a regular basis. As this new professional journey unfolded, one principle was essential: to approach life, work, and relationships in the academy with a more open mind and heart—not open without any fixed point, but open and receptive to new ideas and ways of engaging a diverse community of people. Congruence, empathy, and unconditional positive regard were essential qualities for the Chaplaincy.

We listened carefully to what others had to say about moral and spiritual values. We made a concerted effort to understand other faith perspectives while exploring fresh ways to express our own faith. From lessons of my own Judeo-Christian tradition, I learned the importance of working to break down barriers that divide us, to broaden our worldview, reaching beyond our own kind, our own country, our own religious creed. I believe strongly we must articulate the beliefs and religious experiences that each of us holds dear and share with others the Light by which we live and work and relate. At the same time, we can welcome and acknowledge that our brothers and sisters of other religious traditions surely have a word from God for us to hear.

An open, thoughtful, and discerning mind is an essential principle of ministry on a university campus. Of equal importance is a compassionate and welcoming heart. The old Latin proverb is true, "One person is no person at all." We are creatures of relatedness who grow, mature, and fulfill our own destinies through nurturing and challenging relationships. The life of the mind and critical thinking are informed and enriched when the academy also values the life of the heart and challenges students, faculty, and staff members to reach beyond one's private world of work, study, teaching, and research and engage the interests and needs of others.

Landmarks and Leaders. The physical, visible, and accessible presence of the University Chaplaincy at the heart of the campus was intentional, a statement that the university values and affirms the ethical and spiritual development of fellow humans. Originally situated temporarily in what was called the old Student Center and Military Science Building (now Weinstein Hall), the Chaplaincy moved to the newly constructed Tyler Haynes Commons building in 1976 and later became permanently housed in the new E. Carlton Wilton Center for Interfaith Campus Ministries, constructed in 1990, adjacent to Cannon Memorial Chapel.

The historic Henry Mansfield Cannon Memorial Chapel was constructed in the late 1920s and dedicated on October 23, 1929, when the president of Brown University, Dr. C. A. Barbour, gave the dedicatory address. On the evening of that same day the renowned American poet Robert Frost gave a lecture on poetry in the chapel. A weekly worship place for Protestant and Catholic services and a retreat space for personal, quiet reflection and meditation, the chapel (renovated and refurbished in 1976) hosted an increasing number of weddings, memorial services, and sometimes university-wide lectures. In the mid-1980s former president Dr. George Modlin chaired a committee to replace and transform all Cannon Chapel windows (which were originally installed with amber glass). The theme of these windows became, "Let All the Universe Praise Thee, O God." This splendid project was made possible by select alumni families who donated and dedicated the stained-glass windows. These significant contributions have been instrumental in creating Cannon Chapel as a worthy model of spirituality and the arts. The elegant Rose Window above the Chapel entrance was the first to be added in April of 1984, a gift from Mr. and Mrs. F. Carlyle Tiller.

The architecturally award-winning Wilton Center was a valuable addition to the central campus in 1990 and served as the home base for the Chaplaincy staff and a number of campus ministers/directors of 12 campus religious organizations. With the opening of the center, an alumna and valued supporter of the Chaplaincy, Ms. Betty Ann Dillon, made a commitment to provide the resources for a signature piece of art to be placed on exhibit at the Wilton Center "symbolizing a person's journey toward wholeness through education, personal faith, and service to others." The dramatic crystal sculpture *Pathways* was commissioned in 1993, installed and dedicated in January 1994. It was designed and created by artist Eric Hilton, formerly of Steuben Glass in New York City. The Wilton Center was critical in the successful efforts to bring together various religious groups to foster dialogue, understanding, and service to others. Annual Interreligious Thanksgiving Dinners each fall and Interfaith Seders each spring became annual Chaplaincy highlights as a result.

From this centralized hub of religious planning and activity (Cannon Chapel and the Wilton Center), the University Chaplaincy played an active role in helping address individual crises of loss, illness, and family concerns and brought the university family together for memorial services in times of loss and sorrow with the death of a student, faculty, or staff person. The Chaplaincy staff members always welcomed the professional support of colleagues in the Counseling and Psychological Services Center on campus. In addition, the Chaplaincy was able to provide support services for individual religious organizations representing Christian denominational groups and other World Religions, programs and retreats for interreligious dialogue at off-campus sites, and seasonal celebrations of Christian, Hindu, Jewish, and Muslim High Holy Days. The university was blessed with local campus ministers/religious leaders who served on campus in partnership with the Chaplaincy staff.

A pleasant surprise in these first ten years was the growing interest in these Chaplaincy programs among various university constituencies. University-related persons and university students were looking for ways to participate and contribute. Two excellent examples are illustrative. First was the creation in 1982 of the University of Richmond Chapel Guild. Alumni and friends quickly signed on and became Charter Members of the Chapel Guild. This engaged group of Cannon Chapel friends provided valuable resources for significant physical improvements in the Chapel and the Wilton Center. In addition, the Chapel Guild's Annual Christmas Open House Tour provided generous monetary support for two popular university and community-wide events—the annual Christmas Candlelight Service begun in 1974 and the university choral groups' presentation of Handel's *Messiah* every four years during Advent or Holy Week seasons. Second, in the spring of 1984, three graduating seniors approached me with a request to lead a brief candlelight ceremony at Westhampton Lake (central campus) for graduating seniors on Saturday night before their Sunday graduation. With meaningful changes over the years, the candlelight ceremony at Westhampton Lake has become a sacred tradition for students and family members each commencement weekend.

One other program worthy of mention was the annual observance of University of Richmond Founder's Day in early March with nationally prominent ethical and spiritual leaders presenting a keynote address related to ethical and/or spiritual issues. The address was followed up with faculty-led workshops and small group dialogues—programs that enjoyed university-wide participation. The University of Richmond and the Chaplaincy are grateful for the vision of alumni David and Terry Heilman Sylvester and their generous support in creating an endowment, The David G. and Terry Heilman Sylvester Speaker's Fund, to attract these special guests and support the Founder's Day observance.

The Jessie Ball DuPont Chaplaincy. The University Chaplaincy had become firmly established by the end of the 1970s anchored at the center of the campus. President Heilman's vision for the Chaplaincy was broader than I originally expected. In addition to giving the Chaplaincy visibility and accessibility and adding the chaplain to his Senior Administrative team, he thought, "If I could find some way to endow this position, that would give it influence and respectability just like a professorship." He further reflected, "Where do I get the money and how do I define this position in a way that a foundation would be willing to support it, give it prestige and highlight its significance?" Heilman, in his inimitable way, set out to make the Chaplaincy ministry a permanent part of campus life by leading the university to embark on a $1.5 million campaign to endow the Chair of the Chaplaincy. He placed a call to The Jesse Ball duPont Religious, Charitable and Educational Fund in Jacksonville, Florida, and followed up with a letter detailing his idea, his vision. He believed this goal was so important and unique that he requested a hearing with the executive director and the full foundation board.

Though the request to meet the full board was bold and unusually aggressive, it was granted. Heilman also invited a Richmond alumnus, Mr. Rip duPont (a relative living in the Jacksonville area but not a board member) to accompany him to this meeting. Heilman presented his story and the evolution of the Chaplaincy. His proposal to the Jessie Ball duPont Fund board members was a request to provide a $750,000 grant (50 percent of the $1.5 million goal) to be matched by the university, and the chair would be named "The Jessie Ball duPont Chair of the Chaplaincy." Richmond alumnus Rip duPont spoke up saying, "I think Aunt Jessie would just love this." When the meeting adjourned, each board member thanked Heilman for sharing his dream of an endowed Chaplaincy, and almost without exception board members thought it was a novel idea and that Aunt Jessie would indeed like it. A few months later President Heilman received the first of three $250,000 checks the university was granted of a total of $750,000. Heilman's vision of an endowed Chaplaincy now had the potential of becoming a reality.

President Heilman and Advancement Office leaders developed a creative plan for matching the Jessie Ball duPont Fund challenge-grant. The University of Richmond identified distinguished laypersons and clergymen in Virginia and established endowments to honor and memorialize these leaders. The endowments received wide support from alumni, friends, and families throughout the state of Virginia and beyond. The women and men of the university's Chapel Guild also played a part in this effort.

The foundation's generous gift and a valuable commitment of other significant gifts made it possible to name and establish this university endowment as The Jessie Ball duPont Chair of the Chaplaincy. The income from this chair supports the Chaplaincy ministry in perpetuity. The University of Richmond secured a vital role of spiritual leadership for the campus community.

On Sunday, October 19, 1986, The Jessie Ball duPont Chair of the Chaplaincy was dedicated at a worship celebration in Cannon Chapel. Dr. Gordon Kingsley, a former president of William Jewell College (my alma mater), gave the dedicatory address in which he said of this sacred moment, "It is an occasion which symbolizes all that I value, the conjoining of mind and heart, of faith and learning, of capability and commitment. It is a blending which has built our great universities, our great social institutions, the greatness of our nation itself. Who can adequately extol the duPont Foundation and other generous donors who have again philanthropically taken a stand for what is most to be treasured in America? We Americans, we in education, are grateful to you" (Kingsley 1986).

The Prayer of Dedication was given by the Chaplain's father, Dr. Rollin S. Burhans (minister/educator), who expressed gratitude to God for those, who by their generous gifts and influence, have secured the future of the Jessie Ball duPont Chaplaincy and have affirmed her avowed objective, "to bring wholeness to fragmented, fragile lives by the integrating, life-changing power of Thy Love." And for all those who provide spiritual leadership to the ministry of this Chaplaincy, he prayed, "Give them insight to see life and see it in proper perspective— the big things big, the small things small. In their low moods, recall them to their better selves lest by a cynical attitude they blight the faith of another or by a thoughtless word they poison the air another must breathe. When they are discouraged, lift them up. When they err, correct them. When they are tempted to pride, humble them. When they miss the mark of their high calling of God, forgive them and lead them back to Thee" (Burhans 1986).

Leadership in Civic Engagement. With the Jesse Ball duPont Chair of the Chaplaincy endowed, a significant milestone had been reached in the evolution of Chaplaincy ministry at the University of Richmond. During these critical years of fundraising for the Chaplaincy endowment and the ongoing daily ministries of extensive Pastoral Care and Counseling (from the mid-1970s and into the mid-1980s), profound stirrings of another sort were developing on campus and at other colleges and universities around the country. There was growing concern among college students for reaching beyond college life and their campuses to learn and broaden their education in different city locations with more diverse groups of people.

By engaging the larger community beyond the sacred walls of academe, they were able to offer a helping hand to people and communities who welcomed them. In truth, volunteerism and community service at Richmond had been sponsored and promoted by campus religious organizations, male Greek organizations (sororities were not established until 1986), occasionally by athletic teams, and by campus service clubs such as APO (Alpha Phi Omega), Circle K, and the like for several years prior to the decade of the 1980s. The Chaplaincy leaders praised their efforts and felt a close affinity with these groups and their good work beyond the campus. The high ethical motivation was clear: "So faith by itself, if it has no works, is dead" (The Letter of James RSV, 2: 17).

The idea of volunteerism and service, however, became highly contagious in the 1980s and a community service movement became widespread throughout the campus, aggressively promoted and sponsored by the Jessie Ball duPont Chaplaincy. Representative student service leaders such as Maura Wolf, *W* 1990; Arrington Chambliss, *W 1988;* David Howie, *R* 1990; and Genevieve Lynch, *W* 1989 provided critical leadership for service-focused groups called VAC (Volunteer Action Council) and VA COOL (Virginia Campus Outreach Opportunity League). Soon thereafter a very successful campus chapter of Habitat for Humanity was established and students, faculty, staff, administrators, and alumni were helping build Habitat houses in the Greater Richmond area.

In 1988, under the creative leadership of the new associate chaplain, the Rev. David Dorsey, a University of Richmond bike race on campus would come to be known as the UR Century Bike Race, a major fundraiser for Habitat for Humanity. Under the direction and sponsorship of the Chaplaincy, many students were intrigued with the idea and helped establish one of the most unusual and effective fundraisers many had ever seen. One of these student leaders, Jon Chandonnet, *R* 1992, who participated in and helped lead the UR Century all four years of his college journey, said in recent months, "I was very involved in a number of campus activities to develop intellectually, socially, and physically. I was drawn to the UR Century program to develop spiritually." I was impressed with the number of students who over these years believed their service of providing affordable housing for others (and other service initiatives) were meaningful spiritual exercises and commitments. The annual campus-wide UR Century Bike Race attracted many university student organizations (required to register a team of bikers and make a certain level of contribution to Habitat for Humanity) from Athletic teams to Student Government groups, Greek organizations, Religious groups, to a Faculty Member team, and a Staff-Administrative team. Over the next several years the UR Century raised more than $300,000 for Habitat for Humanity, and the university community not only raised this money but showed up at construction sites with Richmond area residents to help build more than 13 houses. The University of Richmond became one of the leading colleges/universities in the country in fundraising for Habitat for over more than a decade.

By 1991 the University of Richmond students, faculty, and staff and the Jessie Ball duPont Chaplaincy had established a worthy record of servant leadership and civic engagement in the Greater Richmond Area. This was a unique period in the long history of the University of Richmond. Under the encouraging leadership of President Richard Morrill, civic engagement was becoming a defining characteristic of the university, and with each passing year that reputation was greatly enhanced. In fairly rapid succession, new programs were added to the students' Richmond experience, not the least of which was the University's Bonner Scholars Program placed under the guidance of the Chaplaincy. This one program of up to 100 Richmond students each year (25 per class) provided 10 hours of service each week (mentoring, tutoring, assisting nonprofit organizations) in the Greater Richmond Area. Since its inception in 1991, it is estimated that the Bonner Scholar students have contributed over a million hours of service to the Greater Richmond Community.

Another meaningful program of the Chaplaincy was helping university students to partner with Richmond City neighborhoods and assist with small grassroots projects. The program came to be called "In My Back Yard" and popularly known as "The IMBY Awards." Through the generous support of Mr. Marcus Weinstein (an outstanding University of Richmond philanthropist and businessman), this student-led program was able to provide a number of grants to small neighborhood groups who were looking for ways to address needs that would enhance the quality of their communities. One other significant program was a university-wide Community Service Day established in 2001 in which students, faculty, and staff joined forces to paint, landscape, and refurbish selected Richmond Public Schools on a given Saturday each spring. The schools were identified for us through our working-relationship with the superintendent of Richmond Public Schools. These kinds of student-led service initiatives have, over the last four decades, not only closely connected the University of Richmond with its host city but also energized and enriched the educational experience for large numbers of students of the University of Richmond.

As the turn of the century approached, the Chaplaincy staff began to witness the responsibility of growing requests for helping students and student groups identify service opportunities in the Greater Richmond Area. Furthermore, the Jepson School of Leadership Studies (established in 1990) began offering service-learning and other community-based learning courses. And, though for years the University Chaplaincy had been the go-to place for most questions and programing related to service opportunities, it was important the university community understand that service and civic engagement activities not be perceived as only for people of a religious persuasion or commitment. A strong, effective leader, Associate Chaplain Robb Moore, and I began to explore the possibility of a stand-alone center, a place on campus for the centralization of all community service programing and a place where students, faculty, and staff could learn of civic engagement opportunities available to them in Richmond City and the surrounding area.

President William Cooper gladly welcomed our conversations, ideas, and strategies regarding this broader approach to civic engagement and invited Provost June Aprille and Professor Douglas Hicks of the Leadership School to explore with the Chaplaincy staff and a faculty committee the potential development of this plan. As a result, with the generous financial support of the Bonner Foundation, the Corella and Bertram F. Bonner Center for Civic Engagement was launched in the summer of 2004 at the heart of the campus with Professor Hicks serving as the founding director. Currently, under the impressive leadership of Dr. Amy Howard, the center's influence and reach has become a valuable, integral part of the Richmond experience for students, faculty, and staff.

The Ministry of Presence, Landmarks and Leaders, The Endowment of the Jessie Ball duPont Chaplaincy, and Leadership in Civic Engagement capture the heart of the University of Richmond Chaplaincy in its first three decades and brings me back to where I began. That motivating, guiding spirit prevails, *Life is gift: handle this journey with gratitude, with compassion, with humility—gifts of Divine Grace.* There is no substitute in life and relationships for an individual's heart of gratitude. *Gratitude is not only the greatest of all virtues but the parent of all others* (Cicero). Compassionate connection with fellow humans—listening with awareness and creating a culture of caring—gives renewed hope and new meaning to our journey. And, the gift of humility is critical. Theologian Reinhold Niebuhr is helpful when he suggests that we need constantly to reexamine our beliefs and actions and never be too sure of our own virtue.

I stand in awe before the Jessie Ball duPont Chaplaincy enamored by its health and vitality to this day, grateful for the leadership it has attracted. Thoughtful, creative students, faculty, staff, and administrators have shared their knowledge, skill, and wisdom in helping create and sustain a movement of love, compassion, and justice,which has permeated this campus community and the university's host city. For me, the wonder of it all has become identified with the Eternal, consistent with what I interpret as Divine will, a vibrant force for good, for love of neighbor, and for transformative human experiences.

I offer some personal reflections in concluding this Chaplaincy journey. The Eternal God is Infinite Mystery. Yet, in the midst of my own partial knowledge and personal experiences, there has been and continues to be a presence of something far greater than I can comprehend, which loves and affirms me. This presence I call *God*, most clearly revealed to me in Jesus of Nazareth. On this journey, my concept of God has greatly expanded, similar now the concept preached by Apostle Paul, who, when speaking to the Athenians of Ancient Greece, said, "in him we live and move and have our being" (Acts17: 28). This was also reflected in a well-known religion professor's declaration following his address at the University of Richmond (the late Marcus Borg, during Q&A), who, when asked what he believes about heaven, said he could not describe heaven in any definitive way but from his decades of examining/teaching biblical studies was convinced of this, "that when we die, we die into God." Early on in my personal journey, I knew intellectually of this all-encompassing concept of God, but mostly in relation to Jewish and Christian studies. Then I transitioned from a congregation of believers to a world of academe and greater human diversity.

In congregational ministry I believed it was important to speak of God in specific terms, in language familiar to the historic Judeo-Christian (Baptist) tradition with descriptive phrases that helped define God for me and hopefully for others. In truth, this is what I knew best at that time. I needed to proclaim the love of God and encourage others to love the things that God loves. On the way to the twenty-first century, however, I realized how critical my goals, trustworthiness, and skillsets were conjoined with personal congruence, empathic understanding, and unconditional positive regard in shaping healthy relationships, in helping me grow as a spiritual leader, and in becoming an advocate of *faith, unity,* and *reconciliation.* The answers to those early questions—Who am I? Why am I here? What difference can I make? —had come sharply into focus. I met many new people, faced thoughtful ethical questions, engaged devout fellow-believers with different perspectives and different interpretations of Holy Scripture, and became acquainted with people of other faiths (world religions), who shared something of their own faith journeys with language and experiences not all that different from my own.

I began to realize that God's revelation of God's self to these friends was as meaningful to them as were my personal encounters and relationship with God, encounters that led me to embrace as my own the Early Christian Church's confession of faith, "Jesus is Lord." They too had experienced the love and mercy of God with such captivating joy and affirmation that they too believed God had claimed them and was deserving of their allegiance. I discovered over these years that the concept of God I started with was simply too narrow, just too small. The result, wonder upon wonder!

Now I am bold to suggest that anyone who is attuned to moral and spiritual values, who is seeing and listening and paying attention, will likely understand that *wonder* just might be another name for God. The title of this chapter, "The Pursuit of Wonder," may be a worthy human goal. But the ultimate truth is, *wonder* is in pursuit of us! This all-encompassing Spirit of awe and wonder, love and grace, is loose upon the world, a force over which we humans have little if any control. We can, however, be used by it!

References

Oliver, Mary. 2004. "Mindful." In *Why I Wake Early.* Boston, MA: Beacon Press.

Burhans, Rollin. 1986. *Prayer of Dedication.* Worship Celebration and Dedication of The Jessie Ball duPont Chair of the Chaplaincy, Cannon Memorial Chapel, University of Richmond, October 19.

Heilman, E. Bruce. 2008. *An Interruption That Lasted a Lifetime: My First Eighty Years.* Dallas, TX: AuthorHouse Books.

Heschel, Abraham Joshua. 1983. *I Asked for Wonder: A Spiritual Anthology.* New York: The Crossroad Publishing Co.

Kingsley, Gordon. 1986. "Dedicatory Address." Worship Celebration and Dedication of The Jessie Ball duPont Chair of the Chaplaincy, Cannon Memorial Chapel, University of Richmond, October 19th.

PART II

Contemporary Approaches to
Spiritual Leadership

CHAPTER SEVEN

Leading through Reading in Contemporary Young Adult Fantasy by Philip Pullman and Terry Pratchett

ELISABETH ROSE GRUNER

There's a popular bumper sticker in some areas that reads: "God said it, I believe it, that settles it." It is sometimes paired with another one: "Bibles that are falling apart usually belong to people that aren't." The two combine to suggest an approach to reading and religion that are at the core of my argument in this chapter: they suggest that religious reading is fundamentally anti-interpretive; that reading the Bible or other religious texts provides direct access to truth. In the young adult texts I discuss in this essay, however, the opposite is the case: while texts (of many sorts) may provide access to truth, even spiritual and religious truth, such access requires interpretation just as much as, if not more than, any other kind of reading. The *His Dark Materials* trilogy by Philip Pullman and the Discworld novels featuring Tiffany Aching by Terry Pratchett, which otherwise may seem to have little in common, feature young, attentive, skeptical, truth-seeking readers. These novels, while hardly didactic, suggest through their emphasis on critical reading and thinking that no area of development is out of bounds for the reader; that reading, indeed, enables rather than forestalls moral and spiritual development—a development that emphasizes storytelling and caregiving. Storytelling and caregiving in fact turn out to be related gifts, elements of a kind of feminist leadership that has its roots in critical reading.

In an era marked by religious violence and the rise of religious fundamentalism, it is perhaps not surprising that writers from the liberal West would incorporate an anti-fundamentalist message within their texts. Melody Briggs and Richard Briggs suggest, as well, that fantasy literature is uniquely positioned to fill the "gap" between science and religion, as the two dominant modes of meaning making in contemporary life:

On the one hand, science restricts meaning to the empirical, denying people a "sense of their own importance" (42). On the other, religion is marginalized by the relentless march of secularization which relegates religious values to the status of subjective preference. Today's Westerner comes to the point of asking questions about life's meaning and value, and discovers that neither of the culture's dominant traditions gives them the frameworks they need. Instead of finding a way of making sense of things, they find only a gap. If fantasy literature springs in part from such a gap, mirroring the needs of our modern culture, it will also have its part to play in filling that gap. (Briggs and Briggs 2006, 31; quoting Hume 1984)

I will further argue in this chapter, then, that both Pullman and Pratchett are reclaiming the mythic status of their tales, refusing the modern fundamentalism that insists on the empirical truth of religious narrative, and revivifying an older style of reading that focuses on gleaning personal and community meaning from tales (see Armstrong 2000, xiii–xv, for a discussion of the connection between empiricism and fundamentalism). It is a reading intimately bound up with storytelling itself: the protagonists of these texts become leaders by reading, interpreting, and telling stories, modeling the qualities that their implied readers should also be acquiring as they, in turn, read the novels that bear the stories forward.

Young Adult literature has always been controversial, both as a concept and in its contents. Karen Coates writes that YA fiction has often only been recognized "as a house you pass on the way, not a destination in and of itself"—that is, it is defined more by what it is not (appropriate for children and/or adults) than what it is (Coates 2011, 317), while Roberta Trites has argued that what distinguishes YA from children's fiction is, at least in part, its subject matter: sex and death (Trites 2000, see esp. ch. 4 and 5). These generic definitions may offer a general sense of what YA fiction is. But in contemporary YA fiction—written since the mid-90s—young readers are not only learning about sex and death when they read YA fiction: increasingly, they are learning about reading itself. Contemporary YA fiction is centrally concerned with the power-making potential of reading. Rather than being simply objects of passive consumption, books, texts, and reading are part of an interactive exchange in which teen characters and readers can become active agents within, and critics of, their contemporary culture. In the analysis that follows, I focus primarily on the content of the texts in question, rather than their reception; at all times, however, it is important to keep the implied reader of the text in mind as an active agent in the exchange between reader and text, an agent who may be affected by the depiction of other such agents in the texts at hand. I will return to this question of agency in the conclusion.

Narrative Causality, Destiny, and Stories

To be a spiritual leader is to be both bound by, and to resist, a force Pratchett calls "narrative causality"—a near-synonym for destiny, perhaps, or even for the divine. Pratchett defines "narrative causality" as "the idea that there are 'story shapes' into which human history, both large scale and at the personal level, attempts to fit" (Pratchett 2000, 166). In *Witches Abroad* he writes: "the theory of narrative causality... means that a story, once started, takes a shape. It picks up all the vibrations of all the other workings of that story that have ever been.... Stories don't care who takes part in them. All that matters is that the story gets told, that the story repeats" (Pratchett 2002, 2). Spiritual leaders, of course, come to embody stories such as the hero's journey, biblical narrative, fairy tales of epic leaders—but the self-aware leader has read or heard such stories and can, while re-enacting the story, retell and rework it as well. In both Pullman's and Pratchett's series, "narrative causality" is at work, as both Lyra and Tiffany find themselves in the midst of familiar, even sacred, stories. Both are, indeed, the subjects of prophecy, figures who seem to bear the peculiar burden of fulfilling a destiny for a larger community than themselves. In this they may also seem to be stand-ins for their implied readers, or even for all young adults, who bear the burden of fulfilling the future for a generation that is passing leadership on—a generation that may have passed on the stories to them. But narrative causality alone is not a valid substitute for religion, particularly religion in modern crisis—it can seem, after all, simply to replicate the concept of fate or predestination and the concomitant denial of free will. In both Pullman's and Pratchett's series, some kind of destiny seems to

be operative, but it is not absolute—human choice, human intervention, and human agency can all change fate, just as human storytellers
can change the story. The human characters in the series—particularly
the two heroines, Lyra Belacqua and Tiffany Aching—become co-cre-
ators within their texts, storytellers who alter their own destinies by
re-reading, revising, and reworking familiar tales, and by resisting the
extremes of narrative causality. They therefore offer a model of critical
reading to their own implied readers. It is a model of reading useful not
only for fantasy literature but implicitly for religious literature as well,
as I hope to demonstrate further ahead in the chapter.

For readers unfamiliar with them, it may be impossible to summarize
works as dense as Pullman's *His Dark Materials* trilogy or as interconnected as Pratchett's Tiffany Aching novels, a quintet of novels within
the larger Discworld series of books (now comprising over 40 texts).
Key elements are as follows: the *His Dark Materials* trilogy is made up
of *The Golden Compass* (published as *Northern Lights* in the UK in 1995),
The Subtle Knife (1997), and *The Amber Spyglass* (2000). In *The Golden
Compass* we first meet Lyra Belacqua, a seemingly orphaned 12-year-
old girl growing up in a parallel universe to ours, in a version of Oxford
that has seemingly split off from our world at about the time of the
Reformation. References to a Pope John Calvin, to atomic, electrical,
and other modern technologies with different names, and to colonial
enterprises that make Texas a country, defamiliarize the reader's experience while still making the world seem recognizably connected to ours.
It is a hierarchical and patriarchal world, for the most part, dominated by
a Church (always capitalized) that appears to control both the government
and the unversity and that, while it shares elements of Christianity (such
as a priesthood, popes, and a Fall story involving Adam and Eve) lacks
others, including any reference to Jesus. This is the world in which Lyra
comes of age. In *The Subtle Knife*, the action takes place in three distinct
worlds—Lyra's, our own, and a somewhat indistinct waystation known
as Cittàgaze—while *The Amber Spyglass* moves the most freely among a
variety of worlds and creatures the least like our own, including a world
populated by wheeled beasts known as *mulefa*, who, for all their difference from us, share a creation story that has elements of the Genesis tale.
The trilogy as a whole reworks Milton's *Paradise Lost*, recasting the Fall
as fortunate and culminating in a war in heaven and earth that restores
balance to the multiverse in part through the death of God.

The Discworld series is far different. Often read as a satire of our
own world, Pratchett's Discworld is also a comic fantasy, based in a flat
world that balances on the back of four elephants who stand on the back

of a giant turtle. (The elephants and the turtle otherwise never enter into the Tiffany Aching stories.) The inhabitants, though recognizably human, also include witches, wizards, and other fairy-tale type creatures familiar to fantasy readers. Tiffany Aching is a nine-year-old girl when her series begins. Over the course of the series she ages ten more years, becomes a witch (first apprenticing to another, older witch), travels to at least one other world, and learns through a series of adventures the importance of taking control of her own narrative—a lesson that Lyra, too, must learn in her own way. It is through critical reading that both become tellers of their own tales, and thus spiritual leaders—and it is to this aspect of both novels that I now turn.

Reading, Lying, and Telling New Tales

Lyra Belacqua, the heroine of the *His Dark Materials* trilogy, is no reader. Characterized early on as a "coarse and greedy savage" who tries to elude her tutors in order to play in the claypits of Oxford, she is an unlikely poster child for critical reading (Pullman 1996, 36). Yet, when she acquires the alethiometer, a "golden compass" or symbol reader, that gives her access to truth—if only she can both ask the right questions and interpret the answers—she slowly develops the skill. While adult readers of the device use books of symbols to help them both pose their questions and interpret the results, Lyra begins by using it intuitively, and then learns the meanings of the symbols as she goes.

Although the alethiometer reveals the truth, Lyra is also, notably, a liar. I'll discuss her lying in greater detail later in this chapter; here, I'll just note that her lying and her ability to read the truth in the alethiometer are explicitly linked. After Mrs. Coulter finds her in Bolvangar, for example, she lies about her journey there:

> With every second that went past, with every sentence she spoke, she felt a little strength flowing back. And now that she was doing something difficult and familiar and never-quite-predictable, namely lying, she felt a sort of mastery again, the same sense of complexity and control that the alethiometer gave her. She had to be careful not to say anything obviously impossible; she had to be vague in some places and invent plausible details in others; she had to be an artist, in short. (Pullman 1996, 281)

The "complexity and control" Lyra attains through reading the alethiometer and storytelling are centrally connected. Not only does she feel the same way in both cases, but also in both cases she is telling a story. And while there may be transcendental truths that Lyra accesses through the alethiometer, they are by no means transparent: there is no such thing as a fundamentalist reading of the device. So her readings are stories, stories that give her access to truth. As she is first learning to read the device, for example, she explains to Farder Coram: "I can see what it says, but I must be misreading it. The thunderbolt I think is anger, and the child...I think it's me...I was getting a meaning for that lizard thing, but you talked to me, Farder Coram, and I lost it" (Pullman 1996, 152). As she becomes more accomplished, the readings seem transparent—she asks a question, and the answers come back clearly—but there is always interpretation involved, as we see most obviously at moments of stress or loss.

Throughout the series, the same language connects her reading of the alethiometer with her mastery of storytelling—or lying—and the loss of one skill late in *The Amber Spyglass* seems directly connected with the loss of the other. Separated from Pan in the world of the dead, Lyra tries to read the alethiometer:

> How wearily Lyra turned the wheels; on what leaden feet her thoughts moved. The ladders of meaning that led from every one of the alethiometer's thirty-six symbols, down which she used to move so lightly and confidently, felt loose and shaky. And holding the connections between them in her mind...It had once been like running, or singing, or *telling a story*: something natural. Now she had to do it laboriously, and her grip was failing, and she mustn't fail because otherwise everything would fail...(Pullman 2000, 384; emphasis added, ellipses in original)

While Lyra's loss of the ability to read the alethiometer may seem like a consequence of her "fall"—that is, of her sexual encounter with Will—Lyra herself interprets the loss differently. Reunited with her dæmon in the world of the *mulefa*, she tries to read the alethiometer and fails. "It's no good—I can tell—it's gone forever—it just came when I needed it, for all the things I had to do—for rescuing Roger, and then for us two—and now that it's over, now that everything's finished, it's just left me...It's gone, Will! I've lost it! It'll never come back!" The narrator, focalizing Will, notes that "he didn't know how to comfort her, because it was plain that she was right" (Pullman 2000, 490). While it's not clear exactly what she was "right" about—the loss, or its cause, or both?—it does seem plausible that both losses, the lying and the truth-reading, are linked. Lyra has lost her sense of agency, of control, at the same time that she has fulfilled her destiny. What this suggests is twofold: one, that truth and lies are simply two different ways of getting at the same thing and, two, that that same thing is the larger narrative (destiny, fate, prophecy) into which all the characters of the trilogy are bound. The sense of mastery, of control, of free will (as it were) that Lyra's abilities have given her are, to some extent, illusory, given to her only to fulfill her destiny. This is of course literally true: Lyra is a character in a novel, her destiny controlled by an all-powerful author; as the conclusion draws near, her narrative destiny almost complete, her illusory sense of agency must inevitably vanish. As William Gray writes, "Pullman, the 'Author-God' (to borrow Barthes's phrase) might…be accused of exercising the literary equivalent of Calvinist 'double predestination,' with Lyra predestined to salvation and Gomez [her assassin] to perdition" (Gray 2009, 171). Even within the text, though, the link between agency and destiny becomes clear: Lyra's ability to act, to author her own tale, dissipates as the larger narrative within which she participates shifts. Nonetheless, to the extent that she can both read the alethiometer and master storytelling, she functions as a leader, rallying the children at Bolvanger and again, even more importantly, providing hope and direction to the lost souls in the land of the dead.

Stories, lies, and reading work somewhat differently for Tiffany, who is introduced to us from the first as a reader. Confronted with a monster (Jenny Green-Teeth) in the opening pages of *Wee Free Men*, Tiffany turns to the *Goode Childe's Booke of Faerie Tales*, where she finds instructions for defeating it. Soon thereafter, we learn that she has read the dictionary (she has a large vocabulary, though her pronunciation is often somewhat off) as well as the few other books that her family has (Pratchett 2003, 12–13, 30). Much of this reading is primarily informational, and initially Tiffany can take it as directly factual, but as the series continues and she matures, we see her learn not only to read more critically, but to engage with the stories she encounters, reshaping them for her own and her community's purposes. Like Lyra, she becomes a storyteller, engaging with and reworking stories in order to reorder her society.

Rather than rewriting stories out of the Judeo-Christian tradition, Pratchett works in the Tiffany Aching books with the pagan origins of story in England—with fairy tales, tradition, and superstition. In other words, with what are already quite explicitly stories rather than sacred texts. So rather than demystify them as Pullman does with the

Christian stories that are his material, Pratchett reanimates what might have been thought to have devolved into fairy tale, legend, and superstition. Unlike Lyra, Tiffany is not associated with a single text or instrument. Discworld is too disparate, and her adventures too multifarious, for that. As I've noted, the first stories we encounter in her series come from *The Goode Childe's Booke of Faerie Tales,* one of the few books in her parents' sparsely furnished home. And while she finds it useful as a source of information, she is also a highly skeptical reader. This skepticism is initially not productive, however—failing to find the full truth in a tale, she cannot, initially, find any:

> A lot of the stories were highly suspicious, in her opinion. There was the one that ended when the two good children pushed the wicked witch into her own oven. Tiffany had worried about that after all the trouble with Mrs. Snapperly. Stories like this stopped people thinking properly, she was sure. She'd read that one and thought, Excuse me? *No one* has an oven big enough to get a whole person in, and what made the children think they could just walk around eating people's houses in any case? And why does some boy too stupid to know a cow is worth a lot more than five beans have the *right* to murder a giant and steal all his gold? Not to mention commit an act of ecological vandalism? And some girl who can't tell the difference between a wolf and her grandmother must either have been as dense as teak or come from an extremely ugly family. The stories *weren't real.* But Mrs. Snapperly had died because of the stories." (Pratchett 2003, 66–67; emphasis in original)

While Lord Asriel finds the fairy-tale quality of the book of Genesis freeing ("if you include it in your equations, you can calculate all manner of things that couldn't be imagined without it" [Pullman 1996, 372–373]), Tiffany sees the danger in allowing stories that "aren't real" to shape action. Tiffany's suspicions are also aroused because she intuits that there is no place in stories like these for a girl like her. Early on, she asks, "Did the book have any adventures of people who had brown eyes and brown hair? No, no, no...it was the blond people with blue eyes and the redheads with green eyes who got the stories. If you had brown hair you were probably just a servant or a woodcutter or something. Or a dairymaid. Well, that was not going to happen, even if she *was* good at cheese" (Pratchett 2003, 35–36; emphasis in original). Tiffany's gift—and Pratchett's, of course—is to insist that heroism, and leadership, are not limited to those we expect to find at the center of the story: that even the brown-haired nine-year-old can take control of the action.

These are not, of course, religious stories like those that inhibit and constrain the characters of the *His Dark Materials*. Nonetheless, as Tiffany recognizes, they direct behavior—fairy tales may not be "gospel truths" (a term that arises in neither text), but they do influence belief. The people who burn down an old woman's cottage, believing her to be a witch, do not stop to ask the kinds of questions Tiffany asks of fairy tales—although, of course, implicitly they should. Fairy tale, legend, and superstition turn out to have controlling power—narrative causality—despite seeming to be worn out, decayed, obsolete. While Lyra adds reading to her native skill with storytelling, Tiffany works the other way around, learning to reshape the stories that she has critically read, and to retell them with new meanings. Ultimately, however, Tiffany's solution is like Lyra's: to take control of the story, to edit and shape and retell it, a process that goes on throughout the series. As Granny Weatherwax says, "change the story, change the world"—and Tiffany does, repeatedly, both bowing to narrative causality and resisting it (Pratchett 2004, 338). Like Lyra, then, her leadership derives from her facility with story, as both reader and (re)teller.

Re-reading the Fall Narrative in *His Dark Materials*

The most obvious example of narrative causality in *His Dark Materials* comes in a prophecy about Lyra. In a horrific scene near the end of *The Subtle Knife*, Lyra's mother, Marisa Coulter, tortures the witch Lena Feldt to find out who the witches say her daughter is:

> Lena Feldt gasped, "She will be the mother—she will be life— mother—she will disobey—she will—"
>
> "Name her! You are saying everything but the most important thing! Name her!" cried Mrs. Coulter.
>
> "Eve! Mother of all! Eve, again! Mother Eve!" stammered Lena Feldt, sobbing. (Pullman 1997, 314)

If Lyra is, indeed, as the witch says, "Eve, Mother of us all," then we can see the entire trilogy as a revision of Genesis. And certainly in the final pages we get a specific reimagining of the Genesis story in which Lyra and Will come to consciousness, as their forebears did, but with joyful rather than tragic consequences. Despite the "felix culpa" quality of their "fall," however, the story still has its way with them and they choose exile from the garden and separation—much like the joint expulsion Eve and Adam undergo. While throughout the trilogy story both constrains and enables, finally the tale that Will and Lyra find themselves within has intentions for them that they cannot resist. As David Gooderham suggests, the "old myth bit[es] back" when Will and Lyra, like Adam and Eve before them, face "exile" after their "fall" (Gooderham 2003, 170).

By the time Lyra re-enacts the "Fall" toward the end of *The Amber Spyglass*, readers have already encountered two alternative versions of Genesis, although Lyra has only heard one of them. The first, in *The Golden Compass*, changes little from the canonical story but does add the dæmons who have been a central part of Pullman's mythology. The moment of awareness here is significant: after the man and the woman eat the forbidden fruit, "the eyes of them both were opened, and they saw the true form of their dæmons, and spoke with them... [but] until that moment it had seemed that they were at one with all the creatures of the earth and the air, and there was no difference between them" (Pullman 1996, 372). Asriel, reading this to Lyra, calls the story something "like an imaginary number, like the square root of minus one: you can never see any concrete proof that it exists, but if you include it in your equations, you can calculate all manner of things that couldn't be imagined without it" (Pullman 1996, 372–373). That is, for Asriel, this religious creation story is equally "true" and "not-true," rendering the binary distinction somewhat moot. Even in this early scene, then, the novel grants religious story significant value even while rejecting a fundamentalist understanding of it.

The second version, which Mary Malone hears from the *mulefa*, is a significant shift. When the *mulefa* Atal tells Mary her origin myth, two things are particularly significant: first, the story concerns a female, an Eve figure who does not "fall" but comes into self-awareness nonetheless; second, although Atal calls it a "make-like" (metaphor), she also calls it a history; again, like Asriel, claiming for it a significance beyond the literal. As Karen Armstrong notes, premodern people did not distinguish between history and myth: "Historical incidents were not seen as unique occurrences, set in a far-off time, but were thought to be external manifestations of constant, timeless realities" (Armstrong 2000, xiv). The *mulefa* seem premodern to Dr. Malone, no doubt in part because they, too, refuse to distinguish between history and myth. But it may also be helpful here to think of the way feminist theologians have explored the ways in which metaphor can function as an emancipatory strategy:

> Genuine metaphor is not primarily a rhetorical decoration or an abbreviated comparison. It is a proposition (explicit or implied) constituted by an irresolvable tension between what it affirms (which is somehow true) and what it necessarily denies (namely, the literal truth of the assertion)...It forces the mind to reach toward meaning that exceeds or escapes effective literal expression. (Schneiders 1993, 38)

The *mulefa's* story, both true and not-true, both history and metaphor, forces both Mary Malone and, as importantly, the implied reader of the novel into a critical reading position that, as Schneiders suggests, "reaches toward" meaning rather than asserting it:

> *One day a creature with no name discovered a seedpod and began to play, and as she played she—*
> *She?*
> *She, yes. She had no name before then. She saw a snake coiling itself through the hole in a seedpod, and the snake said—*
> *The snake spoke to her?*
> *No, no! It is a make-like. The story tells that the snake said, "What do you know? What do you remember? What do you see ahead?" And she said, "Nothing, nothing, nothing." So the snake said, "Put your foot through the hole in the seedpod where I was playing, and you will become wise." So she put a foot in where the snake had been. And the oil entered her blood and helped her see more clearly than before, and the first thing she saw was the sraf. It was so strange and pleasant that she wanted to share it at once with her kindred. So she and her mate took the seedpods, and they discovered that they knew who they were, they knew they were mulefa and not grazers. They gave each other names. They named themselves mulefa. They named the seed tree, and all the creatures and plants.* (Pullman 2000, 224–225)

In the *mulefa's* story, Pullman retains significant elements from the story of Eve's temptation: a female creature comes into consciousness through the agency of a snake. But this joyful scene carries none of the weight of either our world's Genesis or Asriel's version. Self-awareness brings with it no shame, but is associated with the creative act of naming (which, in Genesis, precedes rather than following the "fall" narrative). By retelling the familiar "fall" story without a fall, the *mulefa* perform what Paul Ricoeur calls "the task of the hermeneut": they help us by "transferring ourselves into another universe of meaning and thereby putting ourselves at a kind of distance with regard to *our* actual discourse" (Ricoeur 1978, 224; emphasis in original). Of course, in J. R. R. Tolkien's well-known formulation, fantasy literature "recovers" our reality for us, making the familiar new; it seems to me that this is another way of saying that it "puts us at a kind of distance with regard to our" consensus reality, and thus, presumably, to our "actual discourse" (Tolkien 1947, 74). But Pullman's text takes things one step further than Tolkien's formulation implies; it recovers and defamiliarizes stories that form the groundwork of faith for many people. As we shall later see, however, Pullman also reintroduces some fundamentalism—or at least determinism—about narrative even as he calls the details of the Christian narrative into question. Nonetheless, in this moment the novel suggests a way of reading that is open to possibility—freeing, rather than constrained or closed down by the text.

Lyra, of course, does not hear the version of Genesis that the *mulefa* tell Mary Malone, and is not fully aware that she has been prophesied to be "Eve, Mother of us all." Unaware of her status, she leads her friend Will into the land of the Dead, where we see perhaps the most obvious demonstration of her leadership and her storytelling capacity—her refusal to stay within a pre-scripted narrative, and her ability to tell a story that both nourishes and frees the listeners.

In her sojourn with the dead, Lyra tells stories that "recover" (in Tolkien's sense) the mundane reality of the world, making it new: for the ghosts who hear it, for the harpies who overhear it, and for the implied readers of the text, who are brought into relationship with the tale as Lyra tells it. Throughout the trilogy, Lyra has been an accomplished liar, a fantasist whose ability to lie has been one of her most salient qualities. She lies easily, freely, even—on at least one occasion— "earnestly" (Pullman 2000, 169). When she lies to the people on their way to the land of the dead, she settles into her role gladly: "as she took charge, part of her felt a little stream of pleasure rising upward in her breast like the bubbles in champagne. And she knew Will was watching, and she was happy that he could see her doing what she was best at, doing it for him and for all of them" (Pullman 2000, 261–262).

But in the land of the dead the facility abandons her. As she begins to lie to the harpies, they attack her, sensing immediately the deceit in her words. Only when she tells them a true story, a story drawn from the world she has come from, do both the ghosts and the harpies acknowledge her as a leader, and as a truth-teller. Here we move from engagement with prior tales to a new tale, to her own story, the one we have been reading: Lyra retells in miniature the story of her life, and she tells it with a particular emphasis, an emphasis on the joys of the material world and on overcoming difference:

> Then she told how the clayburner's children always made war on the townies, but how they were slow and dull, with clay in their brains, and how the townies were as sharp and quick as sparrows by contrast; and how one day the townies had swallowed their differences and plotted and planned and attacked the claybeds from three sides, pinning the clayburners' children back against the river, hurling handfuls and handfuls of heavy, claggy clay at one another, rushing their muddy castle and tearing it down, turning the fortifications into missiles until the air and the ground and the water were all mixed inextricably together, and every child looked exactly the same, mud from scalp to sole, and none of them had had a better day in all their lives. (Pullman 2000, 315)

This brief tale does several things: it quells the fury of the harpies, most significantly and surprisingly, and leads the way to a truce with them which holds throughout the rest of the novel. It also, more subtly, predicts the battle that follows, in which former enemies forget their differences to band together, rejecting the tales that have divided them in order to tell a new story of unity—a unity based on a shared celebration of the material world.

That story of unity comes later, however. For the moment, the focus of the narrative is on Lyra's ability to calm the harpies. Unable to do so with her usual skill of lying, she is surprised to find that telling the truth works:

> "when she spoke just now," [Tialys asks,] "you all listened, every one of you, and you kept silent and still. Again, why was that?"
>
> "Because it was true," said No-Name. "Because she spoke the truth. Because it was nourishing. Because it was feeding us. Because we couldn't help it. Because it was true. Because we had no idea that there was anything but wickedness. Because it brought us news of the world and the sun and the wind and the rain. Because it was true." (Pullman 2000, 317)

No-Name's truth is firmly grounded in the material world but has nothing to do with, for example, Asriel's empiricism, which might seem to oppose the myth-making of the Church. "News of the world" comes to her through story (like the "make-like" or history of the *mulefa*), which, in a telling choice of verbs, nourishes and feeds rather than explaining or proving. It is probably worth noting here that witches and harpies are all female, and the *mulefa* we encounter the most often are also female, although they clearly have two sexes. Rather than the patriarchal world of the Church (it's noted more than once that Mrs. Coulter is unusual in her power within that institution) it is these matriarchies or quasi-matriarchal societies that have access to truth through story. Storytelling is thus linked explicitly here with caregiving, a care that both Lyra or, perhaps even more, Tiffany embodies throughout her series.

Pullman's trilogy, however, centers not on these matriarchal, caregiving societies but on Lyra, who inhabits a far more conventional society—and plot—than these resistant females. Her story-making ability is therefore limited and in the end she seems to be subject to the same narrative causality—the Genesis story of exile—that Pullman's ideology otherwise resists. Tiffany's stories far more explicitly resist and reshape the conventions that would restrict her to either the happily-ever-after of fairy tale courtship (suggested but never fulfilled in her relationship with Roland) or the punishment of witches envisioned by the Cunning Man in *I Shall Wear Midnight*.

Storytelling and the Ethic of Care

The all-female witches of the Tiffany Aching series link story and care even more explicitly than Lyra links them in *His Dark Materials*. But the Tiffany Aching books, as we have seen, initially evince a deep distrust of stories, especially the stories that shape belief. While even in Discworld "fairy tale" means the opposite of "gospel," the *Goode Childe's Booke of Faerie Tales* nonetheless, like a sacred text, directs the behavior and belief of the people who burn down Mrs. Snapperly's cottage. It also furnishes at least some of the monsters deployed by the Fairy Queen in her incursions into Tiffany's world. Like Pullman, then, though working with quite different material to quite different ends, Pratchett refreshes and defamiliarizes stories that may form the groundwork of faith. Although Pratchett does not, as Pullman does, explicitly frame his series' concerns as religious, the language of "sin" and "soul," of caregiving and persecution, is prevalent, especially in *I Shall Wear Midnight*, suggesting an ongoing concern with the functions of religion in society. Learning to read the stories carefully, then, is also a way of engaging with religious stories critically.

Like Lyra, Tiffany Aching frequently finds herself caught in a story not of her own making. In *The Wee Free Men*, this takes a comic turn: brought into the Feegles' clan as their new leader, their *kelda*, she is required to choose one of them for her husband and name a date. This is one of the first times that she uses a story to revise and, in her own way, defeat a story. Choosing Rob Anybody for her husband, she then tells this story:

> "At the end of the world is a great big mountain of granite rock a mile high," she said. "And every year, a tiny bird flies all the way to the rock and wipes its beak on it. Well, when the little bird has worn the mountain down to the size of a grain of sand... that's the day I'll marry you, Rob Anybody Feegle!" (Pratchett 2003, 191)

Adhering to the form of their story—she has chosen a husband and named a date—she has also subverted it, by naming a date that will never be. Her story revises theirs and allows her to become their leader without compromising their tradition. And her reading in *The Goode Childe's Fairie Booke* clearly enables this revision, providing as it does the source material for her new tale.

But later re-readings and retellings turn more serious and more complex. In *A Hat Full of Sky*, for example, Tiffany retells the Genesis story—or *a* genesis story—giving the parasitic hiver that has been occupying her mind a new narrative that ultimately frees both of them:

> "Here is a story to believe," she said. "Once we were blobs in the sea, and then fishes, and then lizards and rats, and then monkeys, and hundreds of things in between. This hand was once a fin, this hand once had claws! In my human mouth I have the pointy teeth of a wolf and the chisel teeth of a rabbit and the grinding teeth of a cow! Our blood is as salty as the sea we used to live in! When we're frightened, the hair on our skin stands up, just like it did when we had fur. We *are* history! Everything we've ever been on the way to becoming us, we still are. Would you like the rest of the story?" (Pratchett 2004, 351; emphasis in original)

This story echoes the narrative movement of the first chapter of Genesis, the familiar "seven days" story that narrates creation from chaos to order, from water to dry land, rather than the later chapters that narrate the Fall, and that form so important a foundation for Pullman. Unlike the story into which Lyra and Will find themselves written at the end of *His Dark Materials*, it is a joyful celebration. And as Tiffany continues the story, she names the hiver (Arthur)—much as Lyra names No-Name the harpy—and in so doing releases him from the "monkey" story of uncontrolled desire that he has been living (and imposing on others). Like the souls of the dead in *His Dark Materials*, the hiver needs a story to free him from an immortality that has become painful:

> *What's on the other side?* asked Arthur.
>
> Tiffany hesitated.
>
> "Some people think you go to a better world," she said. "Some people think you come back to this one in a different body. And some think there's just nothing. They think you just stop."
>
> *And what do you think?* Arthur asked.
>
> "I think that there are no words to describe it," said Tiffany. (Pratchett 2004, 353)

Tiffany releases the hiver—freeing herself from its influence, and, at least temporarily, ridding her community of the evil it represents—through both story and humility: a story of origins, a humility about the future. Tiffany here recasts science as narrative, potentially suggesting a solution—through figurative reading—to the struggles over Genesis that oppose science to religion. In the final words of the story—"I think there are no words"—Tiffany then gestures towards the numinous, the unnarratable aspect of the story she is telling.

The scene also demonstrates what we have already seen in her interaction with the Fairy Queen in *Wee Free Men*, and what we see throughout the series: Tiffany's stories come out of a deep sense of sympathy for others. Hers is clearly what Carol Gilligan and others have called an ethic of care: abstract justice is of far less value to her than responding to immediate human need. She explains, "Well, Dad, you know how Granny Aching always used to say, 'Feed them as is hungry, clothe them as is naked, and speak up for them as has no voices'? Well, I reckon there is room in there for 'Grasp for them as can't bend, reach for them as can't stretch, wipe for them as can't twist,' don't you?" (Pratchett 2010, 28). Pratchett's language here has specific biblical resonances: "Come, you that are blessed by my Father, inherit the kingdom prepared for you from the foundation of this world; for I was hungry and you gave me food, I was thirsty and you gave me something to drink, I was a stranger and you welcomed me, I was naked and you gave me clothing, I was sick and you took care of me, I was in prison and you visited me" (Matthew 25:34–36).

There is, of course, no evidence in the text that Tiffany has read the Bible, or any religious text. Her own critical reading, as we have seen, is limited to the book of fairy tales in her family home. Yet that reading threads throughout the series, perhaps especially in the reshaped narratives that animate *I Shall Wear Midnight*. Here we are not working with a specific myth or legend but with a pattern: the story of the witchfinder and the witch, the story of frightened people swayed by religious language to turn on the women who love and care for them. As Eskarina Smith tells the Cunning Man's story to Tiffany, it seems that Tiffany already knows it:

> "Imagine a man, still quite young, and he is a witchfinder and a book burner and a torturer, because people older than him who are far more vile than him have told him that this is what the Great God Om wants him to be. And on this day he has found a woman who is a witch, and she is beautiful, astonishingly beautiful, which is rather unusual among witches, at least in those days—"
>
> "He falls in love with her, doesn't he?" Tiffany interrupted.
>
> "Of course," said Miss Smith. "Boy meets girl, one of the greatest engines of narrative causality in the multiverse, or as some people might put it, 'It had to happen.'" (Pratchett 2010, 156)

Not only does he have to fall in love with her, as Tiffany quickly learns, he also "has to" kill her—and in his ambivalent resistance to his narrative (and hers) is born the evil she must contend with. It is an evil, again, with a long history, a familiar story:

> Sometimes you got wandering preachers around who didn't like witches, and people would listen to them. It seemed to Tiffany that people lived in a very strange world sometimes. Everybody knew, in some mysterious way, that witches blighted crops and ran away with babies, and all the other nonsense. And at the same time, they would come running to the witch when they needed help. (Pratchett 2010, 58)

Tiffany actively chooses to take on the prejudice against witches that she notes here, overtly marking herself as a witch with hat, broom, and—finally—even a black dress while she goes about caring for her people. Only by inserting herself into the story the people tell—taking on the role of witch, then subverting their expectations—can she change it.

Both as witch and storyteller, Tiffany's work is explicitly gendered. Early in the novel Tiffany's father, at first dismayed by but also proud of the daily care she offers to the people of the Chalk, says it's a "man's job" she is doing (Pratchett 2010, 28); Tiffany demurs silently at the time, but at the end, Granny Weatherwax says "it seems to us that you've done a woman's job today" (Pratchett 2010, 342). The witches know, as most of the men around them seem not to, that caring for others involves both story and dirt, both the "whizzing about" that is part of every story about witches, and cutting old ladies' toenails—which doesn't make it into the stories but is just as important (see Pratchett 2010, 27–28, e.g.). Not only does Tiffany perform the thankless tasks of caring that others neglect, she eschews a sense of abstract moral justice for the here and now. As Mrs. Proust notes, she is one of those "unofficial people who understand the difference between right and wrong, and when right is wrong and when wrong is right" (Pratchett 2010, 138). Carol Gilligan defines her position this way: "morality and the preservation of life are contingent on sustaining connection, seeing the consequences of action by keeping the web of relationship intact. . . . an absolute judgment yields to the complexity of relationships" (Gilligan 1982, 59). Her care for others occasionally threatens to overwhelm her, but it is, as the other witches see, the center around which her steading spins (Pratchett 2010, 342).

In *I Shall Wear Midnight* Tiffany and Letitia come to an understanding through their shared reading. In an echo of Tiffany's earlier complaint about the fairy tale book, Letitia says, "Hah, I wanted to be a witch when I was little. But just my luck, I had long blond hair and a pale complexion and a very rich father. What good was that? Girls like that can't be witches!" (Pratchett 2010, 236). But, as the novel makes clear, narrative causality is not so strong: Letitia is a witch, and cares for her steading just as Tiffany does for hers. As Letitia provides a pumpkin head for the headless ghost, she demonstrates the same kind of humility in her magic as we have seen in Tiffany's: a care for the immediate, the poor, and the sick, that recalls the core teachings of almost all world religions, though they are often imperfectly enacted or forgotten altogether by many adherents of those religions. By performing the tasks of a witch, Tiffany reinfuses her world with a sense of the numinous, with a reverence for creation, that it had lacked, bringing into being a better reality than what had gone before. According to Sallie McFague, "In the picture of the mother-creator, the goal is neither the condemnation nor the rescue of the guilty but the just ordering of the cosmic household in a fashion beneficial to all" (McFague 1990, 256). At the end of *I Shall Wear Midnight*, Tiffany is told that she has written the appropriate endings to the stories that have threaded throughout the novel: "Classic endings to a romantic story are a wedding or a legacy, and you have been the engineer for one of each. Well done" (Pratchett 2010, 340). The "just ordering" of the "household," then, is a kind of storytelling— and Tiffany the witch has become the origin, as well as the subject, of her own story. It is also, to bring us full circle, a kind of spiritual leadership. Tiffany, even more than Lyra, develops as a leader in her community through caregiving, storytelling, and critically rereading and re-engaging with the stories that seem to constrain her.

Stories, it is true, can serve as a constraint on the development of human agency: the stories the church tells in *His Dark Materials*, *The Goode Childe's Booke of Faerie Tales* throughout Tiffany Aching's series, set limits and constrain those who see themselves too transparently reflected in the texts. Rather than binding themselves or others through religious story, however, Lyra and Tiffany learn to tell their own stories and so take on agency, liberating themselves and others. That is—to return to the bumper stickers with which I began—whatever God, the Church, the Bible, or other sacred texts may say, it is up to readers to interpret what they read and to use the language they have gleaned to create new stories that empower them for the worlds they inhabit. These texts suggest that their readers should do the same, reading critically to re-shape the narratives that may constrain, and rejecting the false truths that fail to set their readers free.

Note: Portions of this article first appeared in Gruner, Elisabeth Rose. "Wrestling With Religion: Pullman, Pratchett, and the Uses of Story." *Children's Literature Association Quarterly* Volume 36 Issue 3 (Fall 2011), 276–295. Copyright © 2011 Children's Literature Association.

References

Armstrong, Karen. 2000. *The Battle for God*. New York: Alfred A. Knopf.

Briggs, Melody, and Richard S. Briggs. 2006. "Stepping into the Gap: Contemporary Children's Fantasy Literature as a Doorway to Spirituality." In *Towards or Back to Human Values?* 30–47. Newcastle: Cambridge Scholars Press.

Coates, Karen. 2011. "Young Adult Literature: Growing Up, In Theory." In *Handbook of Research on Children's and Young Adult Literature*, 315–329. New York: Routledge.

Gilligan, Carol. 1982. *In a Different Voice: Psychological Theory and Women's Development.* Cambridge, MA: Harvard University Press.

Gooderham, David. 2003. "Fantasizing It as It Is: Religious Language in Philip Pullman's Trilogy, His Dark Materials." *Children's Literature* 31: 155–175.

Gray, William. 2009. *Fantasy, Myth and the Measure of Truth: Tales of Pullman, Lewis, Tolkien, MacDonald and Hoffmann.* Basingstoke: Palgrave Macmillan.

Hume, Kathryn. 1984. *Fantasy and Mimesis: Responses to Reality in Western Literature.* New York: Methuen.

Kaufmann, Michael W. 2007. "The Religious, the Secular, and Literary Studies: Rethinking the Secularization Narrative in Histories of the Profession." *New Literary History* 38: 607–627.

Lenz, Millicent, and Carole Scott. 2005. *His Dark Materials Illuminated: Critical Essays on Philip Pullman's Trilogy.* Detroit: Wayne State University Press.

Loades, Ann, and Karen Armstrong. 1990. *Feminist Theology: A Reader.* London: SPCK.

Mathews, Richard. 1997. *Fantasy: The Liberation of Imagination.* New York: Twayne Publishers.

McFague, Sallie. 1990. "The Ethic of God as Mother, Lover and Friend." In *Feminist Theology: A Reader,* 255–274.

Pratchett, Terry. 2000. "Imaginary Worlds, Real Stories." *Folklore* 111: 159–168.

Pratchett, Terry. 2002. *Witches Abroad.* New York: HarperTorch.

Pratchett, Terry. 2003. *The Wee Free Men.* New York, NY: HarperCollins Pub.

Pratchett, Terry. 2004. *A Hat Full of Sky.* New York: HarperCollins.

Pratchett, Terry. 2006. *Wintersmith.* New York: HarperTempest.

Pratchett, Terry. 2010. *I Shall Wear Midnight.* New York: Harper.

Pullman, Philip. 1996. *The Golden Compass.* New York: Alfred A. Knopf.

Pullman, Philip. 1997. *The Subtle Knife.* New York: Alfred A. Knopf.

Pullman, Philip. 2000. *The Amber Spyglass.* New York: Alfred A. Knopf.

Ricœur, Paul, Charles E. Reagan, and David Stewart. 1978. *The Philosophy of Paul Ricœur: An Anthology of His Work.* Boston: Beacon Press.

Schneiders, Sally. 1993. "The Bible and Feminism." In *Freeing Theology: The Essentials of Theology in Feminist Perspective.* San Francisco, CA: Harper San Francisco.

Tolkien, J. R. R. 1947. "On Fairy-Stories." In *Essays Presented to Charles Williams,* 38–89. London: Oxford University Press.

Trites, Roberta Seelinger. 2000. *Disturbing the Universe: Power and Repression in Adolescent Literature.* Iowa City: University of Iowa Press.

Wolf, Shelby Anne, Karen Coates, Patricia Enciso, and Christine A. Jenkins. 2011. *Handbook of Research on Children's and Young Adult Literature.* New York: Routledge.

Wood, Naomi. 2001. "Paradise Lost and Found: Obedience, Disobedience, and Storytelling in C S Lewis and Philip Pullman." *Children's Literature in Education* 32(4): 237–259.

CHAPTER EIGHT

Engaged Spirituality and Egalitarianism in US Social Welfare Policy

JENNIFER L. ERKULWATER

On a spring day in late April 2013, police outside the General Assembly building in Raleigh, North Carolina, arrested a group of 17 protesters for trespassing and acts of civil disobedience. Affiliated with 16 organizations representing clergy, labor unions, and civil, women's, and gay rights groups, the protesters staged a sit-in to object to recent legislative decisions that limited the ability of death row inmates to challenge their sentences; denied expanded access to health care for low-income residents; and cut spending on public education, unemployment benefits, and income support for the working poor. The protesters' call for inclusion and equality struck a nerve among progressive activists and everyday voters. By the end of summer, their small act of defiance had grown into a grassroots social justice movement. Each week, on "Moral Monday," hundreds, sometimes thousands, of protesters gathered at the state capitol and in cities throughout North Carolina to march, pray, sing gospel hymns, and occupy public buildings in an effort to make clear their demand that government conform to Christian principles of justice and compassion. Their tactics of spiritual resistance made headlines across the country and inspired similar demonstrations in other states.

There are two ways of viewing the Moral Monday protests. On the one hand, they might be seen as part of the long-running progressive struggle to achieve the rights to social inclusion and a modicum of well-being, a struggle in which religious groups have played a vital role throughout American history. That public debates over the rights of persons would take religious form would not have surprised Alexis de Tocqueville, whose careful observations of American society in 1831 led him to conclude that religious faith made democracy possible by counterbalancing its atomizing tendencies. Otherwise content to live isolated lives devoted to the pursuit of material comforts, citizens needed faith to leave their private selves; faith called upon them to meditate upon their obligations to others and impelled them to enter into public life on behalf of transcendent causes (Tocqueville 2004, 503, also 501–509, 614–616). From this perspective, the Moral Monday movement is just the latest in a long litany of progressive social movements inspired by faith. Of course, faith has not always led Americans toward a more inclusive or just union. Colonial Americans used religious moralism to justify their persecution of women as witches and to enslave fellow human beings, but the religious jeremiad also roused Americans to abolish slavery, extend suffrage to women, create the first organized programs to care for the poor, and dismantle an entrenched system of racial hierarchy. On the one hand, for some historians, accounting for the spread of social and economic equality without reference to the religious principles and institutions that breathed life into American politics and social reform would be unimaginable (Morone 2003). On the other hand, protests are the weapon of the weak, and the fact that Moral Monday takes the form of protests illustrates how tenuous social rights are in the United States, particularly in deeply religious states like North Carolina.

Throughout American history, faith has served as a springboard to collective efforts to grapple with disorienting social and economic transformations, often in ways that led to the application of Christian principles of social justice. Yet today the United States is experiencing a revival of religiosity that, some social scientists argue, fails to challenge prevailing power. Faith-based organizations and the discourse of faith, rather than calling leaders to answer for injustice, have become repositioned as apologists for neoliberalism, a term used to describe broader political and economic transformations that have the potential to undercut political agency and undermine social justice.

Religion as a Staging Ground for Collective Action

Despite the formal separation of church and state in the United States, much of the nation's political life has been animated by the moral fervor borne out of the individual's quest for spiritual perfection. While spirituality denotes an individual's subjective state of transcendence and is not objectively verifiable, an individual's search for spiritual renewal is often expressed as acts of religious devotion, such as church attendance or acts of prayer (Hill et al. 2000). Through participation in organized forms of devotion, the believer is sometimes called upon to act out his or her spiritual transformation in the public arena and, in this manner, is drawn to resolve the political questions in concert with fellow citizens. Thus, although spirituality is inward, the connection it forges among people and the motivation to enter public affairs that it provides are outward manifestations of that inward transformation.

Religious faith facilitates collective political action through three distinct pathways: resources, connections, and salience. First, as sites where faith is enacted, congregations provide individuals with the resources necessary to engage in political activity. Although their purpose is not strictly political, congregations give members an opportunity to learn and practice vital civic skills, such as how to write an article or editorial for a newsletter or a formal letter, how to run a meeting or an organization, and how to plan an event or make a public speech. The participatory structure of Protestant churches, in particular, affords congregants rich opportunities to plan worship; run church groups; and manage church finances, pledge campaigns, and clergy searches. Once learned, these skills easily transfer to the political realm, where they can be used to organize protests, give political speeches, and raise campaign donations (Verba et al. 1995, 228–251).

Second, religious institutions encourage social connections between individuals in ways that increase the likelihood that they will get recruited to political causes. Political involvement is not strictly self-motivated; rather individuals are much more likely to vote, donate, or volunteer if asked to do so (Verba et al. 1995, 97–132). For this reason, "social capital"—that is, the personal connections between individuals—is an invaluable resource to groups that hope to mobilize citizens to collective efforts. Religious institutions supply two types of social capital. By bringing together congregants of similar outlook and religiosity, congregations foster "bonding" connections, networks among people who are similar and who because of that similarity can act with solidarity. While it is the case that places of worship are too often racially and socioeconomically homogenous, congregations can and sometimes do foster "bridging" connections, networks that span differences within a community. Interfaith alliances and partnerships between congregations build the trust between diverse groups that is necessary for cooperative political action (Putnam 2000, 22–24).

Finally, religious faith has the potential to make politics salient for citizens. Sermons that link religious teachings to real-world events can activate congregants' interest in public affairs and catalyze a desire for activism. Such was the case when, in 1913, Social Gospel minister Walter Rauschenbusch warned his congregants of God's vengeance by declaring that "the prophets...said less about the pure heart for the individual than of just institutions for the nation" (Rauschenbusch 1917, 8). Insofar as they offer principles of moral rightness, external to the state, religious teachings serve as a yardstick against which citizens assess the actions of their leaders. Such was the nature of the grievances that Martin Luther King Jr. voiced when he criticized segregation as unjust, nothing more than "a human law that is not rooted in eternal law and natural law" (King 1963). Moral Monday protesters echoed this sentiment when they marched against the state government in 2013–2014. Politically engaged spirituality is never solely a private matter, and for these believers, the actions of government can never be based solely on utility or expediency but must conform to some higher standard of justice—that of God's.

During the twentieth century, two movements brought together faith and political action in an effort to create institutions that would lead to greater social and economic equality. Followers of the Social Gospel entered the new millennium with the firm conviction that righteousness, compassion, and justice were not promises for the hereafter but a call to Christians to realize the kingdom of God while on earth. Their objections to the economic inequality and human misery brought by laissez-faire capitalism led to the Progressive and workers' movements of the early twentieth century. Reformist Protestants also founded a variety of voluntary associations that ministered to the spiritual and material needs of the urban poor. Settlement houses, hospitals, schools, and orphanages, as well as some of the nation's first faith-based social service organizations became models for the public programs that followed (White and Hopkins 1976; Clemens and Guthrie 2010). Similarly, in the 1950s, Christian ethics deeply informed the rhetoric and strategies of civil rights protesters and offered a common language through which African American leaders could forge interfaith coalitions with Jewish groups and white congregations. Meanwhile, local congregations served as recruitment sites for movement leaders and volunteers, meeting houses and shelters for visiting activists, and sites for the training of protesters in the tactics of civil disobedience, community organizing, and lobbying (Marsh 2005; White and Hopkins 1976; Nelson and Nelson 1975).

Faith continues to offer a staging ground for Americans who seek to collectively address the injustices of the contemporary era. Like the Social Gospel and the civil rights movements that preceded it, the living wage movement draws upon religious institutions and the discourse of faith to forge connections and frame its grievances. The groups associated with the movement came together in the 1980s and 1990s to prevent the Religious Right from emerging as the face of political Christianity. Mobilizing around the causes of peace, social justice, and advocacy for the underprivileged, these groups included Protestant, Catholic, and Jewish congregations, nondenominational religious and interfaith groups, and faith-affiliated social justice organizations. Rather than become merely the liberal counterpart of the Religious Right or yet another layer of voluntary services, living wage groups eschewed social services, charity, and electoral politics in favor of grassroots organizing efforts, including the recruitment and training of community-based leaders, the lobbying of local officials, and the mobilization of voters and workers alienated from the labor movement (Snarr 2011, 33, 109).

Leaders of living wage campaigns used the common language of faith to connect people across differences and build local alliances among religious organizations, elected officials, secular liberal groups, and labor unions. Especially where elected officials have a tense relationship with labor unions, faith organizations took the lead on lobbying for wage reform (Snarr 2011, 78–79, 102). Because of its ability to bridge differences among many stakeholders, the movement has been able to turn protest into policy. In 1994, Baltimore enacted a living wage ordinance, the first brought about in the modern era as a result of a grassroots campaign led by a coalition of local churches. Since then, living wage ordinances have passed in over 100 municipalities around the country (Snarr 2011, 18–19).

The Challenge of Neoliberalism

Nevertheless, despite the highly visible Moral Monday and living wage movements, important transformations in American religion and politics call into question the prospects for religiously inspired egalitarian reform of the kind that characterized the Social Gospel and the civil rights movements. Ironically, religious institutions have been brought more fully into the operations of government. Since the 1990s, Congress and the White House have allowed congregations and faith-based organizations (FBOs) to participate directly in the delivery of social services to vulnerable populations, shaping in profound ways how citizens experience the state. At one level, this participation is an extension of the historical role that faith-based voluntary associations have played in meeting the needs of the poor. At a deeper level, however, the contemporary faith-based movement is distinct from its earlier iteration. The faith-based social movements of the twentieth century sought to build national institutions to promote the social rights of inclusion and economic security. Today under the aegis of neoliberalism, American political leaders are dramatically curtailing or at least fundamentally rethinking the nation's commitment to social rights and, rather than resist, some FBOs are complicit in retrenchment.

Neoliberalism is the term that scholars, many of them critical, give to an intellectual movement that, during the years following World War II, sought to resurrect selected classical liberal ideas that extol individualism, negative rights, and the free market. It has since matured into both an economic project designed to privilege capitalism and a political project seeking to remake democratic governance. Citing the power of the market to generate well-being, elected leaders in the United States, Europe, and Latin America have pursued a broad agenda to "unleash free market forces," including eradicating trade barriers and opening domestic markets to foreign competition, deregulating the economy, privatizing state enterprises, and scaling back social welfare protections for vulnerable citizens (Harvey 2005). Neoliberalism, however, is more than simply a platform of economic reform. Because institutions can be difficult to demolish, adherents of neoliberalism have also sought to remake government so that it will ensure that the economy is "directed, buttressed, and protected by law and policy" (Brown 2003, 5). Indeed, insofar as neoliberals treat the market itself as the paragon of all human relations, one that government and society should emulate, merely constraining government so that the free market operates as a separate but co-equal sphere alongside the state is not enough. Rather, government itself becomes a tool of furthering neoliberal subjectivity. Through vouchers, individualized savings accounts, government-constructed markets in health care, and other public programs that elevate individual choice and strategic thinking, public policy trains citizens to think of themselves as consumers and customers, first and foremost. Thus, even when conservatives cannot eliminate entitlements to aid, the way in which citizens experience these rights is radically transformed, from collectively shared protections against risk and poverty to individual rewards for properly made choices (Brown 2003; Brodie 1996; Larner 2000).

In this respect, neoliberalism is a political project that seeks to remake the very essence of self-government and democratic citizenship. While classical liberal scholars presumed that all people were born free and capable of exercising market choice, the neoliberal makes no such presumption. Instead, it is precisely because human beings are not naturally entrepreneurial and calculating that the market needs nurturing and citizens need re-education so that they may become the rational choosers that populate theories of market operations (Brown 2003). While Tocqueville saw religion as moderating the atomizing and materialistic excesses of democracy, some scholars today regard religious institutions as contributing to the neoliberal undercutting of democratic citizenship. Nowhere is that convergence of economic and religious thinking more apparent than in the area of social welfare policy, where Christian values and compassion came to justify the gutting of income support for low-income unmarried mothers as part of the 1996 welfare reform initiative (DeParle 2005; Stryker and Wald 2009). Since welfare reform, religion and neoliberalism have become intertwined in ways that have abetted the restructuring of the nonprofit sector, reasserted distinctions between the "deserving" and "undeserving" poor, and fostered a vision of spiritual self-perfection and economic self-reliance that has depoliticized questions of distributive justice.

Faith-Based Initiatives and Retrenchment of the Welfare State

Faith-based approaches were injected into the debate over welfare reform by Marvin Olasky's book *The Tragedy of American Compassion*, which made a sensation in conservative circles when it was published in 1992. Advocating a policy that made the spiritual uplift of the poor a priority, Olasky argued that private organizations, particularly Christian churches, could be more effective than government in meeting the spiritual and material needs of the poor because of the personal connection made between giver and receiver (Olasky 1992). In 1993, after years of debate about the "underclass," President Bill Clinton entered the White House pledging to "end welfare as we know it," an acknowledgment of the bipartisan consensus that had emerged around ending "welfare dependency." While Democrats hoped to strengthen the support for mothers transitioning from welfare to work, Republicans sought to end aid to mothers entirely, an approach that was facilitated by the veneer of faith that came to dominate discussions of aid to the poor. At the risk of looking mean-spirited whenever they tried to cut aid to the poor, conservatives found in the discourse of spiritual renewal a way of softening the hard edge of their retrenchment agenda. When Republicans seized control of Congress following the 1994 mid-term elections, the new Speaker of the House Newt Gingrich distributed a copy of Olasky's book to every incoming freshman Republican (Hackworth 2012, 39). Five years later, presidential candidate George W. Bush articulated a vision of "compassionate conservatism" that drew heavily from Olasky's thinking. Noting that faith could provide the spiritual succor that bureaucracies could not, Bush singled out FBOs as able to "succeed where secular or government programs fail" because only they could "convince a person to turn their life over to Christ" and therefore "change the person's heart" (Alford 1999, online document).

Provisions within the Personal Responsibility and Work Opportunity Reconciliation Act of 1996 (PRWORA), known as Charitable Choice, gave formal protections for FBOs wishing to use federal monies to deliver aid to the poor. The most divisive aspects of welfare reform act were the work requirements and time limits on cash benefits for needy families. In the vitriolic debate leading up to PRWORA's passage, Charitable Choice was scarcely noticed. Championed by Republican senator John Ashcroft of Missouri, Charitable Choice required federal and state agencies that contract with nonprofits to consider religious organizations and prevented them "discriminating" against sectarian organizations in the awarding of government contracts for social services. States also could not require an organization to "alter its form of internal governance" or "remove religious art, icons, scripture, or other symbols," and each FBO was explicitly permitted to retain "control over the definition, development, practice, and expression of its religious beliefs" (PRWORA, Section 104, Subsections (a)(2) and (d)(1)). While institutions of faith have long been involved in social service delivery, many of these older organizations—the Salvation Army, Habitat for Humanity, Lutheran Services—were theologically ecumenical and humanitarian and were willing to demarcate their social programming from their ministry, to partner with secular organizations, to establish nonsectarian governing boards, and to hire staff in accordance with federal civil rights laws that barred gender, racial, and religious discrimination. Charitable Choice was not aimed at these organizations but at small, congregation-based organizations, many of them evangelical, which had refused to separate proselytizing from service or conform to other federal requirements. Supporters of Charitable Choice hoped that by carving out protections for faith-saturated programs, they could expand both the numbers and kinds of religious organizations on the frontlines of social service delivery and imbue the welfare state with the spiritual uplift and personal transformation that the poor so desperately needed (Hackworth 2012, 18–19; Black et al. 2004, 41–43, 51–59).

Never solely about spiritual healing, however, Charitable Choice also represented the latest salvo in a decades-long effort to shift economic risk from the national government to the private sector and reduce government spending. Part of this effort entailed a restructuring of the voluntary or nonprofit sector to foster competition and efficiency. Although this restructuring began in the 1970s, President George W. Bush invigorated the "marketization" of social policy by actively courting sectarian organizations to participate in public administration. As a cornerstone of his compassionate conservative agenda, Bush widely touted his Faith-Based and Community Initiative during his first term. The initiative included benefits for taxpayers who donated to charity but otherwise did not itemize their taxes, the creation of "compassion capital funds" to help small FBOs comply with federal regulations, and the expansion of Charitable Choice provisions across a range of social policies. Over the next several years, Congress added Charitable Choice to block grants for community services, children's health care, substance abuse treatment, and drug and mental health services. By the end of Bush's first term, social policy informed by faith had gone mainstream, as the centrist Brookings Institution, the conservative Manhattan Institute, and the US Department of Health and Human Services promoted religious involvement in social services beyond welfare (Black et al. 2004, 59–60). Barack Obama's announcement in the summer of 2008 that, if elected president, he would build upon and improve Bush's faith-based initiative signals the continuing appeal of social policy infused with faith (Zeleny and Luo 2008).

The Protection of Vulnerable Citizens

Faith-based organizations have long participated in the administration of American social welfare, with volunteers and a moral fervor that constitute, to borrow Bush's words, "a power that no government bureaucracy can match" (White House 2008). They comprise one-fifth of nonprofit organizations and engage in a variety of activities, from the running of food pantries and child care centers, to the provision of job training and substance abuse counseling. Of the more than 350,000 congregations across the nation, the majority offers some form of social aid to the disadvantaged (Hefferan and Fogarty 2010). In urban areas, congregations are integral to the social safety net and have increased in importance as federal and state support for the poor has contracted. In central Philadelphia, for example, almost every congregation engages in social programming, sometimes with federal help and other times entirely out of private donations and church coffers (Cnaan 2006).

Neither Charitable Choice nor Bush's faith-based initiatives, however, have led to the sort of wellspring of voluntarism or the spiritual renewal of the poor that supporters of the efforts envisioned. Shortly after the enactment of welfare reform, a survey of congregations found that only one-third were open to providing social services through Charitable Choice (Chaves 2001). In the decade following, faith-based policy did not result in a more robust social safety net. Rather than enriching the partnership between government and the voluntary sector, Congress repeatedly cut social service spending, forcing FBOs and other nonprofits into steeper competition with one another for grant funding and requiring them to serve more people with fewer resources. Nor did these initiatives expand service provision beyond the organizations already involved in social services. Moderate and liberal congregations, particularly those that were African American, were much more likely to pursue opportunities through Charitable Choice than their conservative brethren (Schneider 2013). By contrast, because many of the evangelical organizations that had been the target of Charitable Choice viewed government aid as fostering "dependency" among the poor, they refused to accept federal funds lest they too become "dependent" (Hackworth 2012, 102). By the end of the Bush administration, prominent social conservatives dismissed the faith-based initiative as symbolic, designed simply to attract evangelical and African American votes and insufficient to scaling back government spending in any meaningful way (DiIulio 2003; Kuo 2006; Hackworth 2012).

The more lasting impact of these initiatives, though, may be the way in which they reframe the relationship between the public and private sectors, portending, indeed rationalizing, dramatically curtailed federal responsibility for supporting the needy. Bush hinted as much when he characterized his faith-based initiative as indicative of a "new role" for the federal government in which it would be the "supporter, enabler, catalyst and collaborator" of faith-based and community groups (Quoted in Carlson-Thies 2009, 934). In turn, these groups would transform government, opening "a bureaucratic culture accustomed to large programs . . . to localized, community-driven solutions" (Quoted in Carlson-Thies 2009, 938).

The desire for "community-driven solutions," disciplined by market accountability, has paved the way for a restructuring of the voluntary sector, of which the faith-based movement is only the latest iteration. Privatization, devolution, and public administration reforms have inscribed business principles into nonprofit and community groups and reshaped the sector into a semblance of the market environment. In the 1970s and early 1980s, the switch from categorical grants to block grants brought the ethos of competition and accountability to the voluntary sector, as federal and state grant-making agencies began requiring nonprofits to compete for grants and to demonstrate the effectiveness of their programming through the adoption of market-based performance measures. During the 1990s, reform efforts to "reinvent government" led public agencies to adopt business practices of enhancing "customer service," "streamlining red tape," and setting "performance-based goals." Meanwhile, for-profit firms began competing with nonprofits and public agencies for contracts to administer public programs. To survive in an era of increased competition and fewer resources, many nonprofit organizations turned to business strategies of marketing, enhanced customer satisfaction, and performance review and audit (Hasenfeld and Garrow 2012, 301–306). Thus, while devolution freed nonprofit and voluntary agencies from top-down federal directives, these organizations increasingly found themselves "governed" by market-oriented mechanisms of accountability (Larner 2009, 13).

Market mechanisms, however, bode ill for the most vulnerable citizens. Studies of nonprofit behavior suggest that organizations reliant on government contracts avoid devoting resources to developing services that are not likely to receive funding irrespective of client needs (Frumkin and Andre-Clark 2000; Hasenfeld and Garrow 2012). Other studies find that some nonprofits subject the needs of their clients to the "calculus of efficiency and profitability" and therefore seek out the least difficult of the have-nots in order to score well on performance measures (Hasenfeld and Garrow 2012, 307). Indeed, David Rochefort's study of mental health programs following the rise of block grant funding in the 1980s found that community organizations avoided serving people with severe mental illnesses and shifted their staffing from client volunteers to professionals capable of attracting and managing grant money (Rochefort 1993). More recently, Scott Allard's study of the voluntary sector in selected US cities found that residents of high-poverty areas have difficulty accessing social service programs because nonprofits located their programs in neighborhoods where poverty levels were relatively low (Allard 2009). Studies of non-profits in small towns and rural areas come to similar conclusions: high demand for services is rarely matched by the volunteers or resources to meet the needs of the poor and unemployed in the community (Merrett 2001). Bush's faith-based initiative, in short, brought community- and faith-based organizations into a sector already stretched thin. Rather than encouraging the "government [to]...do more to take the side of charities and community healers," as Bush predicted it would in 2001, the faith-based movement has provided further impetus for the state to sidestep its responsibilities to individuals in need (Bush 2001).

Advocacy for the Disadvantaged

Some scholars fear that because of the marketization of social services, voluntary and charitable organizations have been tamed by their dependence on contracts and grants. As intermediaries between government and the poor, these groups historically held public agencies accountable to the citizens they served. In the 1960s, for instance, voluntary associations established through the community action programs of the War on Poverty worked in local communities to mobilize constituents to demand change from local welfare offices and public schools that were discriminatory or unresponsive. These efforts, in turn, laid the foundation for movement organizations, such as the National Welfare Rights Organization (Cazenave 2007). Competition between nonprofits, however, endangers the cooperation and information sharing needed for coalition building and reduces capacity for advocacy and grassroots organizing. Indeed, nonprofits that are heavily reliant on grant funding or contracts are also less likely to challenge or confront governing officials, leading Yeheskel Hasenfeld and Eve Garrow to argue that contemporary human service nonprofits have come to resemble "interest groups that lobby on behalf of their own self-interest rather than on behalf of the public interest." To the extent they engage in political activity, they are just as likely to engage in mobilization aimed at "influencing contract allocation decisions...[not] creating policy change" (Hasenfeld and Garrow 2012, 308–315, quote on 310).

While there are few studies of congregation-based social services, those that exist suggest that faith-based programming is not isolated from the larger changes sweeping the voluntary sector. A field study of African American churches in New York City found that clergy used government grants to consolidate influence with local agencies and amass moral authority within the black community. While clergy members also sought to expand church services to neighborhood residents in need, efforts to enhance personal power detracted from their engagement in grassroots political organizing (Owens 2008). Judith Goode's ethnography of a Philadelphia partnership between a suburban church and an urban one, likewise, reveals the difficulty FBOs face in both satisfying the demands of this new organizational environment and staying faithful to their mission. The partnership initially ran two congregation-based programs, a child-care center and a job-training center. But as program directors increasingly sought to pay for the programs through public and private grants, they shifted resources away from the child-care program, which had been favored by residents, to the job-training program, where administrators could more easily meet the production goals that donors valued. Meanwhile, the board overseeing the programs became increasingly male and white, as the churches sought out members with business expertise to help manage grant money and the growing cadre of college-student volunteers. Residents who had been working in the child-care center left or lost their jobs as the program shrank. Meanwhile, board members counted the job-training program a success so long as it processed clients through the program; whether the clients actually got a job was of secondary concern (Goode 2006).

True, progressives still retain the power of protest and grassroots change. But because authority over income support and social services has been fragmented among state and local governments and nonprofits, the effectiveness of advocacy is also fragmented. Mobilization must occur at the state and local level, thus spatially containing legislative successes. The potential for national mobilization is also stifled because the most well-organized constituents are able to solve problems locally and are therefore no longer motivated to join coalitions on behalf of broad social change (Hasenfeld and Garrow 2012, 309–312). While on the one hand exemplary of the power of faith to bring people together on behalf of shared social justice goals, the living wage movement is also illustrative of the limits of this sort of organizing strategy. Living wage ordinances have been enacted in municipalities around the country, but national legislation is moribund. In the foreseeable future, whether workers are paid a living wage or not depends on arbitrary factors such as their place of residence and their occupation.

The Depoliticizing of Injustice

The marketization of the voluntary sector implicates the solidarity between citizens that makes self-government and faith-inspired social justice possible. FBOs can engage with disadvantaged citizens through acts of charity, social service, social justice, or some combination of these (Harper 1999, 297–309). Radical activists and scholars, however, dismiss charity and social services as acts that both reinforce the distance between "givers" and "receivers" and cement control of the former over the latter. They argue instead for solidarity between haves and have-nots expressed as lives lived side-by-side solving common problems of poverty, crime, and community decline (Perkins 1993; Myers 1994). Yet contemporary faith-based social policy risks undermining collective consciousness by depoliticizing questions of distributive justice.

The rise of a self-consciously faith-based social policy repositions religious organizations, congregations, and religious discourse to express, even inculcate, in volunteers and clients the individualistic orientation of neoliberalism. Witness, for instance, the distinction proponents made between the "deserving" and "undeserving" poor. To tout FBOs as superior to government because faith alone can "change the person's heart" is to suggest that the primary need of people who are disadvantaged is moral or spiritual conversion and those who are unwilling to change are lost causes (Bush quoted in Alford 1999, online document). Indeed, despite acrimonious disagreements among conservatives over whether faith-based initiatives should enhance or simply replace public programs, one point they agreed on was the prospect of FBOs making discriminations among people in need. Lawrence Mead, the intellectual architect of welfare-to-work, argued that assistance for the poor should be conditioned on their proving their moral worth through labor in formal economy, ideas that were codified in PRWORA as work requirements and time limits (Mead 1986). Olasky echoed these sentiments when, defending Bush's faith-based initiative, he argued that because "man is sinful and likely to want something for nothing," the poor needed "internal pressure to live honored and useful lives, modeled after our perfect leader, Christ" (Quoted in Unger 2007, 173).

By channeling assistance and services through local institutions of faith, which would then make distinctions of "deservingness" among the many supplicants for aid, Bush's faith-based initiative provided an institutional mechanism for realizing Mead and Olasky's vision of social rights contingent on moral worth, albeit a moral worth that reified capitalistic valuations of individual worth. Subsequent studies of small, evangelical or congregation-based FBOs found that the organizations tended to view poverty, homelessness, or joblessness as attributable to the personal or spiritual shortcomings of their individual clients rather than as the result of structural injustices. Many required individuals to profess a commitment to "a life change" or to demonstrate a "willingness to work" before being accepted for services (Hackworth 2010, 759; Goode 2006).

Such neoliberal notions of worth are not confined to welfare policy. "Neo-liberal strategies of rule, found in diverse realms including workplaces, educational institutions and health and welfare agencies, encourage people to see themselves as individualized and active subjects responsible for enhancing their own well being." Currently, Wendy Larner argues, "we are all encouraged to 'work on ourselves' in a range of domains" (Larner 2000, 13). This conflation of individual self-discipline with collective self-government, particularly under the guise of faith, risks undermining collective consciousness of societal injustice. Perhaps the strongest example of the confluence between neoliberal ideology and modern spirituality is the Prosperity Gospel. Although a version of prosperity theology has long existed in the United States, the modern version of it exploded in late 1970s, after advances in broadcast technology allowed spiritual leaders to reach a broader audience (Bowler 2013, 77–138). Among white Americans, the Prosperity Gospel thrived as the locus of conservative evangelicalism shifted from local congregations to megachurches and broadcast worship. Through television and, later, the Internet, the celebrity preachers of the modern Prosperity Gospel—T. D. Jakes, Joel Osteen, and Creflo Dollar, to name some of the wealthiest and most well known—merged their ministry with the language of self-help to proclaim a Gospel that rejects the "ethic of self-denial" so often associated with spiritual purity. Urging their followers to embrace the "Gospel's abundant promises," they called on their followers to view unseen faith as manifested through material gain. Rather that await their treasure in heaven, the faithful can enjoy God's promise today (Bowler 2013, 7).

While comforting, the message is enervating of democratic politics. Insofar as the Prosperity Gospel holds that "no political, social, or economic impediment to faith, and no circumstance can stop believers from living in total victory here on earth," its teachings reinforce neoliberal discourse about strategic choices and a well-managed life as keys to spiritual perfection and material success. By denying the need for God's grace and emphasizing only God's blessings to the faithful, the spread of prosperity theology, historian Kate Bowler argues, "represent[s] the triumph of American optimism over the realities of a fickle economy, entrenched racism, pervasive poverty, and theological pessimism that foretold the future as dangling by a thread" (Bowler 2013, 7).

Conclusion

In egalitarian reform movements of the past, spiritual belief offered a wide-ranging critique of the powerful, one that held political, social, and economic institutions accountable to the social justice principles articulated in religious text. Yet, with government and societal institutions organized to mimic the voluntary transactions that characterize market exchanges, citizens risk losing the urgency that this sort of engaged spirituality provides. Indeed, in a neoliberal polity, citizens do not exist in any real sense. As mere consumers of government services, citizens have responsibility for and commitments to no one other than themselves. As rationally calculating individuals, they find freedom and meaning through their actions as entrepreneurs in this transactional universe, not in the collective struggle to achieve shared notions of justice. "The model neo-liberal citizen," theorist Wendy Brown explains, "is one who strategizes for her/himself among various social, political, and economic options, not one who strives with others to alter or organize these options" (Brown 2003, 5, 7). If faith is to serve as a site of resistance, it must seek an engaged spirituality that "not only shapes beliefs but also insists on action," and one that "compels as much, if not more than, it comforts" (Stanczak 2006, 167, 169). It would mean calling on citizens to reflect on solidarity across difference rather than charity to the other and to meditate upon the end times rather than on the good times.

References

Alford, Deann. 1999. "Interview: George W. Bush on Faith-Based Plans." *Christianity Today* 43(12) (October 25). Online document at http://www.christianitytoday.com/ct/1999/october25/9tc020.html.

Allard, Scott W. 2009. *Out of Reach: Place, Poverty, and the New American Welfare State.* New Haven, CT: Yale University Press.

Black, Amy E., Douglas L. Koopman, and David K. Ryden. 2004. *Of Little Faith: The Politics of George W. Bush's Faith-Based Initiatives.* Washington, DC: Georgetown University Press.

Bowler, Kate. 2013. *Blessed: A History of the American Prosperity Gospel.* New York: Oxford University Press.

Brodie, Janine. 1996. "Restructuring and the New Citizenship," in Isabella Bakker, ed. *Rethinking Restructuring: Gender and Change in Canada,* 126–140, Toronto, Canada: University of Toronto Press.

Brown, Wendy. 2003. "Neo-liberalism and the End of Liberal Democracy." *Theory & Event* 7(1). Online document at Project Muse at http://muse.jhu.edu/login?auth=0&type=summary&url=/journals/theory_and_event/v007/7.1brown.html.

Bush, George W. 2001. "Remarks by President Bush in Commencement Address." University of Notre Dame, May 20. Online document at http://news.nd.edu/news/3779-remarks-by-president-bush-in-commencement-address/.

Carlson-Thies, Stanley W. 2009. "Faith-Based Initiative 2.0: The Bush Faith-Based and Community Initiative." *Harvard Journal of Law & Public Policy* 32(3) (Summer): 931–947.

Cazenave, Noel A. 2007. *Impossible Democracy: The Unlikely Success of the War on Poverty Community Action Programs.* Albany, NY: State University of New York Press.

Chaves, Mark. 2001. "Religious Congregations and Welfare Reform." *Society* 38(2) (January/February): 21–27.

Clemens, Elisabeth S., and Doug Guthrie, eds. 2010. *Politics and Partnerships: The Role of Voluntary Associations in America's Political Past and Present.* Chicago: University of Chicago Press.

Cnaan, Ram A. 2006. *The Other Philadelphia Story: How Local Congregations Support Quality of Life in Urban America.* Philadelphia: University of Pennsylvania Press.

DeParle, Jason. 2005. *American Dream: Three Women, Ten Kids, and a Nation's Drive to End Welfare.* New York: Penguin.

DiIulio Jr., John J. 2003. "Inside the Bush Presidency: Reflections of an Academic Interloper." In Fred I. Greenstein, ed., *George W. Bush Presidency: An Early Assessment.* Baltimore: The Johns Hopkins University Press.

Frumkin, Peter, and Alice Andre-Clark. 2000. "When Missions, Markets, and Politics Collide: Values and Strategy in the Nonprofit Human Services." *Nonprofit and Voluntary Sector Quarterly* 29 (Supplement 1) (March): 141–163.

Goode, Judith. 2006. "Faith-Based Organizations in Philadelphia: Neoliberal Ideology and the Decline of Political Activism." *Urban Anthropology* 35(2–3) (Summer/Fall): 203–236.

Hackworth, Jason R. 2012. *Faith Based: Religious Neoliberalism and the Politics of Welfare in the United States.* Athens: University of Georgia Press.

———. 2010. "Faith, Welfare, and the City: The Moblization of Religious Organizations for Neoliberal Ends." *Urban Geography* 31(6): 750–773.

Harper, Nile. 1999. *Urban Churches, Vital Signs: Beyond Charity toward Justice.* Eugene, OR: Wm. B. Eerdmans Publishing.

Hasenfeld, Yeheskel, and Eve E. Garrow. 2012. "Nonprofit Human-Service Orgnaizations, Social Rights, and Advocacy in a Neoliberal Welfare State." *Social Science Review* 82(2) (June): 295–322.

Harvey, David. 2005. *A Brief History of Neoliberalism.* New York: Oxford University Press.

Hefferan, Tara, and Tim Fogarty. 2010. "The Anthropology of Faith and Development." *NAPA Bulletin: Special Issue: Intersections of Faith and Development in Local and Global Contexts* 33(1) (May): 1–11.

Hill, Peter. C., Kenneth I. Pargament, Ralph W. Hood, Jr., Michael E. McCullough, James P. Swyers, David B. Larson, and Brian J. Zinnbauer. 2000. "Conceptualizing Religion and

Spirituality: Points of Commonality, Points of Departure." *Journal for the Theory of Social Behaviour* 30(1) (March): 51–77.

King Jr., Martin Luther. 1963. "Letter from Birmingham Jail." April 16.

Kuo, David. 2006. *Tempting Faith: An Inside Story of Political Seduction.* New York: Simon and Schuster.

Larner, Wendy. 2000. "Neo-Liberalism: Policy, Ideology, Governmentality." *Studies in Political Economy* 63 (Autumn): 5–25.

Marsh, Charles. 2005. *The Beloved Community: How Faith Shapes Social Justice from the Civil Rights Movement to Today.* New York: Basic Books.

Mead, Lawrence M. 1986. *Beyond Entitlement: The Social Obligations of Citizenship.* New York: Simon and Schuster.

Merrett, Christopher D. 2001. "Declining Social Capital and Nonprofit Organizations: Consequences for Small Towns after Welfare Reform." *Urban Geography* 22(5): 407–423.

Morone, James A. 2003. *Hellfire Nation: The Politics of Sin in American History.* New Haven, CT: Yale University Press.

Myers, Ched. 1994. *Who Will Roll Away the Stone? Discipleship Queries for First World Christians.* Maryknoll, NY: Orbis Books.

Nelson, Hart M., and Anne Kusener Nelson. 1975. *Black Church in the Sixties.* Lexington: University of Kentucky Press.

Olasky, Marvin. 1992. *The Tragedy of American Compassion.* Washington, DC: Regnery.

Owens, Michael Leo. 2008. *God and Government in the Ghetto: The Politics of Church-State Collaboration in Black America.* Chicago: University of Chicago Press.

Perkins, John M. 1993. *Beyond Charity: The Call to Christian Community Development.* Grand Rapids, MI: Baker Books.

Putnam, Robert D. 2000. *Bowling Alone: The Collapse and Revival of American Community.* New York: Simon and Schuster.

Rauschenbusch, Walter. 1907. *Christianity and the Social Crisis.* Louisville, KY: Westminster John Knox Press.

Rochefort, David A. 1993. *From Poorhouses to Homelessness: Policy Analysis and Mental Health Care.* Westport, CT: Auburn House.

Schneider, JoAnne. 2013. "Introduction to the Symposium: Faith-Based Organizations in Context." *Nonprofit and Voluntary Sector Quarterly* 42(3) (June): 431–441.

Snarr, C. Melissa. 2011. *All You That Labor: Religious and Ethics in the Living Wage Movement.* New York: New York University Press.

Stanczak, Gregory C. 2006. *Engaged Spirituality: Social Change and American Religion.* New Brunswick, NJ: Rutgers University Press.

Stryker, Robin, and Pamela Wald. 2009. "Redefining Compassion to Reform Welfare: How Supporters of the 1990s US Federal Welfare Reform Aimed for the Moral High Ground." *Social Politics: International Studies in Gender, State, and Society* 16(4) (Winter): 519–557.

Tocqueville, Alexis de. 2004. *Democracy in America.* Translated by Arthur Goldhammer. New York: Library of America.

Unger, Craig. 2007. *The Fall of the House of Bush: The Untold Story of How a Band of True Believers Seized the Executive Branch, Started the Iraq War, and Still Imperils America's Future.* New York: Simon and Schuster.

Verba, Sidney, Kay Lehman Schlozman, and Henry E. Brady. 1995. *Voice and Equality: Civic Voluntarism in American Politics.* Vol. 4. Cambridge, MA: Harvard University Press.

White, Cedric, and Charles Howard Hopkins. 1976. *The Social Gospel: Religion and Reform in Changing America.* Philadelphia: Temple University Press.

White House. 2008. "President Bush Attends Office of Faith-Based and Community Initiatives' National Conference," Omni Shoreham Hotel, Washington, DC, June 26, 2008. On-line document at http://georgewbush-whitehouse.archives.gov/news/releases/2008/06/20080626-20.html.

Zeleny, Jeff, and Michael Luo. 2008. "Obama Seeks Bigger Role for Religious Groups." *New York Times*, July 2, p. A1.

CHAPTER NINE

"A Change Is Gonna Come": Spiritual Leadership for Social Change in the United States

Thad Williamson

On Suffering and Justice

The religious impulse has three distinct dimensions. The first consists of humanity's efforts to *name, confront, and comprehend the ultimate*: that is, the fundamental questions of why anything exists, how that which exists came to be, who or what has set this process in motion (and perhaps even guides it now).

The second consists of humanity's efforts to *come to terms with the conditions of our own existence*. These conditions in turn can be described as falling into two major categories. The first category has to do with the specific attributes of human beings, including our capacity for communication, reflection, abstract thought, and moral language and behavior, as well the limits of these same capacities. The second category has to do with our status as mortal creatures whose very existence is contingent, temporary, and frequently characterized by suffering.

The third dimension consists simply in the effort *to find or make collective meaning out of our peculiar situation* as creatures thrown into a life situation that alternates between the beautiful and wondrous and the absurd and cruel, often in almost the same breath. The existence of multiple religious traditions that have provided human beings of all ranks, from humble illiterates to learned philosophers, with coherent frameworks for not only addressing these questions but also relating them to the practical question of how we are to live must be counted as one of humanity's most magnificent achievements.

It is well beyond the scope and resources of this chapter to delve into these dimensions with equal depth, or to adequately explore the vital question of how the different dimensions relate to one another. Here I focus attention specifically on the concepts of suffering and justice, both as they are found in religious traditions and as they inform secular understandings and practice. To narrow the inquiry yet further, my primary reference point will be instances of Christian social theology as practiced in the nineteenth- and twentieth-century United States.

The problem of suffering is a primary theme in biblical literature, as in religious literature generally. Suffering in turn may have two faces. The first consists of, simply put, bad things happening to people: deaths of husbands, wives, parents, children, entire villages, cities, or even nations; disease; hunger, pain, and poverty. The second consist of inward pain—that is, the pain a human being feels "on the inside," internal to their "soul" or "state of mind." This pain can be concealed and may rarely be manifest through behavior or visible (mental) illness, yet it still permeates the moment-to-moment, day-to-day existence of human beings. What is the source of this pain? Often, the Buddha teaches us, it is frustrated desire: the solution to which must be to learn to restrain and then extinguish desire. Plato's account of the harmonious soul in *The Republic* offers a similar assessment, but a comparatively modest prescription: the well-formed soul, the one that is happy on the inside, is one in which lower-order desires are restrained by reason and rational impulses. (The presumed inability of the majority of persons to achieve the level of self-control needed to be happy without external assistance in turn provides a major justification for Plato's sophisticated scheme for achieving social justice through enlightened aristocratic rule.)

Suffering as such is endemic to the human condition. But the existence of moral language and, in particular, terms such as "justice," presumes that not *all* suffering is necessary, even given the constraints of mortality. Sin, evil, injustice, oppression: these terms name (and condemn) the varieties of suffering that human beings inflict upon one another or upon themselves, needlessly, that is, via avoidable human choices.

Doctrines of Christian social responsibility, in particular the Social Gospel tradition, claim in effect that being faithful witness to Jesus Christ requires concerted effort to reduce needless human suffering perpetuated by unjust social institutions. Here J. S. Mill's account of the evolution of the concept of justice can help clarify terms: in Mill's narrative, the emergence and subsequent evolution of basic social institutions (in particular, law) reflected the functional imperative to establish peaceful conditions of basic human security while minimizing rape, murder, and ransacking. Yet these laws and institutions may create problems of their own and typically become, at least in part, mechanisms for some members of a given community to dominate over others. In Mill's view, it is the responsibility of each generation to critically assess its institutional inheritance, to sort out what practices truly promote utility as opposed to being mere vestiges of outdated traditions, and sift practices that truly promote the common good from those that institutionalize prejudice or reflect the power of vested interests.[1]

In short, social institutions and practices have, even when deeply flawed, a functional utility in establishing and sustaining civilized human life. On the presumption that the primary alternative to civilized human life is continuous violent conflict, this is a good thing from the point of view of reducing needless human suffering. But social institutions can and have evolved in ways that perpetuate suffering. Race-based slavery and oppression, the domination of men over women, class domination, and imperial domination are crucial examples (both in Mill's time and our own).

What's worse, institutionalized forms of oppression in fact normalize suffering, by presenting such suffering as inevitable, a "natural" part of how the world works, and as necessary to prevent yet greater evil. Indeed, the task of figuring what counts as a reasonable institutional practice or policy and what counts as socially unnecessary and unjust is often a demanding one, requiring considerable practical knowledge about both the relevant facts and achievable alternatives. To make a claim that a given practice is unjust and should be reformed is to make a political claim. And even once this work is completed, it is sure to be scrutinized and contested—both by the beneficiaries of existing practices as well as fair-minded observers. Indeed, as a general rule, the more complex the judgment that is required, the less moral certainty is warranted from those engaged in the debate.

The slow machinery of democratic politics stands in stark contrast to the fiery moral passion of the pulpit and related expression of religious moral convictions. The art of getting things done is quite different, and often less pretty, than the work of identifying and expressing what should be done. But this is not, as one might expect, a reason to separate religion and spirituality from democratic politics. It is important to acknowledge that the work of discerning justice and exhorting others to act on behalf of justice is a distinct activity from political negotiation. But the former type of work can and must be connected to the latter if systemic injustices are ever to be addressed and reduced; only passion and deep moral conviction can motivate actual politicians that the slogging through to make a difference is actually worth it.

This chapter examines the role of religious motivations, historically and in the present, in leadership for social change and social justice. Two case studies focus on the historical context of the nineteenth and twentieth century United States by examining the centrality of theological identity and commitment in the writings and actions of Harriet Beecher Stowe and Martin Luther King, Jr. on behalf of ending slavery (Stowe) and advancing racial equality (King). The final section considers what role religious motivation might—or must—have in twenty-first century movements for fundamental social change.

Nineteenth-Century America: Harriet Beecher Stowe's Antislavery Crusade

In the case of the United States, the paradigmatic case to consider is that of the injustice of slavery and subsequent racial oppression. The social ideas of competing brands of Christianity had a profound impact on the way the relevant issues were understood by mid-nineteenth-century Americans. Simply put, secession and war would have been far less likely results had not a vocal, significant minority of voices within the North taken the view that slavery was an abominable evil abhorrent to God and that a revolution in the slaveholding South was required to put an end to the institution.

Consider the theological-political arguments forwarded by Harriet Beecher Stowe in the most influential antislavery text of the 1850s, *Uncle Tom's Cabin*. Stowe's novel offered plenty of melodrama in its depiction of slavery, but it also offered pointed argument and subtle insight. At the philosophical level, Stowe's story turned the traditional (quasi-Platonic) justification of slavery on its head: rather than a kindly system in which the best sorts of people rule over lesser kinds of people to the benefit of all, it was a system that permitted the kindest, bravest, and best souls (Uncle Tom) to be ruled over by the worst kinds of souls (the sadistic overseer Simon Legree).[2] At the political level, Stowe dramatized the contrast between the urgency of offering the basic privileges of humanity to fleeing slaves and the "normal" political calculus that produced the Fugitive Slave Act: normal democratic politics as known in nine-teenth-century America, Stowe's depiction of an Ohio senator shows, was incapable of treating the issue with the moral gravity required. At the interpersonal level, Stowe depicted how various white Americans who thought of themselves as decent people possessing a moral compass none-theless were complicit in both the perpetuation of slavery *and* the worst abuses associated with the system. The financial problems of an undisci-plined Kentucky farmer-businessman sets in motion a chain of events in which families are broken apart and Uncle Tom is sold down the river.

Stowe's storyline and framing of slavery was aimed to shock the nation into action—and to appeal to deeply held religious impulses, particularly of women readers. Stowe describes slavery not primarily as a machine for exploiting black labor, but as a cruel mechanism that tears apart families and hence undermines the most natural of human emo-tional bonds, that between family members and in particular between mother and child. Stowe's account also stresses the way the slave trade appealed to and rewarded greed, violence, and dehumanization—thereby producing not only black victims but wicked white people.

Yet the real target of the book was not "wicked" white people, but complacent white people. Part of the task was simply educational and cognitive: to show readers what slavery actually entailed at the human level. Importantly (and in contrast to the subsequent "Uncle Tom" cari-cature), Stowe's narrative emphasized the dignity, bravery, and potential for accomplishment of enslaved black Americans, thereby undermining racial stereotypes held nearly as deeply in the North as the South. Stowe's book also illustrated the Underground Railroad and depicted the role of whites in its operation, with the strong implication that supporting the railroad would be a helpful practical step for the white reading public.

Importantly, Stowe also held open the possibility of moral and spiri-tual redemption, even within the South. She depicts a New Orleans aristocrat whose ill-fated young daughter's friendship with Tom trans-forms his view of blacks and the problem of slavery, and then a young Kentucky squire, who, showing a courage of which his father had proved incapable, stands up to Tom's tormentor in an effort to reunite Tom with his family and redeem a litany of wrong.

These appeals to conscience and the possibility of moral transforma-tion banked on commonly shared Christian beliefs. More precisely, Stowe intended to show that one could not tolerate, let alone partici-pate in, the evil of slavery and be considered an honest Christian. At the same time, only piety and deep spiritual convictions could possibly sustain individuals (at any level) in efforts to change the system.

Left unstated in *Uncle Tom's Cabin* was the possibility that failure to redress the moral evil of slavery might bring divine judgment upon the nation. Sympathetic readers of Stowe's novel would have comprehended, perhaps for the first time, that blows from a terrible, swift sword might become a worthy price to pay for extinguishing the evil of slavery. (This view would soon be enthusiastically endorsed from the pulpit by Stowe's brother, the prominent revivalist preacher Henry Ward Beecher.)[3] Indeed, Abraham Lincoln himself would go on to depict the Civil War and its fields of blood as just payment for the sin of slavery.

The crux of the issue, from the standpoint of this chapter, is that the anger and passion that fueled antislavery activity in the 1850s cannot be divorced from the theological views of antislavery agitators; nor can the views they expressed be divorced from the theological frameworks in which they were rooted. Stowe is one relatively genteel example of this point; the full-blooded ferocity of John Brown is another. In neither case (Stowe nor Brown) could the motivating theological framework be regarded as liberal (in modern terms), or even as fully rational. But in both cases, these frameworks moved participants to take historically meaningful actions leading ultimately to radical change.

Twentieth-Century America: The Cosmopolitan Christianity of Martin Luther King Jr.

The hope of some antislavery writers that the mass of white Southerners might undergo a fundamental transformation in their views about race were only rarely realized in the South, even after the Civil War. The Reconstruction period brought some remarkable instances of multiracial cooperation in civic and political affairs in the Southern states, but the retreat of federal troops in 1877 was followed by a systematic attack on blacks' political and civil rights over the next generation. The commitment of most whites to a doctrine of white racial superiority found new institutional expression in the combination of legalized Jim Crow regimes and frequent episodes of anti-black terrorism and violence throughout the South over the first half of the twentieth century. The core legal basis for Jim Crow (though certainly not its material effects) was dismantled over an approximately 25-year time period following the end of World War II, primarily as a result of a powerful Civil Rights movement that moved from the margins of Southern society to claiming the moral, legal, and political high ground in a remarkably short period of time.

It is impossible to make sense of the Civil Rights movement in mid-twentieth-century America without reference to the role of religion and the institutional church. The most prominent and influential leader in the movement, Dr. Martin Luther King Jr., was not simply a pastor skilled in community organizing. He was a creative religious thinker, rooted deeply in the African American Baptist tradition but strongly influenced by contemporary cutting-edge Christian theologians and social thinkers like Reinhold Niebhur and deeply impacted by Gandhi's philosophy of nonviolence.[4] For King, religious conviction impacted all three layers of social change: the individual's personal responsibility for enacting social justice; the specific tactics appropriate for use in advancing social justice; and the conviction that God is at work in the world, through the collective agency of human beings.

To be sure, King was more than just a religious thinker; he was also an organizational leader, and by the 1960s had become, in effect, an independent political force who understood and embraced the necessity of operating in political contexts. But a considerable part of his political strategy rested on the assumption that the use of religious language alongside appeals to secular American ideals would find a welcome reception among a significant part of white Americans. As pointedly depicted in the important film *Selma*, King's explicit tactical goal in local struggles was to get on to the front page of national newspapers as well on television news, in expectation that exposing the brutalities of segregation would increase political pressure for more rapid change. But this strategy could not work without the maintenance of a high degree of internal discipline, including a commitment to nonviolence, on the part of civil rights activists. As that film also depicts, even nonviolent strategies impose challenging moral dilemmas upon leaders. King knew that in publicly challenging local police forces in public spaces, unnamed individuals in the movement would likely experience violence, brutality, possibly death. No less than a leader of an army, he knew his tactical decisions could cost the life and limb of the civil rights soldiers—often ordinary persons—enlisted in the cause.

Heavy is the moral weight that falls on any leader entrusted with such responsibility. Near the very end of his life, in March 1968, King offered from the pulpit some extraordinary reflections on both his own personal journey and on his conviction that God was acting in history, then in there in the America of 1968:

> Whenever you set out to build a creative temple, whatever it may be, you must face the fact that there is a tension at the heart of the universe between good and evil. . . .
>
> Now not only is that struggle structured somewhere in the external forces of the universe, it's structured in our own lives. Psychologists

have tried to grapple with it in their way, and so they say various things. Sigmund Freud used to say that this tension is a tension between what he called the id and the superego. Some of us feel that it's a tension between God and man. And in every one of us, there's a war going on. It's a civil war. I don't care who you are, I don't care where you live, there is a civil war going on in your life. And every time you set out to be good, there's something pulling on you, telling you to be evil. It's going on in your life. Every time you set out to love, something keeps pulling on you, trying to get you to hate. Every time you set out to be kind and say nice things about people, something is pulling on you to be jealous and envious and to spread evil gossip about them. There's a civil war going on. There is a schizophrenia, as the psychologists or the psychiatrists would call it, going on within all of us. And there are times that all of us know somehow that there is a Mr. Hyde and a Dr. Jekyll in us... We end up having to agree with Plato that the human personality is like a charioteer with two headstrong horses, wanting to go in different directions. Or sometimes we even have to end up crying out with Saint Augustine as he said in his Confessions, 'Lord, make me pure, but not yet. (Carson 1998, 357–358)[5]

Here King acknowledges the internal struggle that even leaders for social justice continually battle (and by implication, sometimes succumb to). The most important point, however, is King's conclusion:

In the final analysis, God does not judge us by the separate incidents or the separate mistakes that we make, but by the total bent of our lives. In the final analysis, God knows that his children are weak and they are frail. In the final analysis, what God requires is that your heart is right. (Carson 1998, 358)

This conclusion is important for three reasons. First, because actual action for social change requires many, many decisions in real time, not all of which will prove wise or fruitful, no social change agent could be productive if he or she thought God would condemn every failure and misjudgment. Second, the actual work of social change places extraordinary stress on leaders that may induce moral lapses; it is nearly impossible not to read King's comments as a personal confessional, an acknowledgment of his own moral lapses (i.e., extramarital affairs). Third, and most important, it speaks to King's vision of a God who acts on the big stage—the big stage of history.

Indeed, in the extraordinary "I've Been to the Mountaintop" sermon of April 3, 1968 (the eve of his assassination), King imagines a conversation between himself and the "Almighty," in which he is given the opportunity to visit any era in human history. King concludes that given the chance, he would tell the Almighty, "If you allow me to live just a few years in the second half of the twentieth century, I will be happy."
King elaborates:

Now that's a strange statement to make, because the world is all messed up. The nation is sick; trouble is in the land; confusion all around. That's a strange statement. But I know, somehow, that only when it is dark enough can you see the stars. And I see God working in this period of the twentieth century. Something is happening in our world. The masses of people are rising up. And wherever they are assembled...the cry is always the same: "We want to be free."

And another reason that I'm happy to live in this period is that we have been forced to a point where we are going to have to grapple with the problems that men have been trying to grapple with through history. Survival demands that we grapple with them. Men for years now have been talking about war and peace. But now, no longer can they talk about it. It is no longer a choice between violence and nonviolence in this world; it's nonviolence or nonexistence. That is where we are today. (Carson 1998, 359–360)

King's comments thus reveal the convictions that: (1) there is an Almighty God who is involved in human history, even now; (2) that this God is involved in working through human hands and actions; (3) but the course of history is still contingent on human actions, not predetermined, and hence human beings (including King himself) have the obligation to discern God's intention for humanity and then act on it despite (4) the fact that humans are flawed, frail creatures prone to mistakes and moral weaknesses.

But there is still an ambiguity about King's historical-political theology. On the one hand, he famously stated that the "arc of the moral universe is long, but it bends towards justice."[6] This thought is comforting, and indeed probably necessary, for social justice advocates confronting setbacks, mistakes, internal moral failures. We may mess this particular campaign up, but God is still on our side.

Yet on the other hand, King is completely serious about the possibility the human beings may succumb to the war mentality and induce total annihilation of humanity via nuclear war. He cannot help but consider this as a real historical possibility. Such annihilation, if it took place, would clearly stand at odds with his sober but optimistic faith in the arc of the moral universe. But for King, this is precisely the point. The entire project of humanity *and* of God's relationship to humanity is tied up in whether human beings can choose nonviolence over nonexistence.[7]

Twenty-First-Century America: Fueling Passions for Justice in Pluralistic Contexts

Are Martin Luther King Jr. and *Uncle Tom's Cabin* merely instructive historical examples of the relationship between faith and social justice, or might they still have some relevance today? Today we live in a "disenchanted" world in which religion helps define the background of public culture but in which literal theological claims rarely enter the public culture—and when they do, they are almost never attached to attractive, human visions of social justice.

The stakes attached to this question could not be higher, at least from the standpoint of prospects for democratic social justice in the United States. Consider John Rawls's famous 1971 articulation of principles of justice appropriate for a democratic society:

- a commitment to a stable scheme of basic liberties accessible to all, with the political liberties in particular being of "equal worth" to all;
- a commitment to maintaining a social structure in which there is "fair equality of opportunity" for all to obtain "office and positions" (i.e., get ahead), regardless of one's starting point or any ascriptive characteristics; and
- socioeconomic inequalities are limited to those that actually benefit the least well off group (i.e., inequalities resulting from economic incentives that produce a superior standard of living for the entire group may be justified if attempting to remove them would hurt the least well-off group).

John Rawls in 1971 knew that the United States did not then come close to realizing these principles, but he also could not have suspected that the United States of 1971 would come far closer to realizing the third of these principles (distributive justice) than the United States of the late 1990s (date of his last published writings) or of today. Instead, Rawls confidently asserted his principles as the logical implications of commitments he took to be broadly shared in liberal democratic political culture, in particular the commitment to the equality of worth of all persons.

In fact, the achievement of relatively just polities of a social democratic nature in the advanced nations does not rest on principles or ideologies alone, but rather on the presence of adequate social and political forces to advance and sustain such schemes. The well-established consensus among political scientists studying the welfare state is that relatively small state size, a highly organized labor sector, and ethnic homogeneity are the most favorable conditions in which to implement and sustain robustly egalitarian arrangements.

Those conditions are quite nearly the opposite of the fundamental structural features of the United States. Indeed, in the United States, apart from its written principles enshrined in the founding documents, the most promising vehicle for promoting egalitarian social change has often been the religiously motivated social reform movement. While this is quite a heavy weight to place on American religiosity, the historic salience of religious language in reform movements has, at times, been a counterweight to the structural forces militating against social democratic, inclusive politics.

Without the cultural currency of Christianity, and indeed without a convicted faith in God, there could not have been a Harriet Beecher Stowe or a Martin Luther King Jr. But now that shared religious commitments, or even basic biblical literacy, are no longer a binding thread in the dominant political culture, is it still possible that a religiously motivated reform movement with egalitarian commitments could gain substantial traction in the United States? And if such a movement were not to have a strong religious character, on what common threads would it be based? Probably not an academic political philosophy of justice. And probably not on a simplistic concept of "class interests," or on vague concepts of the "American Dream."

Perhaps the best-thought out, most influential answer to this question in contemporary political thought has been provided by, again, John Rawls, in his conception of "political liberalism" (1993). Stated simply, political liberalism takes as its starting point the fact of "reasonable pluralism" about "comprehensive doctrines," including religious worldviews. That is, Rawls takes it as given that in a culturally diverse world that permits freedom of thought and religious expression, different persons will reasonably come to quite different views concerning fundamental questions of meaning and religious belief. To achieve justice in this context thus requires establishing an "overlapping consensus" of shared moral convictions concerning justice that believers (and nonbelievers) can accept and endorse as consistent with their own comprehensive doctrines. To take a straightforward example, Christians, Jews, and nonbelievers alike can easily find reasons internal to their own worldview to endorse the free exercise of religion as a basic tenet of a just society.

Rawls's arguments for political liberalism are compelling, yet they face major obstacles as a general solution. First, as an empirical matter there is a little to suggest that consensus about contested conceptions of (secular) social justice can coexist with deep disagreement about comprehensive doctrines within a given society.[8] Instead, deep-seated disagreements about controversial moral questions often undermine or destroy the possibility of consensus on allegedly less contentious matters of economic distribution.

Second, as Michael Sandel has persistently argued over the past two decades, Rawls's insistence that participants in a liberal democratic society frame public argumentation in terms that all citizens can reasonably comprehend regardless of their comprehensive commitments creates the possibility that some citizens will be forced to "check at the door" fundamental components of their identity. Third, with respect to demands for social justice, removing religious conviction from the debates often will rob arguments for social justice of their motivating moral passion. Sandel thus argues, contra Rawls, for a public sphere in which participants are freely encouraged to draw on their deepest moral commitments, be they of a religious nature or not.[9]

The review of the example of King is instructive on two further points as well. First, in considering the connection between religious conviction and justice, we must consider not only the content of the moral claim, but the motivation and conviction of the individual making the claim. Put another way, putting into practice robust commitments to social justice is an intensely demanding and draining experience. Individual religious conviction as well as relationships with individuals sharing one's moral and religious convictions are typically integral and essential for the sustainability of long-term activist activity, particularly on the scale on which King operated. Spiritual strength thus is typically a prerequisite for actually creating justice in the world.[10]

Second, religious convictions and religious communities historically often have played a critical role in the survival and subsequent liberation of oppressed peoples. The black church in the United States has not simply been a convenient meeting place for organizing civil rights activism. It has been a fundamental source of meaning and support, a bulwark against white oppression (political, economic, spiritual), and a major source of positive black identity, including belief in the very possibility of social change and emancipation in challenging times.

Historically speaking, significant advances in social justice in the United States, particularly with respect to race and class, have been deeply tied to the work and efforts of religious communities. It is hard to imagine a transformational social movement in the United States of the twenty-first century finding the motivation and spiritual will to sustain itself that does not both draw on existing religious communities and express theological commitments. Yet is also hard to imagine a transformational movement in which any single religious view or institution claims a right to lead or guide the entire movement.

This chapter offers no solution to the dilemma presented, save for the insistence that religious convictions be given their due respect in both motivating individuals and communities to fight for a more just society and sustaining them in those fights. But religiously motivated social justice leaders, to be effective and inclusive in the context of pluralism, must be competent and fluent in speaking in multiple idioms—that is, using language and concepts that are explicable to both believers and nonbelievers, as well as believers of multiple religious traditions. Martin Luther King Jr., again, provides an example ahead of his time as a thinker deeply familiar with work from another religious tradition (Gandhi's thought) and who regularly referenced the diversity of world religions in his speeches and sermons, without diluting his distinctively Christian identity.[11]

King's example foreshadows the kind of social justice leadership that will be required in the pluralistic conditions of twenty-first-century United States: thoroughly embedded in a core tradition as well as in a religious community capable of providing an individual with the psychological and spiritual support to sustain arduous, risky tasks; capable of making justice claims in ways legible to nonreligious believers; and capable of building bridges and dialogue across multiple philosophical and religious traditions. The hardest part of this recipe to replicate, however, may not, as in the past, be a comfort with diversity and pluralism; but rather, the character and spiritual formation that comes with being raised in a religious tradition sufficiently robust to counter the saccharine consumerist individualist tendencies in contemporary American culture.

Put another way, the weakening and decline of Christian theological hegemony in the United States has had numerous welcome benefits from the standpoint of the evolution of a more tolerant, inclusive polity, but also significant costs in the weakening of an independent vantage point for providing an internal critique of American culture, a critique that might motivate action for change. In the twenty-first century, serious adherents of religious traditions from across the full spectrum of human religiosity must make common cause with each other—and of course with committed secular humanists—to insist on a higher vision and purpose for human life than that of the disaggregated consumer. Success in that effort is a prerequisite for more ambitious social movements aimed at social transformation to take root in twenty-first-century United States.

Notes

1. See J. S. Mill, *Utilitarianism* (1859), and many related writings.
2. See, among other sources, William B. Allen, *Rethinking Uncle Tom: The Political Philosophy of Harriet Beecher Stowe* (Lanham, MD: Lexington Books, 2009).
3. See Gary Dorrien, *The Making of American Liberal Theology: Imagining Progressive Religion, 1805–1900* (Louisville, KY: Westminster John Knox Press, 2001), 198–207, for discussion.
4. For a short summary of King's theological formation, see James Cone, *Risks of Faith: The Emergence of a Black Theology of Liberation, 1968–1998* (Boston: Beacon Press, 1999), 53–73.
5. These quotations are taken from a March 3, 1968, sermon at Ebenezer Baptist Church in Atlanta.
6. King made this memorable claim in a February 26, 1965, sermon at Temple Israel of Hollywood.
7. This conception of the relationship between humanity and God corresponds to the broader branch of religious thought known as "process theology," in which God's very being is in some sense tied up in the course of events. This stands at sharp odds with the view of an all-knowing, all-powerful, and unchanging God. Among other reasons why the process theology view is attractive is that it provides a potential solution to the "theodicy" problem—the problem of why God allows suffering and injustice—without having to sacrifice the conviction that God is good. If God is all-powerful and all-knowing, and knowingly allows the evils of human existence, how can it also be said God is good? But if God's power and knowledge, even who God is, is in some sense contingent on the unfolding of God's relationship with humanity, this also allows one to consistently hold that God and God's intentions are good.
8. In this context, "comprehensive doctrine" refers to a complete theory of the good, which would imply firm views about the nature of human beings and purpose of human life. To simplify greatly, Rawls argued that it is possible to have society-wide agreement of justice based on merely a "thin" account of the good. Even if we do not agree on the ultimate goods or purposes of life, Rawls believed we can agree that everyone has interests and plans, a desire to pursue them, and need certain things (i.e., resources, education) in order to do so. Michael Sandel, in contrast, believes that an appeal to instrumental self-interest cannot (at least taken alone) be the basis for a robust account of social justice. Specifically,

Sandel argues that a commitment to egalitarian social justice is most securely rooted in an understanding of the human self as intrinsically shaped by communal contexts and communal commitments. Instead of asking what discrete individuals would choose in an abstract, initial situation of fairness, we should instead approach distributive justice by asking what *we owe each other* as fellow citizens, whose fates are intertwined with our own. Taking this approach, in turn, necessarily commits one to a more robust account of the good life. Without a prior commitment to the moral claim that life goes better when it is lived together and that we all have a stake in one another's flourishing, we cannot understand why citizens would agree to enter a procedure like Rawls's original position in the first place. See Michael Sandel, *Liberalism and the Limits of Justice*, Second Edition (Cambridge: Cambridge University Press, 1998), esp. 77–81.

9. See Michael Sandel, "A Response to Rawls's *Political Liberalism*," in *Liberalism and the Limits of Justice*, ed. Michael Sandel, Second Edition (Cambridge: Cambridge University Press, 1998), 184–218.

10. As James Cone puts it with respect to King, "Where he turned when his back was up against the wall and when everything seemed hopeless will tell us far more about his theology than the papers he wrote in graduate school. Engulfed by the 'midnight of despair,' where did he receive the hope that 'morning will come'? The evidence is clear: Whether we speak of the Montgomery bus boycott, the Birmingham demonstrations, the Selma March, Black Power, or Vietnam, King turned to the faith of the Black Church in moments of frustration and despair." Cone, *Risks of Faith*, 60.

11. This point is stressed by Robert James Scofield in a helpful essay, "King's God: The Unknown Faith of Dr. Martin Luther King, Jr." *Tikkun*, November-December 2009.

References

Carson, Clayborne, ed. 1998. *The Autobiography of Martin Luther King, Jr.* New York: Grand Central Publishing.

Rawls, John. 1971. *A Theory of Justice*. Cambridge: Harvard University Press.

Rawls, John. 1993. *Political Liberalism*. New York: Columbia University Press.

CHAPTER TEN

Living a Life of Consequence: How Not to Chase a Fake Rabbit

CRAIG T. KOCHER

The New Testament scholar Fred Craddock tells the hyperbolic story of a conversation he had with an old racing greyhound. Craddock asks the greyhound why he retired. The greyhound responds, "For years I ran around that track, round after round, race after race, chasing the rabbit. One day I got up real close, and you know what? It was a fake rabbit! You know how miserable that made me feel, to discover I had wasted my life chasing a fake rabbit? I didn't retire. I quit!" (Craddock 2001, 29–30).

I have chased a fake rabbit or two for a few rounds of the track in my life, and I know many others have as well. This chapter is an effort to offer some guidance to teachers, mentors, students, and others who are honestly seeking a way to live a life of consequence, who desperately want to pursue the real thing, but may not know where to begin.

Part I: The Three Categories

On the surface my work as a university chaplain involves organizing and leading communities: chapel services, religious programming, university committees, classrooms, and so forth. The real work of my life, however, is bound up in helping emerging adults discover a deeper meaning in their own lives and a sense of place and purpose in the world. There is great irony in this work: my purpose is helping other people find their purpose, and yet that purpose, as with my own, is incredibly elusive, ever-changing with time and place, dependent on individual personality and experience, and shifting life narratives. Academics and practitioners can offer data-driven help in this regard, naming trends about what constitutes a life of happiness (hint, hint: authentic relationships, emotionally satisfying work, and a sense that one's life has a larger significance consistently rank higher than the accumulation of wealth). Yet, the deep spiritual work of discovering meaning and purpose in one's life is not a macro experience but a micro one, imbedded in the uniqueness of every individual, and the rich landscapes that make up their lives. And thus, my work as a spiritual leader is to try and guide others, often young people, into that landscape, or at least name the vast hidden country that exists beneath the surface in the never-ending horizon of the human heart and soul.

In this chapter, I aim draw on my 15 years serving in a chaplaincy role on college and university campuses—a spiritual leadership role—and pull from some of the wisdom I've accumulated in my own life, to narrate several ways to think about one's own meaning and purpose, and to offer a few suggestions for how spiritual leaders might guide others along a path of self-discovery and living a life of consequence.

Wendell Berry's novel *Jayber Crow* tells the fictitious story of Jayber Crow who comes of age in a small Kentucky town in the middle part of the 20th century. Jayber is an orphan who leaves home to find his way in the world, only to find his way by returning home and becoming the town barber and grave digger, and finding at the last, and only in retrospect, that all the deep questions of his life—Will I find a place? Will I have made a difference in the lives of others? Do I believe in God, and if so what might that mean for me?—are answered through his lived experience (Berry 2000). Thus is the challenge in writing about meaning and purpose. Meaning and purpose are intensely personal, and on some level can only be discovered within the contours of one's own life, and must be discovered in living. Yet there are some larger human patterns that do exist, and there is wisdom to be learned from the experience of others. Jayber's life highlights three categories that might be helpful in framing the question.

Category 1: Being the Something of Something

Young Jayber grows up as an orphan in rural Kentucky during the late 1930s and 1940s. Prospects were not so hot for a lad like him, yet he starts out with aggressive aspirations, college, then seminary, then a long career as a minister, preaching in high-status pulpits across the bluegrass state (Berry 2000).

In the last 15 years I have worked on the campuses of three elite academic institutions. On each campus I encounter students who, like Jayber Crow, are brimming with professional ambition, though they are far more likely to come from the privileged suburbs of the Mid-Atlantic than the backwoods of Appalachia. These students are incredibly bright, aggressive, and talented, and also confused, anxious, and depressed. College mental health workers are reporting that more elite colleges (based on entering student GPAs and test scores) also have higher rates of mental health concerns. While the reasons behind this correlation have not yet been identified, I suspect there is a connection between the parental, peer, and social expectations endemic to such places, and internal expectations within a culture of "success" that drive such concerns. Hyper-talented young people have often been driven toward socially acceptable understandings of success from the first moments of their lives.

Devoted mothers and fathers who want nothing but the best for their children, and believe they are offering the best, measure every developmental stage with precision and exude anxious concern if little Johnny and Zoe drop into the "average" range of any category. These are the parents who sign their children up for pre-school before they've emerged from the womb, the same pre-schools that proudly display their Ivy League graduates up and down the hallways. Home life is filled with National Public Radio and regular trips to the zoo and local science and art museums. The refrigerator is filled with phrases like "farm to table," "non-GMO," and "free range organic," and bedtime stories come from the *Wall Street Journal* and the *New York Times*. The message hovering in the background of everything is: Success! And the definitions of success are quite clear: social status and resources, high-profile education, and material accumulation. In order to accomplish, or perhaps accumulate, success in this narrative, these young people are told quite explicitly to go out and be somebody, to become, what a former colleague in higher education called, "a something of something."

A something of something is a title and position easily recognized and exuding social status: Partner at Andrews and Bolton, Primary Care Physician at Mass General, Professor of Physics at Indiana University, Vice President of Technology at Proctor and Gamble, state senator in Oregon, and so forth. Usually, being the something of something involves a string of academic letters, and it always involves responsibility for some combination of organizing, communicating, and managing.

Being the something of something often comes with significant monetary enumeration, and attaining the position is always difficult. Such social stature is rare, and scarcity always produces competition, and the competition is fierce.

Let me be abundantly clear: there is nothing wrong with being a something of something. Indeed, having such a position can be materially and emotionally rewarding. Such opportunities may provide deep purpose, meaning, and lasting satisfaction. Very often the something of somethings of the world are the ones who are able to leverage and sustain social change or use their social and institutional power to do genuine good for others. In my experience, many people in these roles have them because they recognize the opportunities for a larger purpose, or feel a deep sense of calling to the role, and understand whatever success they have attained or received as a complex recipe of privilege, chance, personal ambition, emotional connection, and an opportunity to accomplish a lasting good. However, not all something of somethings have such self-awareness or seek to fulfill their roles to such noble ends.

Category 2: On the Way to Becoming the Something of Something

Almost all the young people I work with understand the trajectory of their lives as becoming a something of something. They genuinely believe in personal freedom, in their ability to choose to be who and what they want, and yet they rarely if ever dare to question the prevailing narrative of success through accumulation. For example, I often ask my students whether the question: "Do you want to go to college?" was ever posed to them. For the vast majority, such a question never entered their minds. The question on the table for them was always: "Which college do you want to go to?" Yet, in the United States, significantly less than half of high school graduates will pursue any form of higher education. These same students regularly tell me their parents are, on the whole, supportive of whatever they want to do, and want them to do whatever makes them happy. Yet again when pressed, they admit that becoming a hairstylist, plumber, or mechanic, even if it might make them happy, would not elicit full-throated support from home. Or, if such an endeavor did receive support on the home front, the social pressure to pursue higher status positions is so acute that anything that might be considered "blue collar" or "vocational" or, God forbid, "less than lucrative" is almost immediately dismissed. In this sense they are not as "free" as they might think, and often are surprised to discover they are living out a socially ordered script that began even before they existed and the script is relentless in its pursuit of becoming a something of something.

The journey to becoming the something of something is not for the faint of heart. Such positions involve a great deal of hard work, perseverance, and natural ability, as well as many kinds of support: family support, professional networking, mentors and advisors, internal inspiration, and external modeling. One of the great myths of the American story is that individual hard work can take one to the top. In rare cases some hyper-talented and motivated people do surmount extraordinary odds to make it as a something of something, and those people should be justly applauded and admired for their pluck and determination. Most successful people, though, rely on the generosity of others, a parent or parents, who were caring and committed, coaches, teachers, and mentors, who offered their time and hard-won wisdom, and professional colleagues a bit further down the path, who were intentional about linking hands with those on the road behind them. Becoming the something of the something can be incredibly demoralizing, and it takes great resiliency to stay the course.

I remember being at a conference for faculty and administrators who were seeking to do a better job of helping young people develop a greater sense of meaning and purpose in their lives when one faculty member from a prestigious liberal arts college who had toiled for years on his way to becoming the something of something he now was said, "I think we too often do a disservice to our students by not telling them life after college is probably going to be really, really hard. We need to tell it to them straight. It's going to suck for a while."

Again, my primary concern is not that young people from elite colleges and institutions are living out this social script. It would take incredible strength, courage, and self-consciousness to deviate too far from the established social story, though some young people do, and begin a new narrative entirely, often suffering copious social loss and personal sorrow in the process. My concern is that young, talented people are not aware of the script they are living. They have been so formed into a particular vision of the world and their role within it they do not recognize any other possibilities. Thus, rather than actively claiming and embracing their lives, which I think is a significant part of living a life of consequence, they are like kayaks in a river being pushed along in the current with agency to make some small changes, to take this channel rather than that one, to avoid the big rock there, to eat lunch on this beach over here, and so forth, but they did not choose the river itself. And there are so many rivers to choose from. No wonder young people often feel so lost.

Category 3: Making the Ordinary Come Alive

Jayber Crow begins his life seeking the high-status job of a learned clergy. Instead, he lives out his life as small town barber and grave digger in the quiet river community of Port William, Kentucky. In that role he finds he is fully immersed in the community's life, taking part in the friendly and often serious conversations about relationships, faith, politics, and civic happenings that flow through his barber shop, cutting the hair of several generations of Port William citizens—a meaningful and necessary service—blessing the bodies of the dead (all of them acquaintances, many of them friends) and gradually becoming more aware that the fabric of his life is fully intertwined with people he knows and loves. In recognizing that his life is rooted in a place and bound up tightly with others, he thus lives out the daily grace of community and obligation, and finds great satisfaction and purpose in his days, even though he does not hold the social status he once imagined he would. In all of these ways Jayber Crow realizes his life has significance precisely because it so ordinary (Berry 2000).

I want to suggest there is a larger narrative than being the something of something, or becoming the something of something, and accumulating all the social trappings and sometimes misery that come along the way. Most of life is not lived on the mountain top of exultation or in the valley of desperation, but rather on the piedmont of the ordinary. The Christian tradition has a word for the ordinary becoming sacred: sacrament. Water is meant for blessing, oil for healing, bread and wine for living an abundant life. Thoreau worried, and rightly so, about the quiet lives of desperation he saw all around him. A quiet life, however, need not be one of desperation. A life lived with mindful awareness, with self-reflection and intentionality, can be shot through with splendor and beauty. After all, the vast majority of the world's population will not be a something of something, nor will they ever be on the road to a title and position that carries social status. Instead, the vast majority of humanity, and the vast majority of our lives—regardless of professional title—are expressed in different kinds of social relationships, as a parent, child, sibling, friend, lover, colleague, acquaintance, and so forth. They are lived out in a time and place bound up in larger surroundings of nation and state and city and region, abounding with fragmented histories and deep wounds and dreams and aspirations that often have nothing whatsoever to do with one's professional position.

If becoming the something of something is the end goal of a young person's aspiration, and in my experience working with college students it often is, there will be, I fear, a great sadness at the end of that journey. The sadness being that one's social status can only offer so much personal satisfaction. For one reason, many people never attain the kind of position they aspire to for all kinds of reasons, some personal: they did not have the right skills, temperament, work ethic, or timing, and others social: the economy changes, institutions shift, or they simply had back luck. For another reason, many people who do attain the position of their aspirations come to discover that it is not enough. That which they believed would bring them happiness now does not, or only does so for a set period of time, or in certain seasons of life. Whether it be social visibility or economic freedom or some other force they thought would satisfy their internal hunger and ambition fails, and what is left?

The ability to interpret and narrate one's own life within a larger context is a critical skill to develop, and one I believe is often neglected in higher education because it feels too soft, like skill building or character development, or seems to lack the accepted modes of academic inquiry that are traditionally built on the story of becoming a something of something.

Mary Oliver's poem *Mindful* offers some insight into how we might live in a way that makes the ordinary come alive. In it, she describes the regularity of every day as beautiful, our small place in the world as filled with extravagant light, and suggests that joy is to be found in "the ordinary, the common, the very drab" (Oliver 2004, 58). If this is the case, that every regular life is sacred and filled with splendor, why then do young people feel so lost? And what can be done about it?

Part II: Purpose and Meaning: Finding the Intersection

The author and Presbyterian minister Frederick Buechner is well known for having said: "Your life's purpose can be found at the place where your deep joy meets the world's deep hunger" (Buechner 1973, 119). I find this a helpful image for discerning one's purpose, and students I share this with do as well. The image is helpful because it is both expansive and specific. It does not regurgitate the typical story of success as accumulation, but nor does it suggest purpose and meaning can be only found in traditional service sectors, or by taking a vow of poverty, or by doing something that is intentionally countercultural.

Discovering one's joy requires an attention to one's interior life and motivations. What are the often hidden and unspoken motives that fire my imagination and shape my calendar and order my relationships? Discerning one's joy goes far beyond being aware of particular interests. Interests come and go, and a particular person may have many, many different interests. Joy is more akin to what Nietzsche called a long obedience in the same direction. Joy may be bound up with feelings. Joy is an extraordinary motivator, but its rewards tend to be intrinsic rather than extrinsic, and experienced over the long view rather than the short. Happiness may be found in the sprinter's flash. Joy is the steady endurance of a marathon.

The needs of the world are overwhelming. Everywhere there are needs. Some of them are personal and explicit: individual people are hungry, thirsty, sick, tired, grieving, bored, lonely, and depressed. Others are macro and social: climate change, lack of access to education or health care, human-trafficking, and adequate natural resources to serve a growing population. Long-esteemed political and social institutions have fallen under suspicion or are failing before our eyes. Income gaps are growing, cultures are clashing, and terrorism threatens. All of these problems point to concerns about the present and the future, and very often the future emerges as a place of fear and scarcity, adding to the personal and social anxiety of the moment.

Assuming one believes that his or her life is meant for something larger than the self, as Buechner does, and I certainly do, choosing between the vast numbers of needs in the world can feel like an impossible task. One concern among the young people I work with is this: I do not fully understand myself, and thus I am afraid I will make a mistake. Therefore choosing a need to elevate above the others may lead me down the wrong path and thus I am afraid to make a commitment to any one road. Another concern, and I sense the most frequent, goes something like this: I am drawn to many different needs. The options are overwhelming and I have no idea where to begin, like standing in the center aisle of a big box mart with a large shopping list and not knowing which way to push the cart.

Attending to Wounds

In the face of this overwhelming challenge, I regularly push my students to invert the question. Rather than asking: What need am I drawn to in the world? I suggest my students ask themselves: What need am I drawn to in my own life? The South African theologian Trevor Hudson says every one of us sits beside a pool of tears (Hudson 2012, 13). Meaning, each person carries hidden wounds, an encounter with another that ended in heartbreak or tragedy, a fundamental relationship that went awry, an experience seared into the mind and soul that forever changed the way they negotiate the world, a family story of tragedy, perhaps from generations past that casts a shadow into the present. Often the wound is received not firsthand, but through the life of someone we love, and is thus all the more out of our control. It can be a debilitating disease, a lack of opportunity, or lack of access to a basic human need or right. It takes courage to look in the mirror, plumb the depths beneath the surface, and confront hidden hurts that often drive our lives beyond our regular awareness.

I believe there is a connection between the visible needs of the world, our personal sense of joy, and the often invisible wounds we carry. Thus, choosing a way to be in the world that connects our deep joy with the world's deep needs does not have to feel like playing darts in the dark. Living a life of consequence can be learned.

Being Chosen by Our Own Stories

The philosopher Alistar MacIntyre says that human beings are fundamentally narrative (MacIntyre 1981, 216). We are not a mere compilation of facts and figures. Rather, the shape of our lives is determined by character, plot, and drama. Understanding narratives requires interpretive skill, historical analysis, and literary insight. Likewise, self-awareness necessitates probing beneath the depths, nosing out moments when the drama turns, patiently looking for patterns to emerge and previously invisible moments of significance to show themselves. The ability to tell stories, especially one's own story with honesty and nuance, does not happen all at once. It takes time, trial and error, testing out the plotlines with friends and family who know us well, patiently looking for a sense of coherence to develop.

This may sound simple, but it turns out learning to tell and interpret our own story is extraordinarily difficult, particularly for young people who lack the advantage of perspective and life experience. The human capacity for self-deception is profound, and thus it is quite easy to simply tell stories that cast oneself as the hero or villain of our own drama. But very often we are both hero and villain at the same time, the cause and effect of our personal fall and redemption. The temptation is to narrate our life in exceedingly different ways depending on the audience. For college students, one image emerges when surrounded by old high school classmates, another appears in anthropology class, another emerges in mom's kitchen, and yet another comes to the fore in a job interview. On some level every story may well be a true account of who they are, and yet if they are to discover a cohesiveness that connects where they have been to who they are in the present to where they might be going, it is critical to be attentive, and look for the dominant themes that continue to appear, in the same way the primary melody of a song may be repeated over and over with different nuance throughout the score.

I suggest the themes that continue to reappear in our life story are the ones that require our deepest attention, and may serve as a kind of GPS to help navigate the future. I regularly push students to talk about their foundational narratives: What are the narratives without which you would not be who you are? Almost always these involve relationships, family of origin, home town, or a lack of a place called home, particular friendships that have stood the test of time, public figures that have been role models, mentors and coaches with whom they develop a particular connection, interests that can be traced back to childhood and remain significant in college. These foundational narratives can serve as the DNA for discerning meaning and purpose and a direction for the future. Why have they been foundational? What is it about the magnetic pull of a particular friendship? The never-ending fascination with photography, or art, or insects, or architecture that continues to hold our attention? What aspects of our home town's culture remain in our soul and shape the way we interact with every other community?

Learning to excavate and interpret our personal narratives is an essential skill, and there are tangible ways to learn and practice that skill. I have used the following three in classes and on retreats with college students.

First, write a one-sentence personal mission statement. It is incredibly difficult to take the vast scope, breadth, and complexity of one's life and put it down in one sentence. The mission should be broad enough to be energetic and aspirational, to involve a sense of value and purpose, yet focused enough to be tangible. Public and private sector leaders have recognized the value of a clear and coherent mission statement for years as a way of organizing complex institutions with all the fiscal, capital, and human resources involved toward a common goal. Doing the same for one's own life can be a helpful way of describing, in the present, why am I here? What am I really working toward in the big picture of my life?

I've discovered that most students have never thought about this before, often because no one has ever really asked them to think about it and articulate it, and find the task enormously challenging. Many students are exhilarated by the exercise which suggests somebody is genuinely interested in their life's trajectory, and engage it with diligence and passion. Other students are demoralized by the assignment, and often end up feeling quite frustrated because they have no idea what to say, or end of feeling sheepish or embarrassed because the best they have simply mimics the dominant narrative of success as accumulation, and the end game feels rather shallow. The point is not that one's purpose at 19 or 20 is chiseled in rock, but rather to serve as a reflective moment, a touch point of self-evaluation, a coordinate on the map.

Second, write your own eulogy. The point here is to begin with the end in mind. When all is said and done, what do you want others to have said about you? How do you want to be seen by your friends and family, a child or spouse, a closest friend or colleague? What might it mean to live in such a way that one's eulogy becomes embodied in one's life? Reading the self-written eulogies of college students regularly brings me to tears. I see in them a depth that is rarely displayed in the hypersocial consciousness of the modern college campus. The eulogies express profound values and ambition, hopes, fears, and aspirations. Once again, this is a devastatingly hard assignment for those who take it seriously. It involves confronting one's mortality, not an easy thing for a college sophomore, and explicitly saying what kind of person they want to become. Again, many students find it an affirming exercise, offering some assurance that they are on the right path. While others find it a painful process, recognizing the gap between who they are and who they genuinely aspire to be. The beauty of the process is that by recognizing that gap, they now might be motivated to close it, and they have articulated a vision of how they might do so.

Third, establish a clearance committee. One of the many gifts of the Quaker tradition is the belief that our truest self is often hidden and ever-changing, and we need to practice regular periods of silence to allow the external and internal noise to quiet so that we can truly listen to our interior lives and tell the story of our lives with integrity. The Quaker assumption is that we cannot do this alone. Rather, we need the presence of a wider community to help us listen and discern. The clearance committee is a way for one person to draw on the trust of close friends to help. The individual brings a significant question to the group: Should I take this new job? Should I get married? Should we have children? Should I pursue a new path? The role of the individual is to listen carefully and respond honestly, to trust him or herself, and those in the community completely. The role of the community is to ask clear and open questions and to withhold any advice or judgment, and to trust that in the process of silence, questions, listening, and responding, the person at the center of the circle will discern the right answer for him or herself. This process involves extraordinary levels of emotional and reflective vulnerability, and should only be practiced when a deep and shared trust and confidentiality exists within the group. It can, however, be an extremely helpful process for someone who is wrestling with a significant question or life choice.

I believe we are regularly chosen by our own stories. Our stories of gladness, relationship, tragedy, and hope have within them the seeds for growing a life of meaning and purpose. The needs of the world are real, and they are legion. Each one of us has the capacity to engage those needs, to help, in the words of the Jewish tradition, "repair the world." In order to do so we need to regularly tell our own stories, listen for the unspoken messages, and recognize repeating themes. And in the process seek a lasting joy by being honest about our wounds, and connecting our joy and our wounds to the needs of the world around us.

Conclusion

Now 75 years in process, the Harvard Grant Study is one of the longest longitudinal studies of human development ever undertaken, following 268 Harvard undergraduate men from the classes of 1938–1940 to the present. Most of these men have died and those living are well into their 90s. The study seeks to probe the deep questions of life over the course of time, and what ultimately makes life worth living. The results are perhaps not all that surprising as consistent themes emerge: Love is really all that matters in the end. Life is more than money and prestige. We have the power to become happier over time. Challenges can bring perspective and meaning. Relationships are crucial. These conclusions strike me as a wise and lived description of what it means to live a life of consequence.

As Jayber Crow comes to the end of his own life, and is reflecting back on the path he has traveled, he reflects similar sentiments to these now old and dying Harvard men. Yet, he also describes a sense of wonder and grace, that his life has not been entirely his own, and there is a wider story at work than he has fully recognized:

Often I have not known where I was going until I was already there. I have had my share of desires and goals, but my life has come to me or I have gone to it mainly by way of mistakes and surprises. Often I have received better than I deserved. Often my fairest hopes have rested on bad mistakes. I am an ignorant pilgrim crossing a dark valley. And yet for a long time, looking back, I have been unable to shake off the feeling that I have been led— make of that what you will. (Berry 2000, 387)

My prayer is that the students I am privileged to walk alongside will not wake up one day at 52 and realize they have been chasing a fake rabbit for 30 years. Rather, I hope they will develop the capacity to recognize the social scripts they have been given, cultivate the skills to interpret their interior lives, the wisdom to understand their own story, the humility to receive grace and goodness as it comes, and the courage to live a life of consequence no matter where it may lead.

References

Berry, Wendell. 2000. *Jayber Crow, Barber, of the Port William Membership, as Written by Himself.* Washington, DC: Counterpoint.

Buechner, Frederick. 1973. *Wishful Thinking: A Seeker's ABC.* New York: NYL Harper and Row, Publishers, Inc.

Craddock, Fred. 2001. *The Cherry Log Sermons.* Louisville, KY: Westminster John Knox Press.

Hudson, Trevor. 2012. *Hope beyond Your Tears.* Nashville, TN: Upper Room Books.

MacIntyre, Alasdair. 1981. *After Virtue.* South Bend, IN: University of Notre Dame Press.

Oliver, Mary. 2004. *Why I Wake Early.* Boston, MA: Beacon Press.

CHAPTER ELEVEN

Suffering and Sacrifice: Individual and Collective Benefits, and Implications for Leadership

SCOTT T. ALLISON AND GWENDOLYN C. SETTERBERG

As the proverbial story goes, a prominent rabbi was once asked to explain the meaning of the word *blessing*. The rabbi gave a roundabout answer, first noting that in the book of Genesis, God took six days to make the heavens, the earth, and all living creatures. After each creation, whether it was light, land, oceans, plants, or the animal kingdom, God pronounced it to be *good*. But on the sixth day, after God created man and woman, this pronouncement from God is conspicuously absent. The rabbi cautioned against concluding that humans are not good, noting that the term *good* is actually a misleading translation of the original Hebrew word, *tov*. Tov means complete, finished, or sufficient.

Humans, the rabbi argued, do not arrive in this world in a finished state. Unlike the earth, the seas, the flora, and the fauna, humans are born incomplete. When a male is born, it takes a lifetime to become a man; when a female is born, it takes a lifetime to become a woman. An entire human lifespan is needed for an individual to achieve wholeness and thus serve the purpose for which he or she was created. The long process of becoming *tov* has been identified by psychologists as steps and stages of growth fraught with challenges and crises. Each necessary entanglement on the human journey represents painful progress toward becoming fully human, each struggle an opportunity for people to achieve the goal of wholeness. Relating this lesson to the definition of a blessing, the rabbi explained that all of our failings and fallings, and the human suffering that results from them, are blessings because they move us toward reaching the fullness of creation that God intended for us.

In this chapter, we review the ways in which suffering and sacrifice are beneficial to human beings. In our review, we draw from both ancient and modern spiritual traditions and a large body of psychological research on the determinants of happiness and mental health. Our review is necessarily an abbreviated one; a thorough treatment of this topic would surely fill an entire volume. This chapter represents an initial attempt to illuminate basic insights, using broad brushstrokes, about the ways in which suffering and sacrifice contribute to people's emotional, behavioral, and spiritual wellness. In addition to describing the psychological and spiritual benefits of suffering, we discuss the implications of these principles for leadership, heroism, and heroic leadership. Our central thesis is that suffering is inextricably tied to two important human drives: the drive for self-improvement, and the drive for improving one's group, community, or nation. Suffering, we argue, is the soil from which good spiritual leadership germinates.

Benefits of Suffering

The Merrium-Webster dictionary's definition of *suffer* is "to be forced to endure pain" or "experience unavoidable unpleasantness." For many people, pain and unpleasantness are destructive experiences to be avoided. From this limited perspective, suffering represents loss, setback, and regression; it is bereft of benefit. Spiritual philosophies throughout the ages, however, have emphasized the counterintuitive benefits of suffering, pointing to the profound gains, advantages, and opportunities that suffering confers to those open to such boons. Our review of the wisdom gleaned from these spiritual traditions reveals at least six ways that suffering can provide benefits to recipients. These six benefits include the idea that suffering (1) has redemptive qualities, (2) signifies important developmental milestones, (3) fosters humility, (4) elevates compassion, (5) encourages social union and action, and (6) provides meaning and purpose. This last benefit is of particular relevance to the genesis of spiritual leadership that aims to elevate groups toward goals that transcend suffering. Below we briefly review each of these six beneficial effects of suffering.

Suffering Is Redemptive

A number of spiritual traditions emphasize the redemptive value of suffering and sacrifice. Buddhism's four noble truths focus on the inevitability of suffering, the source of it, the elimination of it, and the path one must take to free oneself of its ravages. Buddhism points to, and offers antidotes for, the unavoidable suffering of birth, old age, sickness, and death. Centuries later, Sigmund Freud wrote about the inevitability of physical suffering as endemic to the human condition, noting that our fractious relations with others are an additional painful source of suffering (Freud 1930). Buddhism teaches the potential for spiritual awakening, but this awakening requires a willingness to use suffering as a catalyst for going on the further spiritual journey. The Buddha cautioned that the desire for awakening asks much from those who seek it. One must turn *toward* the suffering to conquer it.

Christianity, and Catholicism in particular, most emphatically embraces the redemptive value of suffering. Examples of biblical suffering abound, and so we will limit our review to a few notable examples. Foremost in the Judeo-Christian tradition is the idea that all human suffering stems from the fall of man (Genesis 1:31). The Old Testament also emphasizes the axiom that people reap what they sow, with suffering serving as the natural consequence of defying God's will (Galatians 6:7–10). We witness such suffering when David commits adultery (2 Samuel 11:1–5), when Solomon ignores God's caution about marriage (1 Kings 11:1–5), and when the Israelites experience the natural consequences of disobeying God (Numbers 14:41–45). For Christians, God imparts value into suffering for its own sake, and not as a judgment against sin. For instance, Peter states that "it is commendable if someone bears up under the pain of unjust suffering because they are conscious of God" (1 Peter 2:19). The centerpiece of suffering in the New Testament is, of course, the portrayal of the passion of Christ through the Synoptic Gospels. For Christians, Christ's redemptive death is the ultimate illustration of God's grace. His suffering served the purpose of redeeming no less than the entire human race, elevating Jesus into the role of the Western world's consummate spiritual leader for the past two millennia.

During his ministry as a Christian leader of the early church, the Apostle Paul endured immense suffering. Paul was stoned, beaten, bitten by a poisonous snake, shipwrecked, physically crippled, imprisoned, and executed as a result of his service as a Christian leader (Collie and Collie 2011). The suffering of early Christians always served a larger, higher purpose. According to renowned priest Henri Nouwen (1989), "Suffering invites us to place our hurts in larger hands. In Christ we see God suffering for us and calling us to share in God's suffering love for a hurting world. The small and even overpowering pains of our lives are intimately connected with the greater pains of Christ. Our daily sorrows are anchored in a greater sorrow and therefore a larger hope." Pope Francis (2013) echoed this sentiment in suggesting that the suffering of Christ redeems all of our suffering by allowing the sufferer to share in the redemptive sacrifice of Christ:

> To suffer is to take the difficulty and to carry it with strength, so that the difficulty does not drag us down. To carry it with strength: this is a Christian virtue. Saint Paul says several times: Suffer, endure. This means do not let ourselves be overcome by difficulties. This means that the Christian has the strength not to give up, to carry difficulties with strength. Carry them, but carry them with strength. It is not easy, because discouragement comes, and one has the urge to give up and say, "Well, come on, we'll do what we can but no more." But no, it is a grace to suffer. In difficulties, we must ask for [this grace]. (Kaczor 2015)

The redemptive value of suffering is evident in many striking examples of spiritual leadership both within and outside the realm of traditional religion. Our previous work on the psychology of heroism has identified personal transformation through struggle as one of the defining characteristics of heroic leadership (Allison and Goethals 2011). From the perspective of the heroic journey, suffering plays a pivotal role in illuminating the hero's missing qualities that must be recovered, or discovered, for the hero achieve his or her heroic transformation. Martin Luther King Jr., once said that he would not permit suffering to defeat him or engender bitterness. Rather, King wrote that his goal was to "transform the suffering into a creative force" (King and Armstrong 2007, 97). King understood that the redemptive and transformative power of suffering occurs at two different levels. At the individual level, heroes are personally transformed by their suffering (Campbell 1949). Heroic leaders then use this personal metamorphosis to transform the society to which they belong (Allison and Smith 2015; Goethals and Allison 2016).

Suffering also transformed Nelson Mandela, who endured 27 years of imprisonment before assuming the presidency of South Africa. While imprisoned, Mandela and other inmates performed hard labor in a lime quarry. Prison conditions were harsh; prisoners were segregated by race, with black prisoners receiving the least rations. Political prisoners such as Mandela were kept separate from ordinary criminals and received fewer privileges. Mandela has described how, as a D-group prisoner (the lowest classification), he was allowed one visitor and one letter every six months. Mandela's ability to prevail after such long-term suffering made him an inspirational hero. His remarkable triumph over adversity, occurring before his presidency, propelled him to international fame and admiration. When asked to reflect on Mandela's ordeals, Desmond Tutu opined that "the suffering of those 27 years helped to purify him and grow the magnanimity that would become his hallmark" (Perry 2013).

In the field of positive psychology, scholars have acknowledged the role of suffering in the development of healthy character strengths (Hall, Langer, and McMartin 2010). Paul's figurative "thorn in his flesh" led him to humility and dependence on Christ (2 Cor 12:10): "...for Christ's sake, I delight in weaknesses, in insults, in hardships, in persecutions, in difficulties. For when I am weak, then I am strong." In Romans 5:3, we "glory in our sufferings, because we know that suffering produces perseverance; perseverance, character; and character, hope." Positive psychology recognizes beneficial effects of suffering through the labels of "posttraumatic growth, stress-related growth, positive adjustment, positive adaptation, and adversarial growth" (Hall, et al. 2010, 118).

A study of character strengths measured before and after the September 11 terrorist attacks showed an increase in people's "faith, hope, and love" (Peterson and Seligman 2003). The redemptive development of hope, wisdom, and resilience as a result of suffering is said to have contributed to the leadership excellence of figures such as Helen Keller, Aung San Suu Kyi, Mahatma Gandhi, Malala Yousafzai, Stephen Hawking, Franklin D. Roosevelt, Shiva Nazar Ahari, Oprah Winfrey, J. K. Rowling, and Ludwig van Beethoven, among others.

Suffering Signifies a Necessary "Crossover" Point in Life

Psychologists who study lifespan development have long known that humans traverse through various stages of maturation from birth to death. Models of human development include transitional events that mark the close of one developmental stage and the launching of another. For example, in the physical development of children, the onset of visible secondary sex characteristics signals the end of young childhood and the beginning of puberty. Notable theories of psychological growth include Bowlby's theory of emotional development, Kohlberg's theory of moral development, Gibson's theory of perceptual development, Piaget's theory of cognitive development, and Erik Erikson's theory of psychosocial development. For the purposes of the present chapter, we focus on the work of Erikson, who believed that social development reflects a combination of psychological processes and social experiences. Erikson believed that people do not navigate through a developmental stage until they successfully negotiate a specific crisis that corresponds with that stage. If prolonged or mishandled, the crisis can produce suffering, and it is this suffering that serves as the necessary catalyst for progression to the subsequent stage.

From this perspective, suffering can be a significant stimulus for human growth and development. To illustrate, consider the transition from middle-adulthood to late-adulthood. Erikson was the first psychologist to describe important late-life stages and, in fact, he was the first to address the causes and consequences of the "midlife crisis." According to Erikson, middle-aged people often struggle to find their purpose or meaning in life, particularly after their children have grown and left the house. Erikson surmised that the unhealthy resolution of this struggle is a descent into a life of meaningless, narcissistic, *self-absorption*. Suffering borne of isolation and stagnation is the inevitable result of this choice. The only way to move forward is to carve out a life of selfless *generativity*. A generative individual is charitable, communal, socially connected, and willing to selflessly better society. Generativity is the only antidote to the midlife crisis. Middle-aged and older adults who are able to model healthy generativity serve an important leadership role for their peers and for younger adults. Generative individuals are among society's most valuable human assets; they are often called the "elders" of society.

A recurring theme in world literature is the idea that people must plummet to physical and emotional depths before they can ascend to new heights. In *The Odyssey*, the hero Odysseus descends to Hades where he meets the blind prophet Tireseas. Only at this lowest of points, in the depths of the underworld, is Odysseus given the gift of insight about how to become the wise ruler of Ithaca. Similarly, the *Apostles' Creed* tells of Jesus descending into hell before his ascent to heaven. Much has been written about the meaning of Jesus's surprising descent. Somehow, the author(s) of the creed deemed it absolutely necessary for Jesus to descend before he could "rise" from the dead. In eastern religious traditions, such as Hinduism, one encounters the idea that suffering follows naturally from the commission of immoral acts in one's current or past life. This type of karma involves the acceptance of suffering as a just consequence and as an opportunity for spiritual progress. This process has been called *necessary suffering*, the "way of the wound," and a "spirituality of imperfection" (Rohr 2010). Evolutionary psychologists have argued that suffering may have adaptive value in improving reproductive fitness. Emotional depression, for example, may provide the necessary impetus for people to seek solutions to their personal problems (Watson and Andrews 2002).

The message is clear: we must die, or some part of us must die, before we can live, or at least move forward. This process of going down in order to go up is counterintuitive and thus fiercely resisted by most people. The imagery of the grain of wheat is absolutely clear in John 12:24: "Unless a grain of wheat falls into the earth and dies, it remains alone; but if it dies, it bears much fruit." Some type of dying is a natural prerequisite for living. If we resist that dying—and most every one of us does—we resist what is good for us and hence bring about our own suffering. Psychoanalyst Carl Jung once observed that "the foundation of all mental illness is the avoidance of true suffering." The paradox here is that if we avoid suffering, we avoid growth. Perhaps the great Cistercian monk Thomas Merton summed it up best: "The truth that many people never understand, until it is too late, is that the more you try to avoid suffering the more you suffer because smaller and more insignificant things begin to torture you in proportion to your fear of being hurt." People who resist this type of dying, this necessary suffering, are ill equipped to serve as the leaders of society. Our most heroic leaders have been "through the fire" (Isaiah 43:2) and have thus gained the wisdom and maturity to lead wisely. Notable examples include Franklin D. Roosevelt, who overcame polio; John F. Kennedy, who underwent a near-death experience during World War II and battled life-long illness; Nelson Mandela, who endured a long, brutal imprisonment; and Helen Keller, who overcame deafblindness.

Suffering Encourages Humility

Psychologists believe that psychological "wholeness" depends on realistic self-appraisal. Such accurate self-conceptions are rare, however. The vast majority of people harbor the illusion that they are better than others, more moral than others, fairer than others, and more competent than others (Goethals, Messick, and Allison 1991). Suffering occurs when our pink clouds are burst, when our self-serving illusions are undermined by irrefutable evidence that we are flawed and limited beings who are no better, and often worse, than others. Spiritual traditions tell us that some necessary "pruning" is needed to keep us "right-sized". In Daniel 11:35 we learn that "some of the wise will stumble, so that they may be refined, purified and made spotless." In John 15:2, Jesus is quoted as saying that "every branch in me that does not bear fruit, He takes away; and every branch that bears fruit, He prunes it so that it may bear more fruit." In the end, Jesus's humility before God brought him to accept his suffering rather than reject it, as the crowds dared him to do (Mark 15:29–32, Matthew 27:39–44), because he understood the necessary nature of his suffering. It would seem that some degree of pain and suffering is necessary to keep us all humble.

Spiritual traditions from around the world emphasize that although life can be painful, a higher power is at work using our circumstances to humble us and to shape us into what He, She, or It wants us to be. C. S. Lewis once noted, "God whispers to us in our pleasures, speaks to us in our conscience, but shouts in our pains: It is His megaphone to rouse a deaf world." Richard Rohr (2010) opines that suffering "doesn't accomplish anything tangible but creates space for learning and love" (64). Suffering rouses us out of our inherent spiritual laziness and opens us to growth and maturity. Suffering reminds us that we are not God, thus making us more receptive to the divine. Spiritual leaders teach us, often by example, that suffering serves the purpose of humbling us and waking us from the dream of self-sufficiency.

Humility is a major step toward "recovery" in 12-step programs such Alcoholics Anonymous, Overeaters Anonymous, Gambler's Anonymous, and Al-Anon. Step 1 asks participants in these programs to admit their total powerlessness over their addiction. The spiritual principle at work here is the idea that victory is only possible through admitting defeat. Richard Rohr (2010) argues that only when people reach the limits of their private resources do they become willing to tap into the "ultimate resource"—God, Allah, the universe, or some power greater than themselves. Pain, misery, and desperation become the keys to recovery. Step 7 later asks program members to "*humbly* ask God" to remove personal defects of character (italics added). This humility can only be accomplished by first admitting defeat and then accepting that one cannot recover from addiction without assistance from a higher power. Twelve-step programs begin by focusing on defeat and suffering (Step 1), the possibility of a higher power being the solution (Step 2), trust in that higher power (Step 3), personal self-improvement with God's help (Steps 4–9), and service to others (Step 12). This last step is the step of spiritual leadership. Mentoring others through the steps is a central component of maintaining one's own sobriety and recovery.

Suffering Stimulates Compassion

Arguably the most important role of suffering is to invoke compassion for those who are hurting. Virtually all spiritual traditions emphasize the importance of consolation, relief, and self-sacrificial outreach for the suffering. Buddhists use two words in reference to compassion. The first is *karuna*, which is the willingness to bear the pain of another and to practice kindness, affection, and gentleness toward those who suffer. The second term is *metta*, which is an altruistic kindness and love that is free of any selfish attachment. The expression of these values is crucial to leading a holy life and attaining nirvana. Vietnamese Zen Buddhist monk Thích Nhất Hạnh (1999) emphasizes the compassion-building role of suffering: "When another person makes you suffer, it is because he suffers deeply within himself, and his suffering is spilling over. He does not need punishment; he needs help. That's the message he is sending" (198).

Scriptural references to compassion abound for Christians. According to James 1:27, "Religion that is pure and undefiled before God, the Father, is this: to visit orphans and widows in their affliction." And in Mark 6:34: "When he went ashore he saw a great crowd, and he had compassion on them, because they were like sheep without a shepherd. And he began to teach them many things." Jesus encouraged compassion for sinners, as when he encountered the adulteress about to be stoned in John 8:7, "He that is without sin among you, let him first cast a stone at her." In 2 Corinthians 1:3–4, "Blessed be the God and Father of our Lord Jesus Christ, the Father of mercies and God of all comfort, who comforts us in all our affliction, so that we may be able to comfort those who are in any affliction, with the comfort with which we ourselves are comforted by God." For Jesus, compassion for the poor, the sick, the hungry, the unclothed, the widowed, the imprisoned, the sinful, and the orphaned was at the core of his spiritual leadership.

Psychologists have recently turned their attention toward the mechanisms underlying compassion. Goetz, Keltner, and Simon-Thomas (2010) found that just encouraging people to think about the suffering of others activates the vagus nerve, which is associated with compassion. Having people read uplifting stories about sacrifice increases empathy to the same degree as various kinds of spiritual practices such as contemplation, prayer, meditation, and yoga. Being outside in a beautiful natural setting also appears to encourage greater compassion. Feelings of awe and wonder about the universe and the miracle of life can increase both sympathy and compassion.

One fascinating finding in psychology is that wealthy individuals may be challenged in their ability to show empathic responses to others. In a series of clever studies, Kraus, Piff, and Keltner (2011) observed the behavior of drivers at a busy four-way intersection. They discovered that drivers of luxury cars were more likely to cut off other motorists rather than wait their turn at the intersection. Krouse et al. also found that luxury car drivers were more likely to speed past a pedestrian trying to use a crosswalk rather than let the pedestrian cross the road. Compared to lower and middle-class participants, wealthy participants also showed little heart rate change when watching a video of children with cancer. These data suggest that more powerful and wealthy people are less likely to show compassionate responses to the weak and the poor. Wealthy and powerful people may also be more likely to perform unethical behavior. Over the past decade, numerous executives at Goldman Sachs and other high-powered financial corporations have been convicted for illegal activity borne of excessive greed (Grewal 2012). Research shows that wealthy individuals are more likely to agree with statements that greed is justified, beneficial, and morally defensible. Those with the most seem to be motivated to give the least and to take the most from the poorest among us. Good spiritual leaders somehow are able to guard against letting the power of their position compromise their values of compassion and empathy for the least fortunate.

Suffering Promotes Social Union and Collective Action

Toward the end of his life, Sigmund Freud became increasingly preoccupied with the social aspects of his psychoanalytic theory. His groundbreaking *Civilization and Its Discontents* in 1930 addressed the harsh realities of intergroup conflict and its role in producing unhappiness and suffering in humans. Freud wrote, "We are never so defenseless against suffering as when we love, never so forlornly unhappy as when we have lost our love object or its love" (57). It is clear that Freud viewed social relations as the cause of suffering. In contrast, the spiritual view of suffering suggests the opposite idea, namely, that *suffering is actually the cause of good social relations.* Suffering brings people together and is much better than joy at creating bonds among group members (Rohr 2010). Social psychologist Stanley Schachter discovered this phenomenon in a series of laboratory experiments he reported in his 1959 book,

The Psychology of Affiliation. Schachter told his research participants that they were about to receive painful electric shocks. Before participating in the study, they were asked to choose one of two waiting rooms in which to sit. Participants about to receive shocks were much more likely to choose the waiting room with people in it compared to the empty room. Schachter concluded that *misery loves company.* He then went a step further and asked a different group of participants, also about to receive the shocks, if they would prefer to wait in a room with other participants who were about to receive shocks, or a room with participants who would *not* be receiving shocks. Schachter found that participants about to receive shocks much preferred the room with others who were going to share the same fate. His conclusion: *misery doesn't love just any kind of company; misery loves miserable company.*

Effective leaders intuitively know how to use suffering to rally people behind a cause. We would never dare accuse Adolf Hitler of showing good spiritual leadership, but there is no denying that Hitler showed remarkable skill in rousing the German people to action after their nation suffered from the aftermath of World War I. Leadership that uses suffering to achieve a higher moral purpose can be said to be spiritual leadership. Winston Churchill and Franklin D. Roosevelt were masters at capitalizing on the suffering of British and American citizens to bolster resilience and in-group morale. Suffering can be the glue that binds and heals after everything has seemingly shattered. Romans 12:15–16 advises us to "rejoice with those who rejoice, and weep with those who weep. Be of the same mind toward one another; do not be haughty in mind, but associate with the lowly." This passage reflects God's will for suffering to serve the purpose of building a relationship with God and with others in one's community. Support groups, self-help groups, and 12-step programs are designed to achieve these aims (Miller 1997). There is convincing evidence suggesting that group therapy can achieve a higher rate of effectiveness than individual therapy (Corazinni 2011). Misery doesn't just love miserable company; misery helps alleviate the misery in the company.

Suffering can mobilize people. Mobilization can occur when suffering inspires the emergence of spiritual leadership needed to ameliorate the suffering. Good leaders can invoke suffering as a noble means for achieving a greater end. Franklin Roosevelt used the suffering of impoverished Americans during the Great Depression to justify his New Deal policies and programs. Later, during World War II, both he and Churchill cited the suffering of both citizens and soldiers to promote the rationing of sugar, butter, meat, tea, biscuits, coffee, canned milk, firewood, and gasoline. In North America, African Americans were subjugated by European Americans for centuries, and from this suffering emerged the leadership of Rosa Parks, Martin Luther King Jr., and John Lewis, among others. The suffering of women inspired Susan B. Anthony, Elizabeth Cady Stanton, and a host of other activists to promote the women's suffrage movement.

Three days after the September 11 terrorist attacks, George W. Bush used the suffering of America to galvanize support for military involvement in Afghanistan. Standing amid the rubble of the fallen twin towers, Bush grabbed a bullhorn and shouted to the grief-stricken crowd, "I can hear you. The rest of the world hears you. And the people who knocked these buildings down will hear all of us soon." The crowd roared its approval and, for better or for worse, Bush secured his plan for American military involvement in the Middle East. In our previous work, we have argued that *heroism is in the eye of the beholder* (Allison and Goethals 2011, 2013, 2014; Goethals and Allison, 2012, 2014). The policies and agendas of countless leaders who have invoked spiritual principles, from George W. Bush to Osama Bin Laden, suggest that spiritual leadership may also be in the eye of the beholder. If spiritual leadership serves a higher moral purpose, as we contend here, then we must be mindful that morality can be twisted to serve the psychological needs and goals of the beholder. Sadly, many God-loving nations have waged wars against each other, with leadership on each side proclaiming the spiritually superior upper hand.

Suffering Instills Meaning and Purpose

The sixth and final benefit of suffering resides in the meaning and purpose that suffering imparts to the sufferer. Many spiritual traditions underscore the role of suffering in bestowing a sense of significance and worth to life. In Islam, the faithful are asked to accept suffering as Allah's will and to submit to it as a test of faith. Followers are cautioned to avoid questioning or resisting the suffering; one simply endures it with the assurance that Allah never asks for more than one can handle. This philosophy is not unlike that of Christianity. As Hall et al. (2010) note, "countless Psalms, narratives, and prophetic stories revolve around meeting God in the context of one's suffering or despair" (114). Suffering is endowed with meaning when it is attached to a perception of a divine calling in one's life or a belief that all "events are ordained for God's purposes" (114, 115). Both suffering and divine comfort in the context of suffering mobilize the Christian's identification and connection with Christ. This identification characterizes the phenomenon of *sanctification,* which is the state of growing in divine grace as a result of Christian commitment (115).

Friedrich Nietzche (1886/1992) once observed that "to live is to suffer, to survive is to find some meaning in the suffering" (110). This drive for meaning as a coping mechanism for suffering has been explored by many scholars, including Diehl (2009), Egnew (2005), Frankl (1946), and Gunderman (2002), to name but a few. Gunderman offered that "human beings can endure great suffering if their struggle is shaped by some sense of larger purpose" (70). Frankl suggested that a search for meaning *transforms* suffering into a positive, life-altering experience: "In some way, suffering ceases to be suffering at the moment it finds a meaning, such as the meaning of a sacrifice.... That is why man is even ready to suffer, on the condition, to be sure, that his suffering has a meaning" (145). Diehl (2009) lists "an inability to experience and grasp some meaning of life" among eight primary potentials for human suffering (37). Thus, the search for meaning not only alleviates suffering; the absence of meaning can *cause* suffering.

The ability to derive meaning from suffering is a hallmark characteristic of heroism in myths and legends. Comparative mythologist Joseph Campbell (1949) discovered that all great hero tales from around the globe share a common structure, which Campbell called the *hero monomyth.* A key component of the monomyth is the hero's ability to endure suffering and to triumph over it. As we have noted earlier, heroes discover, or recover, an important inner quality that plays a pivotal role in producing a personal transformation that enables the hero to prevail over seemingly insurmountable obstacles (Goethals and Allison 2016). Suffering is one of many recurring phenomena endemic to classic hero tales. Other phenomena that abound in hero tales include love, mystery, eternity, infinity, God, paradox, meaning, and sacrifice. Richard Rohr (2010) calls these phenomena *transrational* experiences. An experience is considered transrational when it defies logical analysis and can only be understood (or *best* understood) in the context of a good narrative. The legendary poet William Wordsworth must have been intuitively aware of the transrational nature of suffering, sacrifice, and the infinite when he penned the following line: "Suffering is permanent, obscure and dark, and shares the nature of infinity" (Gill 1989, 132). Joseph Campbell (1971), moreover, connected the dots between suffering and people's search for meaning. According to Campbell, the hero's journey is "the pivotal myth that unites the spiritual adventure of ancient heroes with the modern search for meaning" (112).

The Psychology of Sacrifice

Surprisingly, few psychologists have explored the mental underpinnings of self-sacrifice (Allison and Goethals 2008). Individuals who make the ultimate sacrifice by offering their own lives to promote a cause are known as *martyrs*. Droge and Tabor (1992) have outlined three defining characteristics of a martyr's death. First, the death usually occurs as a sign of persecution and is seen by similarly persecuted others as noble and heroic. Second, martyrs die with the notion that others will benefit as a result of their suffering. Third, martyrs make their sacrifice with the expectation of an eternal vindication, which is often their prime motivation.

Martyrdom has its roots in ancient Greek and Roman cultural values. Socrates, called the "saint and martyr of philosophy" by Gottlieb (2000), willingly accepted his death sentence and took his own life to uphold his belief system. The suicide of Socrates "has stood for 2400 years as a symbol of dying for one's principles" (DeSpelder and Strickland 1996, 455). Greeks and Romans valued the idea of meeting death with both courage and acceptance. Romans revered both the bloody deaths in the gladiator arenas as well as intellectual suicides in the tradition of Socrates. The Roman belief system contained the idea that life "was a treasure that gained value or power only when expended" and that martyrdom "transformed weakness into power" (Cormack 2001, 26).

In modern times, martyrdom is probably most often considered in the context of religious extremism, but this religious context also has ancient origins. Two thousand years ago, Christianity was metamorphosed from a peripheral offshoot of Judaism to a beleaguered underdog religious sect. Early Christians were put to death in great numbers for preaching their illegal faith to their fellow Roman citizens. This era of persecution spurred the growth of Christianity, as each publicly executed martyr attracted a new cult of converts. For early Christians, the suffering and death of Jesus held a "fatal attraction" (Kastenbaum 2004, 62) and was a strong advertisement for a threatened faith. "These martyrdoms were a parallel reflection of Jesus' willing choice to suffer an die," according the Gospel of John (10:18): "No one takes my life, but I lay it down of my own accord." The redemptive value of suffering became part of the "Christian heroic ideal" (Cormack 2001, 43). Martyrs did not just expect to be resurrected in the next life, but also for their memories to be resurrected for all of time. The unshakeable determination of these early Christian martyrs shamed the Roman Empire's tactics of brutality, garnered sympathy for the Christian cause, and fueled the growth of Christianity. The spiritual leadership of these early Christian martyrs forever transformed the Western world.

Virtually all religions feature at least some history of martyrdom or suggestion of martyrdom in their belief systems. In Scripture there are numerous accounts of Jewish martyrs resisting the Hellenizing of their Seleucid overlords, being executed for such crimes as observing the Sabbath, circumcising their children, or refusing to eat pork or meat sacrificed to idols. In Hinduism, the term *sati* refers to a woman's act of immolating herself on the funeral pyre of her husband, as remaining alive after one's husband's death carries with it the feared social sanction of being "an alluring or lustful widow who might tarnish the family reputation" (Cormack 2001, 120). Satis are venerated as martyrs for being those who "embody and affirm the truth" (119). The Islamic conceptualization of martyrdom delineates specific rewards for those that would die for their God; the Qur'an specifies that the Muslim martyr, or *shahid*, is spared the pain of death and receives immediate entry into paradise. Islam accepts a much broader view of what constitutes a martyr, including anyone who succumbs in territorial conflicts between Muslims and non-Muslims. There is widespread disagreement in Muslim community about whether suicide bombers should be considered martyrs (Cormack 2001).

Conclusion

"Hardships," wrote C. S. Lewis (1961), "prepare people for an extraordinary life" (54). We began this chapter with the provocative claim that good spiritual leadership emerges out of such hardships. For an individual or a group to move forward or to progress, something unpleasant must be endured (suffering) or something pleasant must be given up (sacrifice). Humanity's most effective and inspiring spiritual leaders have sustained immense suffering, made harrowing sacrifices, or both. These leaders' suffering and sacrifice set them apart from ordinary people who deny, decry, or defy these seemingly unsavory experiences. Great spiritual leaders understand that suffering redeems, augments, defines, humbles, elevates, mobilizes, and enriches us. Enlightened leaders not only refuse to allow suffering and sacrifice to defeat them; they use suffering and sacrifice as assets to be mined for psychological advantages and inspiration. Leaders who successfully plumb the spiritual treasures of suffering and sacrifice have the wisdom and maturity to evolve into society's most transcendent leaders.

Acknowledgment

This research was supported by a John Templeton Foundation Grant (#35279) awarded to Scott T. Allison.

References

Allison, Scott T., and Athena H. Cairo. 2015. "Heroism and Mental Health." In Howard Freidman, ed., *Encyclopedia of Mental Health*. New York: Elsevier.

Allison, Scott T., Dafna Eylon, James K. Beggan, and Jennifer J. Bachelder. 2009. "The Demise of Leadership: Positivity and Negativity in Evaluations of Dead Leaders." *The Leadership Quarterly* 20: 115–129.

Allison, Scott T., and George R. Goethals. 2008. "Deifying the Dead and Downtrodden: Sympathetic Figures as Inspirational Leaders." In Crystal L. Hoyt, George R. Goethals, and Donelson R. Forsyth, eds., *Leadership at the Crossroads: Psychology and Leadership*. Westport, CT: Praeger.

Allison, Scott T., and George R. Goethals. 2011. *Heroes: What They Do and Why We Need Them*. New York: Oxford University Press.

Allison, Scott T., and George R. Goethals. 2013. *Heroic Leadership: An Influence Taxonomy of 100 Exceptional Individuals*. New York: Routledge.

Allison, Scott T., and George R. Goethals. 2014. "'Now He Belongs to the Ages': The Heroic Leadership Dynamic and Deep Narratives of Greatness." In George R. Goethals, Scott T. Allison, Roderick M. Kramer, and David M. Messick, eds., *Conceptions of Leadership: Enduring Ideas and Emerging Insights*. New York: Palgrave Macmillan.

Allison, Scott T., and Greg Smith. 2015. *Reel Heroes, Volume 2: The Villains*. Richmond, VA: Agile Writer Press.

Allison, Scott T., and Jennifer Burnette, J. 2009. "Fairness and Preference for Underdogs and Top Dogs." In Roderick Kramer, Ann Tenbrunsel, and Max Bazerman, eds., *Social Decision Making: Social Dilemmas, Social Values, and Ethical Judgments*. New York: Psychology Press.

Allison, Scott T., and Jennifer L. Cecilione. 2015. "Paradoxical Truths in Heroic Leadership: Implications for Leadership Development and Effectiveness." In Richard Bolden, Morgen Witzel, and Nigel Linacre, eds., *Leadership Paradoxes*. London: Routledge.

Campbell, Joseph. 1949. *The Hero with a Thousand Faces*. Princeton, NJ: Princeton University Press.

Campbell, Joseph. 1971. "Man & Myth: A Conversation with Joseph Campbell." *Psychology Today*, July.

Collie, Robert, and Annelie Collie. 2011. "The Apostle Paul and Post-Traumatic Stress." Lima, OH: Fairway Publishers.

Corazinni, Jack. 2011. "Advantages of Group Therapy." Retrieved from https://healthand-counseling.unca.edu/advantages-group-therapy.

Cormack, Margaret. 2001. *Sacrificing the Self: Perspectives on Martyrdom and Religion*. Oxford: University Press.

DeSpelder, Lynn A., and Albert L. Strickland, A. L. 1996. *The Last Dance: Encountering Death and Dying*. Berkeley, CA: Mayfield Publishing.

Diehl, Ulrich. 2009. "Human Suffering as a Challenge for the Meaning of Life." *International Journal of Philosophy, Religion, Politics, and the Arts* 4(2): 36–44.

Droge, Arthur, and James Tabor. 1992. *A Noble Death*. San Francisco, CA: Harper Publishing.

Egnew, Thomas R. 2005. "The Meaning of Healing: Transcending Suffering." *Annals of Family Medicine* 3(3): 255–262.

Festinger, Leon. 1950. "Informal Social Communication." *Psychological Review* 57(5): 271–282.

Frankl, Viktor. 1946. *Man's Search for Meaning*. New York: Beacon Press.

Gill, Stephen. 1989. *William Wordsworth: A Life*. New York: Oxford University Press.

Goethals, George R., and Scott T. Allison. 2012. "Making Heroes: The Construction of Courage, Competence, and Virtue." *Advances in Experimental Social Psychology* 46: 183–235.

Goethals, George R., and Scott T. Allison. 2014. "Kings and Charisma, Lincoln and Leadership: An Evolutionary Perspective." In George R. Goethals, Scott T. Allison, Roderick M. Kramer, and David M. Messick, eds., *Conceptions of Leadership: Enduring Ideas and Emerging Insights*. New York: Palgrave Macmillan.

Goethals, George R., and Scott T. Allison. 2016. "Transforming Motives and Mentors: The Heroic Leadership of James MacGregor Burns." Unpublished manuscript.

Goethals, George R., David M. Messick, and Scott T. Allison. 1991. "The Uniqueness Bias: Studies of Constructive Social Comparison." In Jerry Suls and Thomas A. Wills, eds., *Social Comparison: Contemporary Theory and Research,* 149–176. New York: Lawrence Erlbaum.

Goethals, George R., Scott T. Allison, Roderick M. Kramer, and David M. Messick, eds. 2014. *Conceptions of Leadership: Enduring Ideas and Emerging Insights*. New York: Palgrave Macmillan.

Goetz, Jennifer, and Dacher Keltner, and Emiliana Simon-Thomas. 2010. "Compassion: An Evolutionary Analysis and Empirical Review." *Psychological Bulletin* 136: 351–374.

Gottlieb, Anthony. 2000. *The Dream of Reason*. New York: W. W. Norton.

Grewal, Daisy. 2012. *How Wealth Reduces Compassion*. Retrieved from http://www.scientificamerican.com/article/how-wealth-reduces-compassion/.

Gunderman, Richard. 2002. "Is Suffering the Enemy?" *The Hastings Center Report* 32: 40–44.

Hall, Elizabeth, Richard Langer, and Jason McMartin. 2010. "The Role of Suffering in Human Flourishing: Contributions From Positive Psychology, Theology, and Philosophy." *Journal of Psychology and Theology* 38: 111–121.

Kaczor, Christopher. 2015. "A Pope's Answer to the Problem of Pain." Retrieved from http://www.catholic.com/magazine/articles/a-pope%E2%80%99s-answer-to-the-problem-of-pain.

Kastenbaum, Robert. 2004. *On Our Way: The Final Passage through Life and Death*. Berkeley: University of California Press.

Kim, JongHan, Scott T. Allison, Dafna Eylon, George R. Goethals, Michael M. Markus, Heather McGuire, and Sheila Hindle. 2008. "Rooting For (and Then Abandoning) the Underdog." *Journal of Applied Social Psychology* 38: 2550–2573.

King Jr., Martin Luther, and Tenisha Armstrong. 2007. *The Papers of Martin Luther King, Jr., Volume VI*. Berkeley: University of California Press.

Kraus, Michael. W., Paul Piff, and Dacher Keltner. 2011. "Social Class as Culture: The Convergence of Resources and Rank in the Social Realm." *Current Directions in Psychological Science* 20: 246–250.

Lewis, Clive Staples. 1961. *A Grief Observed*. London: Faber & Faber.

Miller, Norman S. 1997. *The Principles and Practice of Addictions in Psychiatry*. Philadelphia: W. B. Saunders Company.

Nhất Hạnh, Thich. 1999. *The Heart of the Buddha's Teaching: Transforming Suffering into Peace, Joy, and Liberation*. New York: Broadway Books.

Nouwen, Henri. 1989. *In the Name of Jesus: Reflections on Christian Leadership*. New York: Crossroads Publishing.

Nietzsche, Friedrich. 1886/1992. "Beyond Good and Evil." In *Basic Writings of Nietzsche*. Translated and edited by Walter Kaufman. New York: The Modern Library.

Perry, Alex. 2013. "Mandela's Jailer: 'He Was My Prisoner, but He Was My Father.'" Retrieved from http://world.time.com/2013/12/06/mandelas-jailer-he-was-my-prisoner-but-he-was-my-father/.

Peterson, Christopher, and Martin E. P. Seligman. 2003. "Character strengths before and after September 11." Psychological Science 14 381–384.Rohr, Richard. 2010. *Falling Upward*. San Francisco: Jossey-Bass.

Smith, Greg, and Scott T. Allison. 2014. *Reel Heroes, Volume 1: Two Hero Experts Critique the Movies*. Richmond: Agile Writer Press.

Watson, Paul J., and Paul W. Andrews. 2002. "Toward a Revised Evolutional Adaptationist Analysis of Depression: A Social Navigation Perspective." *Journal of Affective Disorders* 72: 1–14.

CHAPTER TWELVE

Leadership, Spirituality, and Values in a Secular Age: Insights from Charles Taylor and James MacGregor Burns

RICHARD L. MORRILL

Spirituality. This chapter will explore terms and concepts that are famously complex, so they should be carefully considered at the outset. Most theorists find it difficult, for example, to get a fix on the term "spirituality "in relation to leadership, especially outside its use in a specific context. The word refers to many different concepts, doctrines, practices, beliefs, and experiences that no single definition can capture. In effect, "spirituality" operates more as a category than a concept.

An examination of the different threads of belief and practice associated with the term shows several broad themes that are usually in play, though analysts offer parallel but different perspectives. (Astin, Astin, and Lindholm 2011; Bolman and Deal 2001; Crumpton 2011) The motifs of spirituality generally have to do with topics and practices that may operate by themselves or be connected with one or more of the other themes. They all reflect the joys and the burdens of coming variously to terms with the human condition in its finitude and freedom, its fallibility and flourishing, its transience and transcendence. The motifs of spirituality often include (1) a conscious and conscientious search for the ultimate meaning and purpose of life, (2) the experience of a transcendent source of life (however defined) and/or ultimate condition of salvation, peace, and liberation (however defined), (3) a series of practices and disciplines like textual study, ceremonies, rituals, meditation,

and prayer, and (4) a set of religious and/or ethical actions and dispositions based on rules, values, and virtues that are taken to be of defining
importance, such as love, compassion, and justice; the performance of
other moral and religious duties; or the achievement of various forms of
detachment or freedom from the snares, illusions, and sins of the everyday world. Most of these themes have their origins or iconic expression
in the traditions of specific religions. As a result, spirituality occurs
both within and outside institutional religion in various personal, educational, and developmental activities, individually or in groups.

Leadership. The effort to connect the complexity of spirituality with
the well-known complications of understanding leadership makes the
task even more daunting. There is a long tradition of reflection across
many centuries and cultures about various kinds of leaders and leadership, often with a focus on historical exemplars. More recently, several
generations of modern scholars have focused on the many forms and
meanings of leadership. Studies of leadership have provided tools and
constructs with which to build bridges across disciplines, creating an
agenda for understanding leadership as a basic phenomenon of human
social agency and organization. Whatever else might be said about
leadership today, most contemporary scholars would agree that one of
its primary forms is as an interactive social process in which individuals
and groups influence others to achieve common purposes in the midst
of change. In connecting some of the motifs of spirituality to leadership, it will be possible to find themes and questions that we can break
into manageable pieces for closer inquiry.

Values. Many students of leadership would suggest that values represent
one of the pivotal, shared elements that create the reciprocity between
leaders and those who engage with them. The term, again, is ambiguous.
Nonetheless, one common approach in leadership studies is to see values
as the internalized standards and criteria that guide leaders and followers
toward their chosen goals. In doing so, values, especially as master values,
often reach deeply into human experience by displaying what matters
decisively to participants as they struggle to make sense of their lives and
come to terms successfully with change and conflict. In gaining a fuller
and richer understanding of values and how they take hold in human life,
it will be possible to deepen our understanding both of leadership and of
the ways it embodies spiritual motifs. In particular, this inquiry intends
to explore how values gain their authority as forms of human agency,
how they define personal and group identity in the search for meaning,
the ways in which their ultimate sources and foundations are interpreted
and how they illuminate the practices of leadership.

Taylor and Burns. To assist us in exploring this terrain I will draw on the insights of two eminent scholars, Charles Taylor and James MacGregor Burns. The analysis and comparison of their ideas will also at times permit a hypothetical exchange of their differing points of view. The two scholars participated in a common historical and intellectual world, though in different countries (Taylor primarily in Canada at McGill University) and in different fields of inquiry. Burns was a prolific and highly regarded historian and political scientist who had a long career at Williams College, and subsequent appointments at the University of Maryland and the University of Richmond. He died in the year 2014. His studies of leadership have been widely and deeply influential and have helped to create a new interdisciplinary field. Charles Taylor continues to have a deep impact on current thought and scholarship on the nature of human moral and religious experience as a philosopher and historian of culture and ideas. By drawing together their reflections we will be able to frame a number of issues about values and leadership that are not visible from a single point of view.

The Secular Sensibility

Several of the many questions pursued by Charles Taylor in his master and massive works *Sources of the Self* (1989) and *A Secular Age* (2007) will help to set our bearings on human moral experience and values in a secular and postmodern world. The secular age has many features, and Taylor depicts it by using broad cultural, historical, and philosophical analyses, often drawing on monographs and specialized studies done by others. He not only covers vast periods of history with broad strokes, but also digs more deeply into key ideas, frequently using various organizing concepts and metaphors like "the buffered self," which refers to the modern experience of separation from nature and the invisible forces and spirits that threatened or protected our ancestors. He describes the deep and inescapable cultural and historical changes that account for the decline in the public and social authority and the practice of religion, but focuses especially on the changing conditions of belief that characterize a secular age—the mental models and moral frameworks that presuppose immanent frames of causal explanation and reject transcendent references, especially in what he calls the North Atlantic world.

As one form of the conditions of belief in our secular era, Taylor suggests that humans in the contemporary world come to their identities in an "age of authenticity." Unlike our distant forebears who were born into a world that defined them ineluctably by various occupational castes, social stations, and ethical and religious duties, we moderns have a sense of freedom and responsibility to shape our personal, moral, and professional identities through our self-authenticating choices. In a secular age, we choose our own life patterns and life partners and are consistently counseled to find our special passions, and to hone our interests and abilities both within and beyond our work lives to express our individuality and become our best selves.

We also think within an immanent frame in our assumptions about and approaches to knowledge and decision making. Through instrumental reasoning and cost benefit analysis, we bring a calculating mentality to our personal and our organizational lives, the latter often unfolding in large bureaucracies, creating deadening routines that Max Weber called the "iron cage" (Taylor 2007, 719). When it comes to our use of disciplinary methods and personal inquiries about the wider world of culture, history and nature, we automatically reflect through the powers of disengaged rationality. We assume and seek immanent chains of causality that can be measured by evidence-based explanations, as exemplified by the empirical methods of the natural and social sciences. We presuppose an immanent frame and do not look for transcendent sources or supernatural explanations, nor do we invoke the presence of hidden spirits, invisible powers, or divine intervention. The age of enchantment of our ancestors has passed. As Taylor puts it arrestingly in summarizing the temper of secularity in the opening lines of *A Secular Age,* "why was it virtually impossible not to believe in God in, say, 1500 in our Western society while in 2000 many of us find this not only easy, but even inescapable?" (Taylor 2007, 25).

Taylor notes recurrently that for the past two generations or more, much of the intellectual world has as well moved from modern to postmodern interpretations of human moral experience. The Enlightenment's confidence in universal reason has been shattered by ways of showing that our purported rational moral order and enlightened social progress are captive to economic interests, social class, gender, and race. In this form of analysis, the values and beliefs on which modern thinkers have relied to portray moral purpose and experience have been shown to be instruments of social dominance, ways of masking the privileges of power and patriarchy. Postmodern scholars have deconstructed and re-interpreted historical and literary texts and artifacts to display these hidden interests and hierarchies. Much of modern thought in the social and natural sciences has as well described moral and religious experience materialistically or skeptically, from Freud's reductive psychoanalytic theories of religion to sociobiology's genetic explanations of morality.

The moral consequence of this frame of thinking easily leads to the view that any choice of a purpose in life is as good as any other as long as it is made authentically, on the basis of a person's self-choosing. Taylor challenges this view throughout *A Secular Age* and in a smaller work, *The Ethics of Authenticity*, through a central animating concept that he calls the human quest for fullness. As we shall see, he ultimately presses for an adequate source and ground for values beyond a self-authorizing authenticity by connecting fullness with various moral and spiritual experiences of transcendence. "We all see our lives, and/or the space wherein we live our lives, as having a certain moral/spiritual shape. Somewhere, in some activity or condition, lies a fullness, a richness; that is, in that place (activity or condition) life is fuller, richer, deeper, more worthwhile, more admirable, more what it should be" (Taylor 2007, 5). Taylor recounts many examples of how people, whether religious or otherwise, sometimes experience moments of fullness in art, music, and literature, in profound personal and family relationships of love and responsibility, in deep self-awareness, in acts of benevolence and justice, and in exalted experiences of the power and majesty of nature. These kinds of experiences lead people to reach for language that goes deeper, and reaches farther, ultimately toward universal significance and transcendent sources of meaning, what he calls "places" or "conditions" of fullness.

To clarify, Taylor uses the term "transcendence" to refer both to elevated claims and experiences within human life and history, as well as to an ultimate transcendent reality or source. As I see Taylor's approach, he interprets the ultimate source as setting the conditions for the human experience of transcendence itself, giving the experience of the quest for fullness the defining features that it possesses. In the moral sphere, for example, a transcendent source is evident *within* the experience of the depth and breadth of moral motivation, is recognized *in the process through which* we naturally press our moral imaginations toward a universal horizon, and is experienced *as* the ground of the reasons we inherently take many ethical choices to matter with unconditioned importance. The method is often phenomenological, asking implicitly "what are the conditions of possibility for this lived experience (phenomenon) to be what it is?" In effect, Taylor is suggesting that the purposes and values for which we live can be seen as continuously widening in scope as we ask tacitly or explicitly what they stand for and how effectively they meet the challenges of making sense of life. This process of questioning continues to press itself naturally toward a transcendent source, in both experiential and conceptual forms. As he puts it, "If I am right that our sense of fullness is a reflection of transcendent reality (which for me is the God of Abraham), and that all people have a sense of fullness, then there is no absolute point zero. But there is a crucial point where many come to rest in our civilization, defined by a refusal to envisage transcendence as the meaning of this fullness" (Taylor, *A Secular Age,* 769).

Taylor suggests that many modern thinkers are not inclined to move beyond an immanent perspective, such as the moral claims that they acknowledge at the human level; he believes, as he indicates above, that they are conceptually stuck, even arbitrarily, within the immanent frame. Writing primarily as a historian of ideas and philosopher, not as a theologian for believers, he tries to show how moral experience is shaped and how its implications can be meaningfully interpreted in both ontological and religious terms, whether in theistic forms or otherwise.

Taylor often quotes literary texts that in his view reflect traces of transcendence, or that represent "conversions" by thinkers who at a point in their lives turn toward a religious set of beliefs, like Gerard Manley Hopkins or Charles Peguy. He offers a lengthy passage along these lines about spiritual transcendence by the once-imprisoned playwright and later president of the Czech Republic, Vaclav Havel. Havel describes a brief and unanticipated meditation in a prison yard, sitting on a pile of rusty iron, and gazing through wires and bars onto an enormous tree with its leaves "trembling against an endless sky." He suddenly feels a connection to the "sovereignty of Being." Within a much longer statement he says, "I was flooded with a sense of ultimate happiness and harmony with the world and with myself, with that moment, with all the moments I could call up, and with everything invisible that lies behind it and has meaning. I would even say that I was somehow 'struck by love,' though I don't know precisely for whom or what" (Taylor 2007, 728–729).

As Taylor respectfully traces the intellectual courage of several postmodern thinkers like Albert Camus and Jacques Derrida to affirm human rights in a meaningless universe, he also notes the ironies in their posthumanistic ideas, especially in the context of the motif of fullness. They seek to free morality entirely from an exalted humanism, a metaphysical order, or religion. In this perspective, though, the motivation to serve those who suffer seems arbitrary, and could as easily have become an impulse to nihilism or to radical egocentricity. Taylor notes in several ways and different contexts that even the postmodern critique of the various forms of domination amounts to a tacit but inescapable appeal to standards of justice and equality. Otherwise we could not logically conclude that social dominance and exclusion represent any sort of issue about which to be troubled or that needs to be corrected. He suggests that no matter the depth of ethical skepticism and moral self-invention a person may claim in theory, it is not possible to live as a total skeptic. "The utter absence of some (sense of fullness) would leave us in abject, unbearable despair" (Taylor 2007, 600).

Leadership and Values

In the contemporary literature on leadership, signature themes frequently come into play around the questions of human moral experience and values as they are framed by Charles Taylor. (Taylor employs many terms as equivalent to "values" as used here, such as "the good, or "the valuable," or phrases like "moral orientation.") These issues come into sharp focus, for example, in the influential historical studies and leadership theories of James MacGregor Burns. The similarities and contrasts are many, but one of the common points of departure for both Taylor and Burns is the focus on human agency, on life as agents enact it. The aspiration to fullness for Taylor takes hold as a form of life, as standards and patterns of agency that are formed by commitments to a good in one form or another. When construed by Burns as a reciprocal relationship between leaders and followers, leadership occurs precisely as patterns of agency enpowered through an orientation to human needs and values.

One of the contexts in leadership studies where the place of values comes into sharpest relief is in the distinction between transactional and transforming leadership. First developed by Burns in *Leadership,* the motif has been widely applied and adapted by other scholars. In Burns's evolving use of the terms, it is clear that transforming leadership involves deep, systematic, and enduring change in a society or organization driven by fundamental values. Transactional leadership deals with the ordinary decisions of social units that balance the interests of participants and leaders in an exchange of benefits. Leaders and followers transact their relationship through trading on mutual interests and advantages, by bargaining their way to agreement through exchanging rewards, often by compromise. In periods of significant social change and turmoil, however, the needs of constituents may change dramatically and new wants and values arise that must be addressed. Suddenly, leaders in change and crisis may have to develop new policies and practices by reframing basic values such as equality and opportunity, individual freedom, and government authority. Historical change is messy and complex, so the threads of both transactional and transforming change are often bound together on different issues and at different times.

As Burns, the historian and the leadership theorist, reflects on transforming leadership in *Leadership* and even more fully and compellingly in *Transforming Leadership*, the power of values moves center stage. In the latter study he returns time and again to the theme of values–driven change, especially as the catalyst for transforming leadership in challenging periods of change and conflict "…at testing times when people confront the possibilities—and threat—of great change, powerful foundational values are evoked. They are the inspiration and guide to people who pursue and seek to shape change, and they are the standards by which the realization of the highest intentions is measured" (Burns 2003, 29). In *Transforming Leadership,* Burns consistently strikes a resonant, even passionate, note to signal that transforming and creative leadership driven by values, "…can liberate a person from the isolation of frustrated, unacknowledged wants, into the realm of new and shared meanings" and can create a sense of possibility that is…"a mobilizing and empowering faith in the collaborative struggle for real change" (Burns 2003, 169). In terms that parallel Taylor's sense of human flourishing and fullness, Burns asserts, "In sum, values are power resources for the fuller realization of the highest moral purposes" (Burns 2003, 213).

As Burns explores the depths and centrality of values as a theorist of leadership, he addresses some of the questions of the source and durability of values in ways that fascinatingly parallel the philosophical and phenomenological reasoning of Charles Taylor. Referring again to public or foundational values, Burns argues that they "…are the most *powerful* principles because they represent the most *broadly relevant* (relating to *human needs*), *deeply felt, longest lasting, morally grounded commitments* humankind can make" (Burns 2003, 205, emphases added). In this foregoing passage, Burns offers broad phenomenological conditions and criteria by which to make his argument for the power and centrality of values like equality, liberty, and justice, not only historical case studies or theories of psychological development.

This kind of analysis takes us to the outer edge of historical reasoning and represents an argument for human fullness in the form of moral flourishing, in Taylor's terms, since for Burns, they are as the most powerful "commitments humankind can make." As others have noted, these interpretations also appear to cross the line into advocacy for a form of civil and political rights that are embedded in democratic values, such as those found the United States Declaration of Independence and Bill of Rights. In the "Prologue" to *Transforming Leadership* he states explicitly, "I believe leadership is not only a descriptive term, but a prescriptive one, embracing a moral, even passionate dimension" (Burns 2003, 2). In discussing the exhilarating leadership of Eleanor Roosevelt in the adoption of the United Nations Universal Declaration of Human Rights in 1948, it becomes clear that Burns is committed to a statement of universal rights, even though he knows the debate will never end about the specific contents they will have from society to society.

Burns's arguments and advocacy for moral leadership and universal human rights demonstrate that he is not a relativist who classifies moral values as preferences. Nor is he a postmodern theorist, although he is fully sensitive to the issues of social dominance and the lost voices of women and minorities in history, as much of his later writing displays. He is also often a skeptical and critical analyst of the suspect motives of groups and individuals and gives no one a free pass of moral innocence. His critical analysis in both of his leadership texts of some of Franklin Delano Roosevelt's manipulations and duplicity suggests that even a powerful and sometimes heroic transforming leader should be subject to intense moral scrutiny.

The psychological sources to which Burns turns to explicate human motivation and values suggest that he is open to broad interpretations of human moral commitments and development in a style that many postmodern thinkers, empiricists, and experimental psychologists would be likely to question. In relying heavily for some of his insights about human motivation on the stages of human need and motivation advanced by Abraham Maslow, he shows an unusual openness to cross the lines of disciplines in search of a comprehensive picture of human behavior and, ultimately, a general theory of leadership. In *Transforming Leadership* he qualifies his reliance on Maslow's theories since they have a predominant focus on individual self-actualization versus social experience and motivation, and research has not established their explanatory power for leadership in broader organizational and societal contexts (Burns 2003, 143–144).

In spite of these reservations, Burns's broad openness to interdisciplinary, normative theories is evident in his use of Kohlberg's theory of cognitive moral development, which relies on Kantian ethical reasoning and even motifs of spiritual development at its highest stages.

In drawing on the theories and research of Milton Rokeach on values, Burns again turns to an integrative interpretation of human development and behavior. Rokeach understands values in ways that are largely parallel to Burns's descriptions of them, both in *Leadership* and especially in *Transforming Leadership*. The supposition in all these perspectives is that moral development is tied to the sequential organic, social, and cognitive development of human beings.

If we place Burns's conclusions about values within the framework of some of Taylor's categories we gain new insights about transforming leadership. Burns suggests, in effect, that human flourishing and fullness are pursued historically in the satisfaction of wants and needs that define human life everywhere and that include the affirmation of fundamental and universal rights and values. Burns's exalted language, his explicit moral criteria for powerful "public values," and his reliance on developmental psychology, create what we might call a theory of transforming moral humanism as a form of fullness. Burns's humanism offers its own type of intra-human transcendence in his argumentation for the power of moral values, and in affirming the movement to higher stages of human moral experience and development.

Some would see his vision of transforming moral leadership as itself a form of spirituality (Astin, Astin, and Lindholm 2011) since it is focused on beliefs that bestow a sense of possibility, and affirms what makes life worth living It is appropriate to see the striving for justice, the affirmation of human dignity, the endless search for enlarged human rights, as defining causes for Burns the historian, the leadership scholar, the political activist, and the person. In the "Epilogue" of *Transforming Leadership*, Burns proposes ways that society's leaders across the globe can and should address the alleviation of poverty as a central task of leadership for the twenty-first century. Human rights and values are deep and real within the elemental forms of being human. In Taylor's terms this is a rich and textured, passionate and authentic, but incomplete version of human moral transcendence and fullness.

Burns does not give attention to the possibility of an ontological ground or external transcendent source for human values themselves. This might not have direct relevance for a historian, but it does for a leadership theorist. As Taylor puts it, paraphrasing French philosopher Luc Ferry, what is "le sens des sens," the "meaning of the meanings"— the ultimate significance of all the meanings in life that values mediate and convey, and all the relationships and possibilities that they open up for us in the total circumstances of experience (Taylor, *A Secular Age*, 677)? Put another way, it is the question, where does the "dignity and worth of the person" come from in the first place? In effect, values offer meanings *in* existence, but not *of* existence. Burns's work does not draw significantly on philosophical thinkers from Plato and Aristotle onward who have reflected in depth about the good life and its ultimate sources. Nor does he explore religious sources that present agape love or its parallels, or creation in the *imago Dei*, as motivating and grounding human rights. When the opportunity is at hand in writing, for instance, about the Declaration of Independence in *Transforming Leadership*, Burns does not pursue the Declaration's claim about a transcendent source for inalienable rights. As another obvious case in point, Burns's discussions in both of his leadership books of Mahatma Gandhi's psychological formation and his uncanny skills as a leader do not broach the spiritual sources of the nonviolent movement.

Drawing on the perspectives of Taylor, several issues come clearly into view. In general terms, Burns does not explore the way in which spiritual wants and needs, whether illusory or otherwise, drive so much of human experience and history and condition the expectations for leadership. He provides a cursory but skeptical perspective on the way religions paradoxically teach love but create conflict, often in violent forms (Burns 2003, 186–187). Even granting these points, it remains clear that all forms of human artistic and cultural expression and the record of political history itself show a universal human yearning for a benevolent and indefectible source of truth, love, and justice. Those essentially spiritual wants and needs set criteria both for what humans live in hope to find in fullness, and that decisively shape their expectations of what they want and need from one another and from their leaders. This remains the case even as the religions they have created spin out of control and inflict violence and suffering on those outside the circle of their beliefs.

A Phenomenology of Valuing

Burns and Taylor have provided us with ways of thinking about values in terms of identity and fullness and transforming leadership. Some questions need further exploration to enlarge the understanding of what Burns calls the "power of values," and to analyze more fully what Taylor intends when he continues to press toward transcendence in human moral experience. A place to begin is with a descriptive phenomenology of values that tries to describe the conditions of possibility, the defining elements that appear in the ways that values, as engaged forms of valuing, take hold in human experience.

It may help to get inside the intricacy and scope of the agent's experience of valuing if we give an extended example of a central moral value like respect, not in terms of the motif of social deference but with regard to its meaning as "esteem." In respecting other persons, we live out the Kantian imperative of treating others as having intrinsic worth or value, as ends, and not as an instrumental means to another goal. In everyday language, we say that we respect others when we treat them as persons, not as objects.

In sum, the value of respecting the other presses claims on us, shapes our unconscious and explicit intentions, and inhabits our inwardness. As it takes hold in conduct, it creates a mutual sense of trust and confidence. Through mutual respect, we trust and affirm the value of the other, and in turn receive a sense of our own worth and trustworthiness. We come to count on the other for actions that demonstrate loyalty to us, and in turn of we to them. We know as well the power of values in their breach. Should we turn a deaf ear and fail to listen, ignore someone in need, stereotype another person through a label, show disrespect in word or deed, or break a promise, we experience a broken relationship and a sense of self-reproach that normally weigh heavily in our interior dialogues and self-appraisals.

In valuing, we are both affirming a valued other and shaping a pattern of conduct that has value. We do so always as agents, as selves, who integrate thoughts, feelings, and actions. No matter at what point one penetrates into the life of a self or a culture, one finds that values lead to action, that they enforce claims and standards of expectation, and create as well a set of desires and aspirations of the best possibilities for our choices. The self becomes the point of unity for the values that are chosen to be enacted, though always in, through, and with the forms of thought, feeling, and action on which valuing also depends. Valuing emerges, to be sure, through the activity of all the intricate neurological networks of the brain, by means of physiological and psychological processes and internalized cultural norms and expectations, and through the deliberations of logic and reason. Yet it is the self as agent that provides both meaning and integration of these factors as it, as the "I," takes ownership of and responsibility for its feelings, thoughts, and actions (Morrill 1980).

Reflecting on a value like respect in this way, as the engaged respecting of the other through the centered actions of the self, brings other factors to mind. Respect for the other is not simply a concept that we entertain, but a relationship into which we enter. Affirming the worth and rights of others requires an enacted belief in their intrinsic value that typically resonates beyond our explicit awareness. It represents a commitment, a form of life that also takes shape under the tacit awareness of the total circumstances of the human condition as lived within cultural forms, the vastness of nature, and the passage of time, including our own finite time. These inclusive circumstances are always registering in our experience, and we constantly, if usually unconsciously, read and interpret their meaning. Whether often in doubt and anxiety or sometimes in joy and confidence about what it all means, we cannot live without valuing and believing in the worth, the real and unquestioned worth, of the other. And we learn time and again that it is only through these relationships with the other that we also come to confirm our own sense of value. The reciprocal worth of self and other and, we might add of leaders and followers, then, is something that we discover, but do not invent *ex nihilo,* and that at the least is in the nature of things human, whatever our religious and spiritual beliefs. Though not using the same language, Burns assumes this much about valuing, while Taylor wants to explicate the wider spiritual meaning of these defining moral experiences.

Values and Moral Identity

Our effort to dig a bit deeper into the experience of valuing helps us to understand more fully the resonance that they take on in the oeuvres of Burns and Taylor, and the motivational power that they attribute to them. Taylor reminds us repeatedly that the pursuit of fullness draws us toward richer, deeper, and more enduring master values and narratives, and comes to form our identities as selves. He suggests that the question of identity, of "Who am I?," is no longer answered by genealogy, or class, or occupation, or tribe. "What does answer this question for us is an understanding of what is of crucial importance to us. To know who I am is a species of knowing where I stand" (Taylor 1989, 27). The quest for fullness is enacted over a lifetime, and the intense and unrelenting effort to make sense of our lives, necessarily takes a narrative form. Taylor suggests that... "we must determine our lives in narrative form, as a 'quest'" which is an "inescapable structural requirement of human agency" (Taylor 1989, 52).

Benevolence and Justice in a Secular Age

As Taylor works and sometimes meanders his way through *A Secular Age,* he often makes it clear that what he calls "exclusive humanism"

(humanism that excludes a religious or ontological foundation) has emerged as one of the primary forms of contemporary secularism. It is a pattern of moral beliefs and practices that reflects earlier religious and philosophical origins, but is now shorn of any extra-human transcendence. Its system of human rights and justice is woven into most patterns of culture and systems of law in the West and elsewhere, and its belief in benevolence to those suffering is widely affirmed in global philanthropic initiatives. Taylor wonders repeatedly whether a humanistic ethic can be sustained without a deeper foundation and a stronger base of motivation. Ours, for example, is also a time when altruism is understood as a form of evolutionary genetic adaptation among kindred gene pools, when values are defined as personal preferences or as the instruments of dominant groups, when massive greed is a virtue in the marketplace, and when extremes of violence become purported holy duties. Taylor suggests that we are living on borrowed moral capital in the secular age. We are trading on inherited notions of agape love that have been inherited from a religious source, ideas of human dignity established by belief in a creator who formed humans in the image of the divine, and on the remnants of metaphysical reasoning about natural rights.

In neither of his major works does Taylor suppose that argumentation alone can give morality and ethics an apodictic and widely accepted transcendent foundation, but he presses hard on the questions that modern notions of moral self-sufficiency leave unanswered. In particular, he believes that exclusive humanism fails to answer the question of its sources of motivation. As Taylor puts it, "High standards need strong sources" (Taylor 1989, 516). He argues that the modern history of self-sufficient humanism as a moral concept is not promising since high standards of benevolence by themselves can quickly produce fatigue in those serving the needs of recalcitrant and imperfect human beings. When disappointments or big problems occur among the beneficiaries, the benefactors may soon decide to leave those in need to their own devices, blaming them for their shortcomings as they seek cover for their own guilt. Commonly, too, Taylor notes, especially in considering one-regime Marxist societies, that the limits of a utopian humanistic ethics show up in impatience to effect the changes that the exalted vision demands, so leaders become rulers who are tempted to re-shape the resistant stuff of humanity by control, by force, and by tyranny.

Taylor suggests that when an image of the divine is seen in the human person, both the interpretation of the circumstances and the motivation to respond to even the most wretched conditions are moved to a different plane. The shift is made to a sustaining commitment to meet the needs of persons who have inestimable value, not to fulfill expectations for recognition or to display righteousness. "Wherever action for high ideals is not tempered, controlled, ultimately engulfed in an unconditional love of the beneficiaries this ugly dialectic (of control and guilt) risks repeating itself" (Taylor 2007, 697).

Continuities and Discontinuities

Our analyses of values and leadership in the thought of James MacGregor Burns, and of values and transcendence in Charles Taylor, have shown both striking continuities and discontinuities. Each of the authors makes the question of the good a key to understanding human experience, which in turn takes on broad significance for the ways humans search for what Taylor calls "fullness" and Burns "transforming leadership" through foundational values.

Burns is fixed squarely on values as his Rosetta stone for understanding transforming leadership. He does not link values to a transcendent source, which he may see as not relevant or not possible, or both; nor does he pursue leads or linkages to historical cases and moral theories that display a connection between leadership, values, and religious or spiritual sources. Nevertheless, he uses values to display how humans make sense of their lives in historical contexts and how they are the most morally compelling historical form of human wants and needs. In fact, he says as much as one might say about the meaning of human moral experience and of life itself in terms of the power of values, especially in *Transforming Leadership*. These concepts of human moral flourishing become, in Taylor's terms, a form of fullness.

Where Taylor and Burns differ most is in their divergent conceptualizations of the similar things they see taking place in human moral experience. Taylor would suggest that the power of values, as Burns actually describes them, requires a larger frame of reference than history and humanistic psychology and phenomenology can provide. In sum, Taylor would see Burns's account of values as valid, but in need of a wider framing and deeper interpretation to be adequate for the transcendent content it actually includes.

Burns in turn would be likely to see Taylor's philosophical and religious reflections as needing fuller and more demonstrative historical, textual, and empirical support, as well as more evident predicative and explanatory power in understanding historical change. Taylor offers evidence from a variety of historical and cultural studies, but they take on their meaning within the broad set of theories and arguments that Taylor provides. For Burns, the place of religion in history is morally ambiguous, but Taylor would insist that the extraordinary influence of religion on human life and aspiration through centuries and across cultures cannot be so easily bracketed.

Taylor's thinking about transcendence is clearly informed by his deep knowledge of the Western philosophic tradition, historical inter-pretations, and reflections concerning Christianity and other religions, and his own participation in the Catholic tradition. He uses theology at times to illustrate and explore the moral meaning, possibilities, and consequences of religious beliefs, ideals, and practices, but bases his arguments on philosophical and historical analysis.

Values and Leadership in Practice

What bearing do these reflections on values have on the exercise of leadership in the many contexts in which it occurs? In the everyday work of leadership many of these thoughts will appear as too abstract and theoretical to have much impact on making decisions or solving problems. That is too easy a conclusion. The insights of disciplinary and interdisciplinary studies of leadership are appropriated through theory and in practice, just as are studies of other large and complex ideas and forms of agency such as democracy, law, language, or other fundamental forms of human capability such as education and human development. We shape our self-understanding and our expectations of ourselves and others as moral agents and citizens when we enrich our knowledge of leadership in relation to values. When we examine leadership in the context of the deep currents of the ways humans make sense of their own commitments and life purposes, we fund a whole range of actual and potential connections to practice.

With regard to the practice of leadership as a relationship of both influence and of authority, we know that the deep self-awareness of the leader is a critical aspect of the process. As both Taylor and Burns argue, and I have tried to show, human moral identities are shaped through the distinctive constellation of values that embodies what matters to us and orders our choices. To the extent that we deepen our sense of our own commitments, goals, and ambitions, we are much better able to decide if we should take on the responsibilities of leadership, and if we do, to what end. In considering a leadership responsibility, the first questions to be asked and answered are, "What values are to be served, what purposes fulfilled?" We should inquire of ourselves: "What do I want to do," not "What position do I want to hold?" As we critically assess what we care about and why, we are better able to know both what we might be able to accomplish and to contribute, and where false images and compulsions may take us off track. Values awareness is both a practical and theoretical process that can be improved in the practice of it, in learning how to decipher and to spell out features of our commitments in the centering and re-centering of self.

The knowledge that we gain of ourselves through values awareness applies as well to our understanding of those with whom we engage in a leadership process. We benefit greatly by having the ability to see below the functional roles in organizations to understand what motivates groups and individuals in terms of what they care about deeply. As leaders we can focus on better ways to communicate, more effective ways to develop rewarding tasks and to enlarge individual and group capabilities, if we consider the meanings that matter to people. In leadership interactions with others we learn that people want to be part of something significant, that they desire to develop new talents and hope to be part of a community that makes a difference, a place of inclusiveness, affirmation, and of high expectation. These are the values around which leaders and participants interact. At their base all the most effective relationships between leaders and participants are born of mutual respect that is grounded in deep convictions about the worth of persons. However it is framed, whether in spiritual or other terms, respect is a matter of human faith as trust and confidence in the value of the other.

The rewards for understanding the depth dimensions of values connect with a large series of other facets of the responsibilities and expectations of leadership. We know that leaders and followers come together around an evocative sense of the mission of the organization, and a belief in its vision—its best possibilities for the future. As Burns and Taylor both understand deeply, knowing the history and recounting the narrative of identity and aspiration of any organization or social system is a critical element of leadership. To tell the story effectively and with integrity means that leaders have to grasp, articulate, and live the values that are at the core of the narrative. This task has to be done by listening as much as telling, and with sensitivity to dissenting voices that may communicate a counternarrative, in which exclusion or unfairness may be part of the story that needs to be heard.

In times of crisis and change, there is always a need for leaders to connect controversies, failures, and challenges to the basic values that underwrite the organization or the society. They must assure that distortions or violations of norms and values will be vigorously addressed and problems solved in the most transparent ways possible. When deep forces of change press on the society and the organization, leaders have to delve into their own deepest sources of worth and rely on their integrity and confidence. They have to summon the courage to help themselves and others face the hard realities of change. Leadership in negative circumstances takes deep patience, the capacity for detachment and perspective, empathy for the struggles of those suffering a sense of loss, and insights into the emotional distortions that people experience under stress, including leaders. Values count more than ever.

These lessons are especially true when it becomes clear that the culture of an organization or a social system needs to be changed, often when a controversy or crisis, or a process of self-appraisal, shows that shifts in the culture are required. Culture is a thickly interconnected web of norms, practices, and expectations that rest on basic values about what an organization and its people take to be important. Culture is formed through successful adaptation to the challenges and opportunities that presented themselves in the past. The self-esteem of individuals and groups usually lodges in the practices and beliefs that proved effective. Getting a hold on the values and routines that need to be altered becomes a critical element of any change process, especially when it touches the way people have come to define what it means to belong and to be accepted. Leadership through values awareness and criticism and a powerful vision for the future can become the ingredients for effective cultural transformations.

The depths to which they reach in the lives of individuals and groups show values to be both conceptually and practically central in leadership. Values make both inescapable claims and inspire high aspirations. They press their adherents to come to terms with an ever-widening horizon of choice as life moves from the small circles of family and neighborhood to larger social and national settings, and then to ever-enlarging global, universal, and environmental contexts. As they press toward widening contexts and circumstances, they also push more deeply into the depths of human moral and spiritual experience that underwrites leadership. As both James MacGregor Burns and Charles Taylor argue, humans finally have no choice but to commit themselves over time to foundational values that lead toward personal and social transformation and human fullness in a just and benevolent, a comprehensive, and an enduring community.

References

Astin, Alexander W., Helen S. Astin, and Jennifer A. Lindholm. 2011. *Cultivating the Spirit: How Colleges Can Engage Students' Inner Lives*. San Francisco, CA: Jossey Bass.

Bolman, Lee G., and Terrence E. Deal. 2001. *Leading with Soul: An Uncommon Journey of Spirit*. San Francisco, CA: Jossey Bass.

Burns, James M. 1978. *Leadership*. New York: Harper and Row.

Burns, James M. 2003. *Transforming Leadership*. New York: Atlantic Monthly Press.

Crumpton, Alice D. "An Exploration of Spirituality within Leadership Studies Literature." Online document. www.inter-disciplinary.net/wp-content/uploads/crumpton-paper.pdf.

Maslow, Abraham H. 1971. *The Farther Reaches of Human Nature*. New York: Viking Press.

Morrill, Richard L. 1980. *Teaching Values in College: Facilitating Development of Ethical, Moral, and Value Awareness in Students*. San Francisco: Jossey Bass.

Niebuhr, H. R. 1960. *Radical Monotheism and Western Culture: With Supplementary Essays*. New York: Harpers and Brothers.

Taylor, Charles. 1989. *Sources of the Self: The Making of the Modern Identity*. Cambridge, MA: Harvard University Press.

Taylor, Charles. 1992. *The Ethics of Authenticity*. Cambridge, MA and London: Harvard University Press.

Taylor, Charles. 2007. *A Secular Age*. Cambridge, MA and London: Belknap Press of Harvard University Press.

Afterword

A young marine corporal in Iraq, with his hands blown off and with a serious wound in his leg, continued to lead his men. When later asked why he didn't pass out, his response was, "I couldn't pass out. I was in charge." That Marine embodied the best of the value of responsibility, strength of character, and commitment to purpose. Somewhere, either at home, at school, in his church, or in the Marine Corps, this value was developed and, when called upon, the mind and thus the body responded automatically to the responsibility at hand. Because the situation asked for the impossible, the result was to get the best possible.

"The flesh may be weak" but it is stronger if the spirit is willing. The level of energy, and the resulting action, is to a large extent determined by the level of passion toward the committed purpose. State of mind has much to do with why some far outpace others. It makes a vast difference in how we deal with problems and opportunities. The spirit with which we face challenges is often more important than technique and know-how.

Longfellow (1858) expressed the resulting rewards of a willing spirit in his *The Ladder of St. Augustine*: "The heights by great men reached and kept/Were not attained by sudden flight./But they, while their companions slept,/Were toiling upward in the night."

Clearly, the spirit is a component of the human condition which is the dynamo that propels actions while spirituality introduces the complexity of personal faith or religious convictions. The commentary embodied in the chapters of this book bear upon the simplicity and the complexity of the above consideration.

Writing the postscript to this publication on Spirituality and Leadership has provided me the opportunity for reviewing some interesting and provocative manuscripts. As a result, I compliment these colleagues for having joined together to present their perspectives on a subject and at a place that invites diverse opinions, which might go unappreciated elsewhere.

These chapters, prepared by capable colleagues, have made me aware that I am not capable of challenging what is written even if I wished to do so, but I am comfortable in complementing what is conveyed by each. It is not easy to interpret or even to critique such a package of ideas, but it is satisfying to reflect on my actions of 44 years ago that likely helped to create an environment conducive to such a publication as this.

As president and chancellor at the University of Richmond for 44 years, it is no surprise to me that a book such as this could become a reality. In its almost 200 years of history, the university has developed traditions within which such collaborative endeavors as this can be comfortably carried out. The spirit of the institution, emboldened by its faculty, students, and alumni, fosters such activity.

The essence of this publication is that it serves many avenues of thought. The ideas are not just reinforcements of each one's perspective but suggest alternatives. The special character of the book is that each one of these who have written chapters are presenting studied impressions and not just articulating long-held prejudices. Their ideas are bound by objective and thorough investigation. In response, it's not my purpose to summarize, draw from, add to, reinforce, or question. My response is intended only as a general impression of what I have read.

In the chapter "The Pursuit of Wonder," Dr. David Burhans tells the story of how the University of Richmond came to have a Chaplaincy. Of course, that's real to me because early in my presidency that position was my idea and my creation. Many at the university at that time questioned whether or not it was a good idea. Nonetheless, I judged to bring into the university community a person spiritually motivated, with religion being a focus but who understood the need to be tolerant of people of all faiths or none. David Burhans represented what the Chaplaincy would become, and now Craig Kocher represents in the Chaplaincy a new era in age and perspective broadening its scope.

Because the presidency of the United States is used by one writer as an example in leadership, I acknowledge that presidents of universities have many responsibilities and a level of authority similar in character to that of the president of the United States. Each has a community for which he or she is responsible and has vested authority to function within that community.

I used my authority as president to establish the position of chaplain to the university. I did that out of my own background of learning, of living, of understanding, and out of my sense of responsibility for the fact that there is a spiritual depth to everyone irrespective of what they believe or don't believe.

I used my authority and was engaged with others in selecting the person who was to carry out that responsibility, but it was mine alone to initiate what became an operating position, administratively cloaked, which created an environment that could result in a publication such as this. I doubt that it would have happened without there having been a Chaplaincy that acknowledged the reality of the spirit and the spiritual.

Some of what we do as leaders is to make judgments. In a university the judgment might not always be supported by the faculty, staff, students, alumni, or the community, and it may not prove to be the right action for years to come. Thus one must have the long view in order to hold the position. Spirit is essential along with deep convictions in order to operate against opposition, which many times is strong but in the end the leader is selected to lead, not to follow the opinion of the community.

In reading this material, I have concluded that this is not a manual for applying spirituality in leadership, but rather it is a lesson of learning about the subject matter, and the expanding of one's thinking and allowing each to further address what the subject of spirituality and leadership is all about.

I am aware of the fact that the attempt is to deal with the subject assigned from different perspectives by writers from different academic disciplines. Thus the outcome is to cast light on the subject by reconciling different perspectives and opinions.

I attempt no evaluation from my reading of the drafts; rather, I draw from the works of these colleagues some impressions of my own, adding to or deducting from all the work, the ideas, and the rationalizations presented.

I make the following conclusions:

1. That my judgment in establishing of the Chaplaincy at the university was unique and helped to create an environment conducive to such collaboration as this book.
2. That the university interdisciplinary activities make natural the cooperative deliberations of subjects of interest in multiple disciplines.
3. There is within this community of scholars a spirit of collegiality and challenge in selecting ideas to pursue.

4. That individuals are not hesitant to attack subjects dissimilar to their own and to draw valued results from interdisciplinary thinking.
5. Only at an institution founded upon spiritual motivations within an environment of seeking the truth with an appreciation for a variety of ideas, opinions, and interpretations could such circumstances result in learning.

And a thought by J. R. Tolkien (1955) confirming Merriam Webster's definition of spirit seems relevant to my closing: "It is not the strength/ Of the body that counts/But the strength/Of the Spirit."

E. Bruce Heilman
Chancellor, University of Richmond

References

Longfellow, H. W. 1858. *The Ladder of St. Augustine*, stanza 1. Oxford: Oxford University Press.
Tolkien, J. R. 1955. *Lord of the Rings*. Wilmington, MA: Mariner Books.

CONTRIBUTORS

Scott T. Allison is professor of psychology. He has published extensively on heroism, leadership, and prosocial behavior. His other books include *Heroes, Heroic Leadership, Reel Heroes, Conceptions of Leadership,* and the *Handbook of Heroism and Heroic Leadership*. His work has appeared in *USA Today,* National Public Radio, the *New York Times,* the *Los Angeles Times, Slate Magazine,* MSNBC, CBS, *Psychology Today,* and the Christian Science Monitor. He has received Richmond's Distinguished Educator Award and the Virginia Council of Higher Education's Outstanding Faculty Award.

David D. Burhans is chaplain emeritus of the University of Richmond. He has served the university for 40 years, as chaplain, special assistant to the Office of Advancement, a member of the president's senior staff, and a teacher in arts and sciences. A graduate of William Jewel College in Missouri, he received his doctoral degree at the Southern Baptist Theological Seminary. Because of his special interest in the ministry of pastoral care, his work often involves people in crisis situations. He is an active counselor and speaker to diverse groups of people. In the community, Burhans is chairman emeritus of the Virginia Center for Inclusive Communities' State Board and also serves on boards for Volunteer Emergency Families for Children and Virginia Holocaust Museum.

Henry L. Chambers, Jr. is professor of law. He teaches and writes primarily in the areas of constitutional law, criminal law, law and religion, employment discrimination, and voting rights. His most recent scholarship has focused on the president's executive power under the Constitution and what role an employer's religious beliefs may play in its employment decisions. A recipient of the University of Richmond's Distinguished Educator Award, he also frequently lectures on constitutional law through the program "We The People," which provides civic education instruction to K-12 school teachers, students, and the public.

L. Stephanie Cobb is associate professor of religion and the George and Sallie Cutchin Camp Professor of Bible. Her current research interests focus on the interrelationship among paganism, Judaism, and Christianity in the first and second centuries CE. In particular, she works on martyrdom and persecution, gender and sex constructions in antiquity, and the function of texts in communities. In addition, her teaching interests include: magic and religion in antiquity, women in early Christianity, studies of the historical Jesus, the spread and growth of Christianity, and the battle between orthodoxy and heresy in early Christianity.

Jennifer L. Erkulwater is associate professor of political science. Her research focuses on social welfare, poverty and inequality, public policy, American politics and government, and civic engagement. She is the author of *Disability Rights and the American Social Safety Net* (2006) and coauthor, with Rick Mayes and Catherine Bagwell, of *Medicating Children: ADHD and Pediatric Mental Health* (2009).

George R. Goethals is the holder of the E. Claiborne Robins Distinguished Professorship in Leadership Studies. He has held academic and administrative appointments at Williams College and visiting appointments at the University of Virginia, Princeton University, and Amherst College, among others. At Williams College he served as the chair of the Psychology Department for eight years, acting dean of the faculty, provost, and finally founder and chair of the program in leadership studies. He has served as an editor or on the editorial board of the *Personality and Social Psychology Bulletin,* the *Journal of Experimental Social Psychology, The Leadership Quarterly,* and *Rhetoric & Public Affairs.*

Elisabeth Rose Gruner is associate dean, School of Arts and Sciences, director of the Academic Advising Resource Center, and associate professor of English. She teaches children's and young adult literature and Victorian literature, as well as Creative Nonfiction Writing. Her current research is on young adult literature and the "crisis in reading"; more broadly, she is interested in the relationships between children's and young adult literature and education.

E. Bruce Heilman is Chancellor at the University of Richmond after serving as President and Chief Executive Officer for 17 years. A US

Marine during the World War II Pacific Campaign, Dr. Heilman later received his BA, MA, and PhD from Vanderbilt University. He has held teaching positions at Belmont University, Kentucky Wesleyan College, and Peabody College of Vanderbilt University. He has served as chief business and financial officer at Kentucky Wesleyan College, Georgetown College and Peabody College, where he also served as Vice President of Administration. He also served as Coordinator of Higher Education for the State of Tennessee, and as Vice President and Dean of Arts and Sciences at Kentucky Southern College. Dr. Heilman holds membership in Phi Beta Kappa, Omicron Delta Kappa, Beta Gamma Sigma, Pi Omega Pi, Kappa Phi Kappa, Lambda Chi Alpha and Kappa Delta Pi. He has been listed in numerous publications including *Who's Who in the World, Who's Who in America, Who's Who in American Education, Who's Who in College and University Administration, Leaders in Education, Leaders of the English Speaking World, and Personalities in the South.*

Peter Iver Kaufman is professor and George Matthews & Virginia Brinkley Modlin Chair in leadership studies. His scholarship examines the political cultures of late antique, medieval, and early modern Europe and North Africa. He has written 8 books and more than 40 articles on authority, religious conflict, and literary history, which have appeared in, among other journals, *The Journal of Late Antiquity, Harvard Theological Review, Archiv für Reformationsgeschichte, Journal of the American Academy of Religion, Clio,* and *Mediaevalia.* He is editor-in-chief of *Religions* and editor of a series of monographs on the religion around iconic figures from Dante and Dürer to Virginia Woolf, Billie Holiday, and Bob Dylan. He has also edited five books, ranging from studies of charisma to others on leadership and Elizabethan culture.

Craig T. Kocher is university chaplain, Jessie Ball duPont Chair of the Chaplaincy, and lecturer in the Jepson School of Leadership Studies. Dr. Kocher has received many awards for his work and in the pulpit including the Jameson Jones Preaching award given by Duke Divinity School, the John Wesley Preaching award from the Finch-Hunt Institute of Homiletics, and the ODK award for service to Davidson College. In 2012 he received the Administrator of the Year award from the Richmond College Student Government Association and in 2013 he was given the Servant Leader Award by the Jepson School of Leadership Studies Student Government Association.

Richard L. Morrill became chancellor and Distinguished University Professor of Ethics and Democratic Values at the University of Richmond on July 1, 1998, following his 10-year presidency of the University of Richmond from September 30, 1988, to June 30, 1998. On his retirement from the presidency, the university's board created the professorship he now holds that is to carry his name. Prior to his association with the university, he served as president of Centre College from 1982 to 1988 and as president of Salem College from 1979 to 1982.

Gwendolyn C. Setterberg is a graduate of the University of Richmond Psychology and Latin American and Iberian Studies Departments. A member of Phi Beta Kappa, her culminating research investigated parental involvement among minority-language speakers in US public schools, and she is the recipient of a Fulbright English Teaching fellowship to Argentina.

Sydney Watts is associate professor of history and WGSS. Her current research is on the history of Lent in early modern French cities. This study examines Lenten practices and beliefs and how they changed with the development of the Enlightenment self. She focuses on the quotidian negotiation of the laws and customs of Lent, in light of metaphysical questions of how the temporal meets the spiritual, to illuminate the complex relationship between food, the body, and belief. The convergence of both scientific and holy circles brings into focus one of the central problems in the history of religious life: how piety and self-discipline changed with the rise of secular ideas and scientific discoveries about nutrition and digestion. This project compares the regulation and disciplining of Christian life across several centuries, among various social groups, in a number of urban contexts.

Thad Williamson is associate professor of Leadership Studies and Philosophy, Politics, Economics and Law (PPEL). A sought-after professor and civic activist, his research focuses on urban politics and sprawl, community economic development, politics in the city of Richmond, and sports, justice, and ethics. He writes regularly on current issues for a wide variety of popular and scholarly publications. Williamson was on leave from the university during 2014–15 to oversee the Mayor's Office of Community Wealth Building and take the lead in implementing comprehensive poverty reduction strategies identified by the Mayor's Anti-Poverty Commission and the Maggie L. Walker Initiative for Expanding Opportunity and Fighting Poverty, which he has cochaired.

INDEX

Lightning Source UK Ltd.
Milton Keynes UK
UKOW06n0623260416

272982UK00014B/345/P